COERCIVE MILITARY STRATEGY

COERCIVE MILITARY STRATEGY

Stephen J. Cimbala

Texas A&M University Press
College Station

The paper used in this book meets the minimum requirements
of the American National Standard for Permanence
of Paper for Printed Library Materials, z39.48–1984.
Binding materials have been chosen for durability.
ff

Library of Congress Cataloging-in-Publication Data

Cimbala, Stephen J.
    Coercive military strategy / Stephen J. Cimbala. — 1st ed.
        p.   cm.
    Includes bibliographical references and index.
    ISBN 0-89096-836-5
    1. Strategy.   2. United States—Military policy—Case studies.
    I.   Title.
U163.C53   1998
327.1'17—dc21   98-22791
                                                                          CIP

Contents

Tables

Acknowledgments

I gratefully acknowledge the following perons for helpful insights and references pertinent to this study: for the introduction, Colin Gray, University of Hull; Sam Sarkesian, Loyola University Chicago; and Robert Wendzel, U.S. Air War College; for chapter 1, Paul Davis, RAND; Lawrence Korb, Brookings Institution; and John Allen Williams, Loyola University Chicago; for chapter 2, Raymond Garthoff, Brookings Institution, and Richard Ned Lebow, Ohio State University; for chapter 3, Don M. Snider, U.S. Military Academy, and Barry Watts, Northrup-Grumman Aerospace; for chapter 4, Richard Schultz, Fletcher School of Law and Diplomacy, Tufts University, and Sam Sarkesian; for chapter 5, John Arquilla, U.S. Naval Postgraduate School, and Richard Betts, Columbia University; for chapter 6, Michael Lytle, Science Applications International Corporation, and Donald Snow, University of Alabama. None of these persons bears any responsibility for contents of this study.

The interest and support for this project by the staff of Texas A&M University Press is gratefully appreciated. I also acknowledge with thanks Penn State Delaware County Campus for administrative support. I also want to thank Joanne Clendenen for her exceptional work on the index. This work is dedicated to my wife, Betsy, and to my sons Chris and David, with all my love.

Coercive Military Strategy

INTRODUCTION

Military Strategy and Coercion

The study of military strategy attempts to explain how armies and states ought to set out to win or prevent wars and why they succeed or fail. There is no universal "correct" strategy: all is dependent upon time, place, and circumstance. This variability of conditions under which fighting or prevention of war takes place is itself a constant, if an elusive one. Military strategy is inseparable from political, social, cultural, and historical context.

In this study, I develop the idea of *coercive military strategy*, explaining why mastery of the principles of military coercion is a necessary condition for success in war or diplomacy. In brief, an understanding of coercive military strategy is a necessary condition for policy makers, military leaders, and scholars who hope to understand and to manage favorably the forces at work in the post-Cold War world.[1] Appreciation of the context for successful or failed military coercion is a necessary constituent for obtaining political or military objectives at an acceptable cost.

Theories about the coercive use of military power have suffered from disbelief on the part of military professionals and charges of American ethnocentrism laid down by scholars. There are good reasons for the skepticism: coercive military strategies have been wrongly presented, and mistakenly applied, more than once. Nevertheless, this introduction and the chapters that follow argue that coercive military strategy is not necessarily a culture-bound product of American political and social theory. More emphatically, this book rejects the argument that coercive strategy is of little importance to politicians and commanders. Coercive military strategy has the potential to contribute to the best, and the worst, results in war and policy; the skill of the swordsmith cannot be separated from the sharpness of the blade.

3

I. COERCIVE STRATEGY AND THE PAST

In one sense there is "no news" in the observation that strategy, or the connection between the ends of policy and the military instruments used to obtain those ends, must be selective. No state can achieve all of its objectives during any crisis or war, and few combatants exhaust all their resources trying to do so. On the other hand, whether limits on ends and means are purposeful and well thought out in relation to the immediate context is not so clear. One can blunder into a limited war or a small crisis just as one can blunder into a larger one. A coercive military strategy is one that explicitly seeks to employ deliberately calibrated means in order to accomplish policy objectives, while adjusting its ends and means relationship to the evolving situation and context. In the following propositions of his classic study *The Art of War* (dated between 400–320 B.C.), the noted Chinese military theorist Sun Tzu Wu called attention to the importance of selectivity and calibration related to context in war:

> For to win one hundred victories in one hundred battles is not the acme of skill. To subdue the enemy without fighting is the acme of skill.

> Thus, what is of supreme importance in war is to attack the enemy's strategy. . . . Next best is to disrupt his alliances. . . . The next best is to attack his army. . . . The worst policy is to attack cities. Attack cities only when there is no alternative.[2]

According to Sun Tzu, victory comes to those who know how to invite it: (1) the commander who knows "when he can fight and when he cannot" will be victorious; (2) the commander who understands how to use both small and large forces will prevail because there are circumstances in war when "the weak can master the strong" and one must "manipulate such circumstances" to win; (3) the commander whose ranks "are united in purpose" will achieve victory; (4) the commander who is prudent and "lies in wait for an enemy who is not" will be victorious; and (5) the commander whose generals are able and "not interfered with by the sovereign" will win.[3]

Each of Sun Tzu's five principles of war can be illustrated by historical examples occurring subsequent to his writing. Successful application of the first principle (knowing when and when not to fight) is shown in Mao Zedong's campaign against Chinese nationalist forces, which led to the seizure of power by the Chinese Communists in 1949.[4] North Vietnamese military strategist Vo Nguyen Giap demonstrated mastery of the second principle (the alternation of small and larger forces), during the Second Indochina War in the 1960s and 1970s.[5] U.S. President George Bush and Gen. Norman Schwartzkopf conducted a successful coalition war against Iraq using the third principle (that of "ranks united in purpose") in 1991. The American Civil War defeat inflicted by the Army of Northern Virginia on the Army of the Potomac at Fredericksburg in December, 1862, illustrates the fourth principle (one side that is prudent laying in wait for another side that is not),[6] a principle also illustrated by the decisive sea battle of Midway in 1942. The fifth principle (that of generals not unduly interfered with), is best understood in its absence: this principle was not observed by the United States during the Vietnam War between 1965 and 1973, and especially from 1965 to 1969, with disastrous results for policy and strategy.

An important relationship exists between Sun Tzu's conditions for victory and what he referred to as "moral influence."[7] Moral influence is a sense of harmony among people, their rulers, and their fighting forces. When moral influence is operating, both the purpose for which fighting is undertaken and the means of fighting are commonly understood and approved. Sun Tzu quotes with approval his interlocutor Chang Yu: "When one treats people with benevolence, justice, and righteousness, and reposes confidence in them, the army will be united in mind and all will be happy to serve their leaders. The *Book of Changes* says: 'In happiness at overcoming difficulties, people forget the danger of death.'"[8]

Karl von Clausewitz, in what many regard as the most philosophically important study of war by a Western military theorist, also emphasized the significance of moral influence.[9] According to Clausewitz, war is a "chameleon" whose dominant tendencies make up a "remarkable trinity": first, the people, who are the source of passion, violence, and emotion; second, the commanders and armed forces, who operate in the realm of risk, probability, and chance; and, third, the government, which is responsible for rational direction of warfare according to its political objectives.[10] Any viable theory, according to Clausewitz, must maintain a "balance" or equilibrium among these three tendencies. This trinitarian concept of war's essence is just one illustration of Clausewitz's recognition of the importance of moral—to include psychological—forces in war.

Clausewitz's compelling descriptions of the psychological climate of battle emphasize how the commander's mind is plagued by: (1) uncertainty about what is actually taking place and about future events; (2) concern about the welfare of troops assigned to his or her command; and (3) questions about how to minimize the amount of "friction" in war that creates a discrepancy between war plans and the actual outcome of battle.[11] Since war is an act of force, Clausewitz cautions, emotions "cannot fail to be involved":

> In the dreadful presence of suffering and danger, emotion can easily overwhelm intellectual conviction, and in this psychological fog it is so hard to form clear and complete insights that changes of view become more understandable and excusable. . . . Nowhere, in consequence, are differences of opinion so acute as in war, and fresh opinions never cease to batter at one's convictions. No degree of calm can provide enough protection: new impressions are too powerful, too vivid, and always assault the emotions as well as the intellect.[12]

Commanders must master this environment by maintaining a sense of self-control despite suffering inevitable reverses in battle. Commanders who display this kind of character will have moral influence on those under their command. The Civil War provides many positive, and negative, examples of moral influence on the part of commanders and politicians; sometimes one person assumed both roles, usually to the detriment of fighting power. It is moral influence that makes many troops reluctant to commit atrocities that are against human nature as well as contrary to their military law. It is often moral influence that makes troops accomplish the seemingly impossible.

For example, some years ago the U.S. Marines attempted to recreate the movements of the Army of Northern Virginia on the second day of the battle of Gettysburg. The Marines began at 4 a.m. and marched throughout the day, assaulting Little Round Top and concluding their recreation at 6 p.m. The Marines were exhausted by the time activities had concluded. The Army of Northern Virginia on July 2, 1863, had marched the same route and then assaulted Little Round Top not once, but three times. Most Confederate soldiers had not had water for hours. Some fought without shoes. Many were sick from having eaten too many green apples. The exhausted Confederates repeatedly pushed an attack that had delayed too long against Union defenses that were only at the last minute fortuitously deployed.[13]

Equally fortuitous for the Union was the presence on the extreme left flank of the Union defensive line on Little Round Top of the 20th Maine Regiment, under the command of Col. Joshua Lawrence Chamberlain. No better example exists of the power of moral forces to motivate superior performance in combat. The prominent role of Chamberlain's 20th Maine in the defense of Little Round Top is so well known that it has become memorialized in screenplay. Subsequent to the dramatic events of July 2, 1862, his activities are less publicly known, but equally impressive. After Little Round Top he was wounded six times, once almost fatally; his obituary was published twice (mistakenly) in newspapers. He was promoted to brigadier general by commission, promoted to brevet major general by the end of the war, and selected by General Ulysses S. Grant to preside over the Confederate surrender of arms ceremony at Appomattox. In a speech at Gettysburg decades after the fighting had ended, Chamberlain gave eloquent testimony to the significance of moral forces in war:

> The inspiration of a noble cause involving human interests wide and far enables men to do things they did not dream themselves capable of before, and which they were not capable of alone. The consciousness of belonging, vitally, to something beyond individuality; of being part of a personality that reaches we know not where, in space and in time, greatens the heart to the limits of the soul's ideal.[14]

II. COERCIVE STRATEGY AND THE CONTEMPORARY ENVIRONMENT

Sun Tzu's and Clausewitz's arguments outline some of the components of coercive military strategy, but they stop short of identifying all of the necessary aspects of coercive military strategy today. The international system is now a global community, military technology has undergone many scientific revolutions since 400 B.C. or even since 1832, and cultures are no longer as isolated from one another as they were when the great Chinese and Prussian theorists wrote down their maxims on war. These changes are obvious: less so, are the more immediate, short-term changes in the context for making policy and strategy that the United States and other military powers must identify since the end of the Cold War and the demise of the Soviet Union. The impact of these more immediate and specific coercive factors on future U.S. and allied coercive military strategy will be the focus of this study. This study treats as working assumptions the reasons why coercive strategy is a necessary part of any diplomatic-strategic recipe for U.S. military success in the post-Cold War world. These reasons are as follows:

1. Although combat soldiers are not typically trained for peace operations and other operations apart from war, an important mission for U.S. and other professional militaries in the post-Cold War world will be soldiering for peace. This will include humanitarian rescues, traditional peacekeeping, intervention in civil disorders, and other politico-military assignments loaded with cultural and social bear traps. The political objective in these situations will almost always be one that calls for the coercive, but effective, use of force, with minimum destruction and loss of life to nonmilitary targets and civilians.

2. The end of the Cold War and the demise of the Soviet Union virtually eliminate the problem of great-power war in Europe. Now instability results from smaller conflicts between hostile states outside of Europe or within states, including failed states that have lost popular legitimacy and the ability to govern themselves. Smaller conventional wars and civil wars call for U.S. and allied NATO intervention strategies and military capabilities that are more discriminating in their military effects, but politically self-defeating when too little is too late.

3. Combat soldiers of today who are assigned to peace operations or to other nontraditional missions are diplomats on

the march. Their discretion with regard to factors on the ground will influence the likelihood of successful termination for civil conflicts in locales from Bosnia to Tajikistan. How roadblocks are set up, when and to whom medical services are delivered, how housing is allocated, and under what auspices elections can be held are items now added to the agenda of peacekeepers and other militaries. This calls for a velvet glove clothing a mailed fist, and perhaps for a split military personality. Soldiers still carry weapons, and when push comes to shove, they have to "do" the bad guys.

4. Fighting smarter means persuading your opponent that its current losses are only a prelude to greater, and inevitable, losses unless it complies with your demands. Persuading your opponent may require, depending on the circumstances, *either* rapid and decisive escalation *or* slow and deliberate steps toward tightening the screw.[15] Choice of the correct strategy is always situational, and situations are always highly politicized, although they vary in what can be called their political "specific gravity." Perpetrators of ethnic cleansing in Bosnia, of massacres in Liberia, and of genocide in Rwanda were all engaged in doing bad things, but the specific gravity of their political situations varied enormously. So, too, did the likelihood that outsiders could bring to bear efficient and effective force to solve the problem.

5. Although the question of *whether* to use force can be separated analytically from the question of *how* to intervene, the two considerations are inseparable in action. As Richard N. Haass has explained, the question whether to use force "can never be divorced from the question of how to use it effectively. If there is no satisfactory answer to the latter question, there can be no commitment to the former."[16] In the face of widespread humanitarian disasters, on the heels of civil war, and in the wake of failed states, the overwhelming temptation to "just do something" is understandable but misguided; the case for doing *something* is not necessarily a case for doing something *military*.

This list is not exhaustive but it does outline the major guideposts to understanding why military coercion is often central to, and not apart from, a successful politico-military strategy.[17] Coercive military strategy, like all strategy, must adapt to the existing and anticipated future international *environment*. This "environment" includes the various state and nonstate actors and their numerous political, military, economic, social, and cultural attributes. Some aspects of this environment impose constraints on the choices and opportunities available to heads of state and to military planners. In particular, the sources of military threat to a state, including other states with potentially or actively hostile intentions and their military capabilities, loom large as a part of the environment relevant to coercive military strategy.

In brief compass, the international environment of the Cold War years relevant for coercive military strategy can be summarized thus: Technology more or less enforced interest in coercive strategy, while politics helped to enable it.

Technology *enforced* interest in coercive strategy by making nuclear weapons of mass destruction available in large quantities to the major powers, especially to the Americans and Soviets. The result was to preclude any large-scale war at an acceptable cost even for the "victor." Once both the United States and the Soviet Union had survivable retaliatory forces capable of inflicting unacceptable levels of damage even after absorbing a surprise attack, general war between them and their allies became infeasible. In addition, because no one could guarantee that even a small war in Europe or elsewhere involving Americans and Russians would not escalate into a larger and possibly nuclear one, it became necessary for Washington and Moscow to impose some restraint on the military provocations of their allies. Limited wars had to be sealed off from any direct U.S.-Soviet military engagement. The nuclear stalemate also inhibited the spread of nuclear weapons to non-nuclear states during the Cold War, as the Americans and Russians joined with other members of the nuclear club in support of the Nuclear Non-Proliferation Treaty and other measures to limit the spread of weapons of mass destruction.

Politics, on the other hand, also *enabled* interest in coercive military strategy. It did so in two ways. First, the international system was basically bipolar in its distribution of military capability; only the United

States and the Soviet Union were "superpowers" capable of global military influence and war fighting. Two could comprehend one another's policies and strategies at a faster rate and with fewer misunderstandings than could many. Second, politics enabled coercive military strategy because of the education about crisis management and limited war that took place, especially on the part of the Americans and the Soviets, between 1946 and 1990. Although the Cold War adversaries did not always learn the same lessons, a set of norms and expectations developed over time that helped to keep both Washington and Moscow well shy of a direct shooting war between their combatant forces. The same lessons about crisis management and limited war also helped both the United States and the Soviet Union to avoid any outbreak of accidental or inadvertent nuclear war.

In contrast to the period between 1946 and 1990, the post-Cold War years have already reversed the relationship between technology and politics pertinent to military strategy.

Now politics *compels* or requires an interest in coercive military strategy. The end of the Cold War and the demise of the Soviet Union virtually eliminate the threat of global war or general war in Europe. At the same time, a larger variety of small wars, including wars resulting from failed states, dots the international landscape. Even for great powers, then, future wars are likely to emphasize the *coercive* use of military power.

The coercive, but effective, use of military power was the problem that the United Nations and NATO failed to solve in the former Yugoslavia from 1992 through 1995 until the Dayton peace accord of December, 1995, and NATO's undertaking of Operation Joint Endeavour in Bosnia. Russia's military embarrassment in Chechnya never did solve the same problem, as indicated by Russian acquiescence in 1996 to a peace agreement leaving open the political future of Chechnya. Studies of "failed" states show that regimes that lose legitimacy (the sense of rightful rule accepted by the population) also frequently lose the ability to employ force selectively.[18] Lawful use of force descends into praetorianism and profiteering on the part of armed factions, including those who are in theory charged with the responsibility for order and public safety. Post-Cold War examples in 1997 included Zaire (renamed Democratic Republic of the Congo after the ouster of former President Mobutu Sese Seko), Cambodia, and Sierra Leone.

Table 1
Compelling and Enabling Factors in Coercive Military Strategy

	Compelling Factors	Enabling Factors
Cold War	Unwinnability of nuclear war Fear of nuclear weapons spread	Bipolarity focuses U.S. and Soviet attention on one another Nuclear learning/ crisis management
Post-Cold War	Growing number of small wars, including civil wars Need for operations other than war	Technology for precision guidance and command/ control, reconnaissance, and surveillance

Source: Author

If politics compels interest in coercive military strategy, technology now *enables* it. Operation Desert Storm previewed emerging and future technologies of the first-rank militaries: precision long-range weapons; superior reconnaissance, rapidly turned into information for prompt attack; improved intelligence and command and control systems; stealthy weapons-delivery platforms; and other not-entirely-foreseeable technologies and military applications based on a wide-ranging information revolution. This "Revolution in Military Affairs" (RMA) will, according to experts, make possible the accomplishment of military objectives with more discrete force and less collateral damage to unintended or incidental targets.[19] The revolution in precision weapons and in C4ISR (Command, Control, Communications, Computers, Intelligence, Surveillance, and Reconnaissance) may make it possible for one side in a future military conflict to obtain a comprehensive picture of the war on land, in the air, and at sea while denying vital information of the same sort to its opponent.[20]

Table 1 summarizes the preceding discussion about environmental factors and their probable impacts upon the level of interest in coercive military strategy.

Throughout this study I discuss various prominent components of

Table 2
Types of Coercive Diplomacy v. Deterrence/Compellence
(George model)

Deterrence	Coercive Diplomacy Type 1	Coercive Diplomacy Type 2	Coercive Diplomacy Type 3
Persuade opponent not to initiate action	Persuade opponent to stop before accomplishing goal (compellence?)	Persuade opponent to undo action already begun (compellence?)	Persuade opponent to make changes in government or regime

Source: George, "Coercive Diplomacy: Definition and Characteristics," 9.

coercive military strategy, particularly "coercive diplomacy," "deterrence," and "compellence." These possible parts of any coercive military strategy must not be confused with the whole. Although each of these has stood alone as the subject of important theoretical and policy studies, I am presenting them here within a more general framework for analysis.

For example, the following chapters make repeated mention of *coercive diplomacy* as an instrument of crisis management. As Alexander L. George has explained it, coercive diplomacy is a strictly *defensive* strategy intended to accomplish one of three possible objectives: (1) to persuade an opponent to *stop* an action already in progress short of its accomplished purpose; (2) to convince the opponent to *undo* or retract an action already taken or a commitment previously made; or (3) to persuade an opponent to make changes in its *government or regime* in order to accomplish the defender's political objective (table 2).[21]

George excludes deterrence from his types of coercive diplomacy. *Deterrence* aims to persuade potential or actual opponents not to *begin* actions that they are thought to be considering, but have not yet undertaken.[22] And, although its meaning is very similar to his definition of "type A" and "type B" coercive diplomacy, George prefers not to use the term *compellence* because compellence "implies exclusive or heavy reliance on coercive threats, whereas I wish to emphasize the possibility of a more flexible diplomacy that can employ rational persuasion and accommodation as well as coercive threats to encourage the adversary either to comply with the demands or to work out an acceptable compromise."[23]

These distinctions are suitable for George's purposes, but in his theory, coercive diplomacy offers an *alternative* to military action. If force is used in coercive diplomacy, it takes the form of "an exemplary or symbolic use of limited military action" to help persuade the opponent to back down.[24] By "exemplary" George means "just enough force of an appropriate kind to demonstrate resolution" and "to give credibility to the threat that greater force will be used if necessary."[25]

My concept of coercive military strategy includes, but is not limited to, coercive diplomacy. *Coercive military strategy* shares with coercive diplomacy the explicit mixture of political and military actions toward the end of conflict termination or victory, but I would include some "deterrence" and "compellence" as well as some uses of conventional military action within the compass of coercive military *strategy*. My preference for being so inclusive is captured nicely in Robert Jervis' discussion of the problem of crisis instability:

> A decision maker with even a modicum of sanity will prefer even a very unsatisfactory peace to war, but this choice might not be available. In a crisis of unprecedented severity, one may come to believe that the choice is between war right now and war in the immediate future, between a war one's own state starts and a war the other side initiates. If the former is seen as preferable to the latter, war can result even though both sides want to avoid it.[26]

In his discussion of the ends and means of military action, Clausewitz explains that destruction of the enemy's combat force is not always the object of military action. But even when it is not, the military potential to bring about such destruction lies in the *background* of all prewar and wartime calculation:

> The combat is the single activity in War; in the combat the destruction of the enemy opposed to us is the means to the end; it is so even when the combat does not actually take place, because in that case there lies at the root of the decision

the supposition at all events that this destruction is to be re-garded as beyond doubt.[27]

Coercive military strategy is also more inclusive than coercive diplomacy because the latter implies a preference for de-escalation of the pace and scope of fighting: coercive military strategy is *open-ended* as to whether it is better to escalate, or to de-escalate, in order to accomplish policy objectives. For example, I argue that one of the dilemmas of peace operations, including UN peace enforcement or peace imposition as in Bosnia, is that it is sometimes necessary to escalate immediately with large troop deployments and stiff diplomatic démarches in order to bring about later reduced tension and fighting.

There is an explicit or implicit threat of coercion in all military strategy. And successful diplomacy is often backed by the credible threat of military action, as in the Dayton peace accords on Bosnia in December, 1995. Drawing the line between coercive and noncoercive actions in coercive military strategy is therefore somewhat arbitrary. Table 3 offers some examples about the moving line between coercive and noncoercive uses of force.

In addition to making clear the distinction between coercive military strategy and coercive diplomacy, I also want to distinguish coercive military strategy from deterrence. Deterrence and coercion are related: each is a kind of influence process intended to affect the behavior of another state or nonstate actor. But the primary intended effects of deterrence and coercion differ in important ways. As Robert A. Pape has explained, deterrence seeks to maintain the status quo by preventing an action that someone might otherwise undertake. Coercion, on the other hand, is an effort to make an opponent alter behavior that is already taking place.[28] I would not draw such a hard-and-fast line between deterrence and coercion. But the distinction between deterrence as a relatively passive and status-quo-oriented form of coercion, in contrast to other more assertive, and more risky, forms of coercion, is fair. Coercive military strategy borrows from any combination of deterrence and coercion as called for by political and military objectives and by the nature of the situation.

According to Pape, strategies for military coercion can be divided into strategies of punishment, risk, denial, and decapitation. *Punishment* campaigns attempt to raise the cost of continued resistance to one side's

Table 3
Coercive and Non-Coercive Uses of Armed Force

Basically Coercive	Basically Non-Coercive
Information warfare (offensive) (e.g., attacking another state's computers, communications and command/control systems, including netwar and cyberwar)	**Information warfare (defensive)** (e.g., protecting one's computers, communications, and command/control systems from disruption or destruction)
Coercive bargaining/compellence (e.g., Kennedy's imposition of a blockade against Soviet missle shipments to Cuba in 1962)	**Civic action** (e.g., construction of roads, schools, and hospitals)
Ultimata (e.g., Kennedy's insistence upon removal of the Soviet missiles by a certain deadline)	**Plate glass window** (e.g., interpose neutral force between or near combatants to prevent renewal of fighting or war-widening, as in the UN's numerous buffer-zone forces during the Cold War)
Maneuvers accompanied by threat (e.g., U.S. and Soviets during several Berlin crises)	**Demonstrations not accompanied by explicit or strong threat of actual war** (e.g., reconnaissance intrusive and apparent to the state being watched; some movements of naval forces near the vicinity of conflict to establish "presence")
Faits accomplis (e.g., incursion of forces into territory previously off limits, as in Hitler's invasion of Rhineland)	**Military diplomacy** (e.g., confidence building measures to increase transparency against surprise attack or cheating on arms control agreements)

Source: Classifications are the author's. The taxonomy is influenced by: Schelling, *Arms and Influence,* 69–108; George, "Strategies for Crisis Management"; Cohen and Gooch, *Military Misfortunes;* George and Simons, *The Limits of Coercive Diplomacy,* esp. chaps. 1 and 2; Arquilla Ronfeldt, *Cyberwar Is Coming!;* and Waller, "Onward Cyber Soldiers." See also Cimbala, "Military Persuasion and the American Way of War."

demands by inflicting direct or indirect suffering on civilians. Like punishment strategies, *risk* strategies target the civilian economy and society in order to coerce the opponent's government, but whereas punishment strategies inflict sudden and comprehensive attacks, risk strategies emphasize the gradual increase of punishment, and the promise of more to come. *Denial* strategies seek to coerce an opponent by demonstrating one's ability to defeat the opponent's military strategy in battle, and thereby one's ability to deny the opponent's political and military objectives at an acceptable cost to the coercer. Finally, *decapitation* strategies attempt to either (1) kill or to overthrow top leaders in the hope that their successors will be more willing to stop fighting; or (2) inflict sufficient destruction on the opponent's military command and control system that effective prosecution of a coordinated war effort becomes impossible.[29]

One of the important issues raised by this taxonomy is to identify the conditions under which one form of coercive military strategy or another may be employed most successfully. One would anticipate, for example, that denial strategies would be more applicable to conventional warfare than to nuclear crisis management; risk and punishment strategies, more suited to nuclear crisis management than to conventional campaigns.[30] As Bernard Brodie notes, with regard to the Cuban missile crisis of October, 1962:

> From beginning to end, the confrontation that we call the Cuban missile crisis—the most acute crisis of any we have had since World War II—shows a remarkably different quality from any previous one in history. There is an unprecedented candor, direct personal contact, and at the same time mutual respect between the chief actors. Normal diplomatic formalities of language and of circumlocution are disregarded. Both sides at once agree that their quarrel *could* lead to nuclear war, which is impossible to contemplate and which would leave no winner.[31]

III. PLAN OF THE STUDY

Chapter 1 explains how the United States came gradually, and grudgingly, to a greater awareness of the significance of coercive military strategy. The evolution of U.S. strategy for limited war from Korea to the Gulf War of 1991 was not a history of cumulative progress. Although the Korean War indicated a need for rethinking the entire problem of limited war, its stalemated outcome diminished its appeal as a source of lessons for the future. U.S. thinking about coercive military strategy instead came predominantly from another source: concerns about controlling the risks of nuclear war or escalation. The United States was thus no better equipped to apply coercive military strategy to conventional war fighting in Vietnam than it had been in Korea. The outcome of the Gulf War of 1991 did not accomplish all U.S. and allied war aims, but it did demonstrate that the United States' policy and military establishments had learned some valuable lessons about fighting a limited conventional war in a single theater of operations. And President George Bush also handled the diplomacy attendant to limited war better than did his predecessors Harry Truman and Lyndon Johnson.

Chapter 2 considers the Cuban missile crisis and its significance for students of coercive military strategy. This is much plowed terrain, and I accept more or less the conventional wisdom about the crisis handed down by those who have made a career of studying it. My own purpose is to ask more specific questions. There is no doubt of the success of U.S. coercive diplomacy, one aspect of coercive military strategy, in the Cuban missile crisis.

But the story is more complicated than that. The crisis appears much more manageable and U.S. and Soviet behavior much more restrained to *post facto* readers than it did to participants and real-time observers. It was a dangerous confrontation between two opponents that had not yet taken advantage of the nuclear "learning" that decades of arms control negotiations and political détente would teach. The United States and the Soviet Union learned the rudiments of coercive military strategy "on the street" in those tense thirteen days of October, 1962. Each was required to comprehend under duress the apparent motives of the other, and each political leadership was forced to confront *explicitly* the relationship between its own military standard operating procedures and the (sometimes contradictory) requirements of coercive military strategy.

In Chapter 3 I consider the Gulf War of 1991 as an example of some U.S. and allied success in applying coercive military strategy. Iraq's military forces were expelled from Kuwait and Kuwait's sovereignty restored. The more ambitious objectives of dislodging Saddam Hussein from power in Baghdad, of destroying or rendering inoperative all of his most modern armored forces, or of completely eliminating all of Iraq's nuclear weapons manufacturing complex, were not accomplished. These objectives were not necessary to the American administration's strategy, nor to that of its allies. The first objective, in particular, was not one in which other members of the coalition would have joined; President Bush placed coalition unity ahead of an enhanced politico-military aim and the additional operations needed to achieve that aim. The coalition waged a war of limited political aim within a single theater of military action. Within that theater, maximum, but coercive and carefully targeted, force was permitted to U.S. commanders.

The successful use of coercive strategy in the Gulf War was in contrast to the unsuccessful application of U.S. military power in Vietnam. Coercion was important but hardly recognized for what it was in most assessments of U.S. Gulf War strategy. In contrast, coercive military strategy has been assigned a significant amount of blame for the inability of U.S. policymakers to achieve their aims in Vietnam. The critique has some merit, as Chapter 4 explains, if coercive strategy is equated with a gradualist approach to escalation. But coercive strategy and military gradualism are not the same: coercion, as in Operation Desert Storm, can involve dramatic and sudden escalation, under the constraints of a particular policy objective and within the confines of a specific theater of operations. In addition, the complaint of gradualism against U.S. strategy in Vietnam carries small weight compared to the more fundamental conceptual and operational problems in U.S. strategy and policy formulation. U.S. policy vacillated among conflicting objectives that were never clearly explained to the public or consensually understood within the government. U.S. military strategy emphasized the conventional aspects of war fighting, especially battlefield attrition, in contrast to the less tangible but decisive sociopolitical and cultural contexts within which the fighting took place.

The case against gradualism in Vietnam is, if valid, an argument against the limitation placed upon U.S. policy objectives there, and not a correct indictment of the performance of the U.S. armed forces. The U.S. Army can be truly said to have been given a "mission impossible" by being expected to defeat an insurgency in South Vietnam aided by North Vietnam while the U.S. president attempted to conduct "business as usual" in domestic politics and in other foreign policy matters. Nor, in contrast to the claims of some critics, would a sudden campaign of annihilation against North Vietnam have brought about a solution to the conflict consistent with declared U.S. policy objectives. The U.S. objective in Vietnam did not include conquest and postwar occupation of Indochina, nor the plausible risk of war with China and Russia.

In Chapter 4, however, I make the harder argument. Even if permissive international conditions had favored a more escalatory strategy in Vietnam, U.S. leaders were driven by fundamental politico-strategic misconceptions about war and politics. I use the views of former Secretary of Defense Robert S. McNamara, shared with other high Kennedy and Johnson officials, to illustrate the argument about political and military misconceptions, including misconceptions about coercion.

The problem of collective security is bound up with the definition of coercive military strategy. In Chapter 5, I explain how historical approaches to collective security, and probable future approaches, must make use of coercive strategy. Collective security occurs either on the "concert" model of a standing committee of the great powers, or on the "balancing" model of ad hoc coalitions called together against individual cases of aggression. Collective security can only work if the power of revisionist states is weak relative to that of those states favoring the status quo. Either concert or balance of power (alliance) approaches to collective security depend upon a coalition of the willing to take charge of restoring peace and order.

Few, if any, circumstances exist under which members of such coalitions will make open-ended commitments. Coalition management of collective security must take place in an environment that assumes coercive, and contingent, contributions from relevant members. This makes all the harder the decision when and whether to escalate or to threaten overwhelming force against aggressors. The contingent character of coalition management makes equally difficult the pacing of deescalation in order to bring interstate conflicts or civil wars to a conclusion satisfactory to all parties, as apparent in Bosnia from 1992 until the Dayton peace agreement of December, 1995.

One test of whether collective security will succeed or fail in the post-Cold War world is whether the leading states can collaborate in peace operations, including those peace operations requiring the use of coercive military strategies. In Chapter 6, I consider the problems presented by military operations "other than war," especially for the United States and other democratic and developed military powers in the post-Cold War international security environment. The problems group themselves into several main categories. First, operations other than war involve U.S. or other military forces in complex sociopolitical milieus that defy easy intelligence gathering, test military professional mindsets, and compound the fog of war with additional cultural barriers to understanding. Second, the "enemy" or opponent in peacekeeping or other nonwar operations is a set of activities to be deterred or overturned, not a group or force as such. Third, publics and media have a hard time understanding and explaining this kind of conflict and the role of U.S. or other external interventionary forces.

In the concluding chapter, I summarize the findings of preceding chapters and draw inferences about the wider implications of those findings for the place of coercive military strategy in war and politics.

1

The Cold War and U.S. Limited War Strategy

The Cold War has ended, but the intellectual legacy of the intensive, bipolar U.S.-Soviet competition between 1946 and 1990 remains. For U.S. and allied leaders, nuclear weapons technology created a compelling interest in both ways to limit war and military strategy involving the calibrated use, and threat, of force. The Cold War demanded of U.S. leaders an untested capacity for the coercive application of military power, and they groped about for the handles of an effective strategy of military limitation appropriate to the context of a bipolar, nuclear world. It was a clear case of on-the-job training, and very much against Americans' instinctive way of war.[1] Success, as explained below, was elusive.

This chapter explores some of the challenges presented by limited war to U.S. political leaders, military planners, and academic strategists caught off-guard by the unexpected milieu of Cold War. The chapter begins with a mostly chronological review of the story from Korea through the Gulf War of 1991. The chapter continues with a consideration of the United States' Cold War experience, the lessons U.S. leaders learned from that experience, and what that learning may portend for the future.

I. THE COLD WAR AND U.S. LIMITED WAR STRATEGY

After World War II, the United States' extension of peacetime defense commitments to Western Europe and decision to station permanent American garrisons there formed a politico-military strategy for Cold War competition. But that strategy also froze the status quo in the center of Europe, thereby reducing the risk of inadvertent war between the

United States and the Soviets.[2] The North Atlantic Treaty Organization (NATO) came to symbolize both the absence of proclivities among the British, French, and Germans to fight with one another and the presence of the United States should Europe's calm be threatened by another aspiring hegemon. Although the fact is still not fully appreciated even now, NATO's early political roles were as important as its military task of deterring Soviet attack.

Most U.S. foreign-policy leaders did not anticipate another actual shooting war during the latter 1940s or early 1950s. What they expected, as George F. Kennan had predicted, was the slow squeeze of Kremlin pressure against American and allied interests both directly, as in the Berlin crisis of 1948, and through surrogates. What they did not expect, however, was that one of those surrogates would be Korea. The eruption of North Korea's forces across the 38th parallel in June, 1950, began an improbable war for which American strategic planners had scarcely prepared. Believing that any global war against the Soviet Union would begin in Europe, U.S. planners had given little consideration to the possibility of American involvement in limited wars supported by the Soviet leadership but fought by other governments and forces outside of Europe.

Shortly before the outbreak of hostilities in Korea, the Truman administration had completed NSC-68, a high-level policy study calling for major U.S. rearmament in view of an imminent Soviet military threat.[3] At that time the administration had found it difficult to convince Congress that the United States should commence a military buildup, including a rapid expansion of the U.S. nuclear arsenal. Now, however, U.S. defense spending shot across the previous ceilings imposed by the Truman administration. The Chinese entry into the war further convinced many Americans that a Sino-Soviet bloc now threatened U.S. global interests.

Korea posed strategic and policy-making dilemmas in Washington, and the Truman administration's decision to fight a limited war was controversial on several grounds. The U.S. field commander, Gen. Douglas MacArthur, chafed at political restrictions on military operations. Truman neglected to ask for a formal declaration of war against North Korea or against China after Chinese troops later entered the fighting on the Korean peninsula (thereby setting a precedent for commitment of U.S. forces to limited war without a Congressional declaration of war, a precedent that would be repeated to disastrous effect in Vietnam). And although the war was fought under the auspices of a UN collective security operation, it was not exemplary of truly multilateral collective security operations, because it was in fact a U.S. military operation terminated according to U.S. requirements. Thus the Korean War provided no model for future uses of U.S. military power on behalf of collective security missions. To the contrary, the Korean War led to the militarization of containment and to the hardening of Cold War fault lines between the communist and capitalist worlds.

American military thought and doctrine treated the Korean War as an exception and an aberration, and drew few appropriate lessons from it about how to fight a limited war. In fact, the greater availability of nuclear weapons during the Eisenhower administration supported a U.S. policy shift to a declared strategy for a general war of massive retaliation. While administration officials were eventually forced to retreat from this formulation in cases of less-than-total war, Eisenhower's defense planning for global war against the Soviet Union relied mainly upon massive and promptly delivered air atomic offensives. NATO's declared objective of ninety-six active-duty and reserve divisions was far beyond any commitment its members were actually willing or able to provide, which made reliance on nuclear weapons for extended deterrence all the more necessary as a result of allied as well as U.S. domestic budgetary priorities.

The U.S. Army emerged from the 1950s as the fourth wheel of a defense establishment whose preferred military doctrines favored the more technical and less manpower-intensive services. Army officials chafed at the allocation of defense resources within arbitrary ceilings and under planning assumptions favoring air force and navy procurement. Special study committees such as the Gaither Committee pointed to the need for a larger menu of military responses, and under the new Kennedy administration things began to change. Kennedy preferred the strategy known as *flexible response,* which sought to raise the nuclear threshold in Europe by calling for improved U.S. conventional forces for crisis response, forward presence, and, if necessary, actual fighting. This last rationale was pushed hard within NATO by Kennedy's secretary of defense, Robert McNamara, to the detriment of alliance solidarity on doctrine until the French departure from NATO's military command structure in 1966 and the promulgation of flexible response in 1967. Although flexible response arguably allowed a greater role for the ground forces in U.S. military doctrine and force planning, the lines between Cold War "east" and "west" had solidified by the time it became official NATO doctrine, at which point neither side seemed interested in even limited probes against the other.

Civilian and military strategists, as well as some policymakers who recognized the inappropriateness of massive retaliation for other than all-out nuclear war, struggled during the latter 1950s and early 1960s to define a concept of selective military strategy more suited to the variety of challenges to U.S. security, a strategy that would become known as *limited war* strategy. Robert Endicott Osgood, for example, called for increased sophistication in U.S. academic and public understanding of the requirements of limited war in the nuclear age.[4] Henry A. Kissinger, an academic strategist who was later to serve as National Security Advisor to President Richard M. Nixon and as Nixon's Secretary of State, examined the potential role of nuclear weapons in U.S. limited war strategy.[5] Thomas C. Schelling applied bargaining theory to the study of military strategy in several influential works.[6] William W. Kaufmann explained the military strategy of the Kennedy administration as an effort to provide an extended menu of military options even for nuclear war.[7] Maxwell Taylor, writing as former U.S. Army chief of staff, critiqued Eisenhower's strategy as negligent of preparedness for limited war and as insufficiently attentive to the needs of U.S. ground forces.[8] These and other varieties of limited war theory were not without shortcomings, however. As Robert A. Doughty and his coauthors noted:

> Limited-war theory had numerous flaws. It was primarily an academic, rather than a military concept, and it drastically misunderstood the dynamics of war. Its authors seemed to say that since limited war was mainly about bargaining and diplomacy, it required no knowledge of military matters and indeed military considerations should not affect its conduct. . . . In terms of bargaining theory, moreover, they [limited war theorists] assumed a greater capacity than was warranted on the part of a gigantic bureaucracy like the United States government to send clear, precise signals, and

they reduced the behavior of potential enemies to that of laboratory rats.[9]

If strategic deadlock reigned in Europe, Khrushchev's insistence that wars of national liberation should be unleashed against Third World regimes supportive of U.S. policy called forth from the Kennedy administration a burst of doctrinal innovations. "Special operations" and what would be later be called "low-intensity conflict studies" led to an emphasis on subconventional warfare, with psychological operations and nation-building as constituent elements of U.S. military strategy.[10] But only a small minority of the armed forces officer corps, such as the Green Berets, committed themselves to careers along these lines. The more traditional services lacked serious interest in special operations and regarded their counterinsurgency brethren with undisguised distaste. In Vietnam, as the U.S. commitment escalated well beyond the engagement of special operations forces and intelligence operatives, conventional military mind-sets displaced the political side of the politico-military equation on which special operations had been predicated. U.S. conventional forces in Vietnam, on the evidence, fought well against North Vietnamese conventional forces and Viet Cong units when the latter were willing to stand and fight pitched battles.

However, by 1968, it had become apparent even to the Department of Defense that the United States could not win the counterinsurgency or conventional wars at an acceptable cost; Lyndon Johnson's resignation and Nixon's phased disengagement followed. Having decided that it was necessary in South Vietnam for the United States to escalate from limited commitment to a major U.S. military campaign, Johnson nonetheless sought to balance the requirement for military escalation against his other priorities in domestic politics, especially his cherished Great Society programs recently passed by Congress. Johnson's "guns and butter" policy filled armed forces enlisted personnel requirements by expanded draft calls instead of mobilizing the reserves. The result of this approach was to create nationwide dissent against the war first across U.S. college campuses, and then more widely.

The domestic turbulence on the home front, in part due to Johnson's lack of any apparent strategy for victory, brought U.S. military escalation in Vietnam to a stopping point. When U.S. Commander-in-Chief

William Westmoreland asked for several hundred thousand additional troops in 1968, Johnson's Secretary of Defense Clark Clifford suggested that Johnson pull the plug. Johnson did so, also announcing his intention not to seek another term of office and thereby conceding the failure of U.S. policy and strategy in Vietnam. However, Johnson left the nation with a major force and policy commitment to a war that would continue without complete U.S. disengagement until 1973, and continue between the Vietnamese until 1975. Along with military disengagement from Vietnam came an examination of U.S. conscription policy; the Gates Commission's recommendation to end conscription was adopted and ordered into effect beginning in 1973. In effect, the United States had come full circle to its pre-twentieth-century peacetime standard of raising armed forces by voluntary enlistment (with the exception of the Civil War, during which both sides drafted).

The onset of the all-volunteer force coincided with post-Vietnam doctrinal revisionism. The Nixon administration changed the 1960s goal of being able to fight two and one-half wars simultaneously to that of one and one-half wars and emphasized to besieged allies that U.S. support would stop short of involving American ground forces. Voluntary enlistment dictated a strategy of selective rather than ubiquitous military engagement. Selective engagement was also facilitated by the full-blown emergence of U.S.-Soviet détente and Sino-American rapprochement during the 1970s. U.S. foreign and defense policy elites perceived that diplomatic containment of Moscow's ambitions was more cost-effective than overpromising U.S. military involvement in regional conflicts. U.S. and Soviet leaders worked to stabilize the Middle East and to create new expectations about their mutual interests in avoiding nuclear war and inadvertent military escalation. In addition, under the direction of Chief of Staff Gen. Creighton Abrams, army planners during the early 1970s implemented the "total force" concept so that future presidents could not avoid substantial reserve callups during any national mobilization for war.[11]

U.S. military planners who contemplated how to prevail in a war between NATO and the Warsaw Pact, and who were confounded by the commingling of conventional and nuclear forces in Europe, found a more amenable theater of operations for the application of U.S. military power in the Gulf War of 1991. A five-month period of grace for military buildup in Saudi Arabia did no harm to U.S. readiness for war in January, 1991, and U.S. air-land battle doctrine played successfully before a packed house. The results of the Gulf War seemed to vindicate not only U.S. conventional military strategy and technology, but also the decision in favor of the all-volunteer force taken decades earlier. Columnist Charles Krauthammer, rejecting arguments of U.S. "decline," and celebrating the "unipolar moment" in which the United States had allegedly found itself by virtue of the collapse of the Soviet Union, noted that

> in 1950 the U.S. engaged in a war with North Korea: it lasted three years, cost 54,000 American lives, and ended in a draw. Forty-one years later, the U.S. engaged in a war with Iraq: it lasted six weeks, cost 196 American lives, and ended in a rout. If the Roman Empire had declined at this rate, you would be reading this in Latin.[12]

Experts, however, recognized the ironic character of the vindication of U.S. strategy. The Bush administration had already commenced a defense builddown prior to Iraq's attack on Kuwait; revisions resulting from Clinton's "Bottom-Up Review" would diminish active-duty forces even more. Table 4 summarizes U.S. military active and reserve personnel and strengths from 1987 through 1997 (as projected in 1996).

U.S. forces were nevertheless required, according to Clinton national military strategy published in 1996, to deter or, if necessary, to fight with allies and "decisively win" in two "nearly simultaneous" major regional conflicts (MRCs).[13] The option of fighting and holding on one front while prevailing on another, the initially proffered one-and-one-half or "win-hold-win" strategy first adumbrated by Clinton's Secretary of Defense Les Aspin, was shot down by Pentagon and Congressional opponents. Some dubbed it "win-lose-lose" or "win-hold-oops."[14] In addition, the Congress and some politico-military strategists in the executive branch were also planning to employ U.S. military capability for nontraditional or noncombat missions, including operations designed to preserve sanctuary from attack for besieged ethnic or national populations (such as Operation Provide Comfort for the Kurds in Iraq). As well, both Bush and Clinton strategies for more traditional uses of U.S. military power emphasized the performance of forward-presence and crisis-response missions intended for regional contingency operations

Table 4
Department of Defense Personnel
(End of Fiscal Year, in Thousands)

	FY 1987	FY 1996	FY 1997	Percent Change 1987–97
Active Military	2,174	1,482	1,457	–33
Army	781	495	495	–37
Navy	587	424	407	–31
Marine Corps	199	174	174	–13
Air Force	607	388	381	–37
Selected Reserves	1,151	931	901	–19
DOD Civilians	1,133	841	807	–27

Source: Adapted from Perry, *Annual Report to the President and the Congress,* 254, table V-4.

outside of Europe, not for global warfare or for large interstate wars within Europe.

Some experts contended that the Clinton defense program based on Aspin's Bottom-Up Review was already underfunded by 1995, placing an expected crimp in future modernization and other aspects of support necessary for the strategy of two nearly simultaneous MRCs.[15] Real (inflation-adjusted) Department of Defense spending between 1990 and 1995 had fallen by 25 percent, around $85 billion in 1995 dollars. The Clinton Future Years Defense Program (FYDP), introduced in February, 1994, proposed cutting real defense spending by another ten percent between 1995 and 1999: a 1995–99 reduction of about $25 billion. If enacted exactly as proposed, the February, 1994, FYDP would have decreased the share of U.S. gross domestic product devoted to national security to 2.9 percent—the lowest share of GDP devoted to national security since before World War II.[16] In December, 1994, the Clinton administration asked Congress for an additional $25 billion for defense in the period 1996–2001; of this, some $10 billion would be spent during the 1996–99 period against any shortfall. This and other proposed adjustments to the original FYDP would, according to the Congressional Budget Office, reduce its estimate of the DOD shortfall to around $47 billion, about four percent of total planned spending in 1995–99.[17] The U.S. military force structure projected for September, 1997, and expected to meet the requirements for two nearly simultaneous MRCs (compared to earlier baseline years), is summarized in table 5.

II. U.S. MILITARY CHOICES AND THE FUTURE

According to military historian Martin Van Creveld, large-scale conventional war is mostly obsolete; the future of warfare lies in low-intensity conflict, terrorism, and the like.[18] The reasons are that large-scale warfare does not pay political and military dividends relative to its costs. Van Creveld argues that this trend represents the dismantling of the Clausewitzian paradigm that dominated military-strategy formation from the Peace of Westphalia until the end of the Second World War. In Clausewitz's model of the relationship between war and policy, a trinitarian unity among people, government, and army support the conduct of war on behalf of state interests. War is something done on behalf of the state, and only on behalf of the state. The adoption of this model was an important marker in Western military and political history, for it made possible, along with the political theories of Machiavelli and Hobbes, the "realist" tradition in international politics that informed generations of scholars and students.

This prejudgment of the obsolescence of Clausewitz's theory of war, and the assumption that the territorial state is headed for the ash heap of military history, should not be accepted without question. Clausewitz's great work, *Vom Kriege* (*On War*), is not "theory" in the form of a list of timeless axioms or answers about war. Its theory is, instead, a set of guiding questions for instruction. Clausewitz's purpose is to open the mind of the soldier to the subtleties of the scholar, and that of the scholar to the uncertainties and hard realities of soldiering. Clausewitz's description of the essence of war as consisting of violence, chance, and reason thus remains pertinent to the conduct of war in modern times, whether by state or nonstate actors.[19] Nor does his insistence upon the subordi-

Table 5
U.S. Conventional Force Structure (Selected Years, Compared with "Bottom-Up Review" [BUR])

	1990	1993	1995	1997	BUR
Land Forces					
Army divisions					
Active	18	14	12	10	10
Reserve[a]	10	8	8	8	5 or more
Marine Corps divisions[b]	4	4	4	4	4
Naval Forces					
Battleforce ships	546	435	373	357	346
Aircraft carriers					
Active	15	13	11	11	11
Reserve	1	0	1	1	1
Navy carrier air wings					
Active	13	11	10	10	10
Reserve	2	2	1	1	1
Air Forces					
Tactical fighter wings					
Active	24	16	13	13	13
Reserve	12	11	7	7	7
Airlift Aircraft					
Inter-theater[c]	400	382	374	345	
Intra-theater	460	380	428	430	no goal set

Source: Adapted from U.S. Congressional Budget Office, *Reducing the Deficit: Spending and Revenue Options,* 99, table 3–1.

[a] Army reserve totals exclude 15 enhanced-readiness brigades.
[b] Marine Corps totals include one reserve Marine Corps division.
[c] Stated as 49–52 million ton-miles per day of transport capability.

nation of military ends and means to policy lose any of its relevance, even if the monopoly of the state over the use of violence has become less habit-forming after the Cold War.[20]

Two points are noteworthy here. First, the monopoly of the territorial state over the *legitimate* use of military force is not the same as its ability to monopolize *all* uses of force. State assertions of legal monopoly have coexisted with antistatist and other violence on the part of individuals and groups, notwithstanding state claims to the exclusive right to use military power. Internal wars of various descriptions, including rebellions intended to overthrow the state itself, have contested the legitimacy of states and their military monopolies since the very founding of the modern state system.

Second, it is not entirely clear that wars between states have been supplanted by wars within states, if the criterion being used is one of the overall significance for the international system as a whole. It cannot be denied that, since 1945, there have been many more wars within states than between states.[21] The incidence of interstate and domestic wars per state and by region from 1945 to 1995 is summarized in table 6.

But it cannot be inferred from the greater *frequency* of internal wars that states are less important *politically.* In some ways, the rising frequency of intrastate wars is testimony to the growing, not weakening, significance of states as international actors. Many of these intrastate wars have resulted from the desire for a state of their own by ethnonational, religious, and other groups who feel displaced within the confines of their existing political order; Palestinians and Kurds provide excellent contemporary examples. The state is not suffering from apparent lack of demand, but from insufficiency of supply relative to demand. In addition, interstate war has changed its cast of characters in the last half of the twentieth century; relatively speaking, war is no longer the resort of the great powers, but of the medium and small powers.[22] Whether this is a Cold War artifact or a more permanent feature of international politics is a subject for reasonable disagreement.

Unless the next few decades are less turbulent than many suppose, U.S. policymakers will be forced to consider the involvement of U.S. forces in both conventional and unconventional wars. These "wars" may include multinational peace operations, for which the U.S. Army has now written official doctrine. Whether future U.S. armed forces will be

Table 6
Interstate and Intrastate Wars (Per State) by Region, 1945–95

Region	Number of States	Interstate Interventions Wars	Internal/ Domestic Conflicts
Western Europe	18	0	0.16
Balkans/Eastern Europe	8	0.38	0.25
Former USSR	15	0	0.47
Central America/ Caribbean	20	0.20	0.50
South America	12	0.08	0.67
Africa	43	0.16	0.86
Middle East	18	0.61	1.22
South Asia	7	0.57	2.00
Southeast Asia	11	0.45	1.82
East Asia	6	0.50	0.50
Average		0.30	0.85

Source: Adapted from K. J. Holsti, *The State, War, and the State of War,* 24.

able to wage high-intensity warfare, low-intensity conflict, both, or neither is as much dependent on the American public's understanding of the American way of war as it is on military-technical issues such as force size and weapons modernization. Public perceptions of international threats are notoriously fickle, and Cold War policymakers deliberately exaggerated the degree of threat in order to obtain defense commitments from the U.S. Congress. Defense scholar Robert J. Art argues that the United States was virtually free from serious threat of invasion and conquest, slow strangulation through global blockade, or nuclear attack during the Cold War years.[23] His comparison of threats to U.S. security during three eras is summarized in table 7.[24]

Many would argue that Art's definitions of possible dangers in the Cold War and post–Cold War eras are adequate to address worst-case scenarios. But at levels of threat or potential conflict below those worst

Table 7
Threats to U.S. Security in Three Eras

Type of Threat	Geopolitical Era (pre-1945)	Cold War Era (1945–90)	Post-Cold War Era (after 1990)
Invasion and conquest	Quite difficult after 1900	Practically zero probability	Practically zero probability
Slow strangulation by global blockade	Of indeterminate feasibility	Practically zero probability	Practically zero probability
Nuclear attack from Soviet Union	N/A	Not probable	Highly improbable
Nuclear attack from states other than Soviet Union or subnational groups	N/A	Highly improbable	Not probable

Source: Art, "A Defensible Defense," 11, table 2. My slight revision of Art's category labels has no effect on his intended meaning.

cases, Cold War experience and events since 1990 offer less reassurance that other security objectives can be guaranteed at an acceptable cost. As John Lewis Gaddis has noted,

> Victories in wars—hot or cold—tend to unfocus the mind. They encourage pride, complacency, and the abandonment of calculation; the result is likely to be disproportion in the balance that always has to exist in strategy, between what one sets out to do, and what one can feasibly expect to accomplish. It can be a dangerous thing to have achieved one's objectives, because then one has to decide what to do next.[25]

Some lessons can be derived from Cold War history. One is that forces which are optimized for high-intensity conflict against industrial-strength armies cannot simply be reduced in size and reassigned to low-intensity warfare. During the 1960s and prior to the Vietnam escalation, for example, it was assumed by planners that forces adequate for war between NATO and the Warsaw Pact would easily brush aside smaller and less-heavily armed foes.[26] In contrast, it is now acknowledged that low-intensity conflict or unconventional warfare, including counterinsurgency and counterterrorism, is qualitatively different from larger-scale warfare.[27] One result of the U.S. military's experience of having been forced to face the unique environment of unconventional warfare was the reorganization of special operations forces, under Congressional prodding (see table 8).

A second lesson is that low-intensity conflicts involve ambiguous political missions for which U.S. popular support cannot be assumed, and must therefore be assiduously built. Third, the U.S. armed forces' sense of military professionalism is compromised by missions outside the competency of military training and experience.[28] Assigning to military forces the mission of "nation-building" confuses a military mission with a broader political one, to the probable detriment of both types of objectives. Nonetheless, the post-Cold War world is already witnessing U.S. military involved in a number of peacekeeping, peace-enforcement, humanitarian-assistance and other nontraditional operations.

Future war is likely to be marked by a mixture of high-technology equipment and low-technology strategy. This syncretic approach to war accepts from Clausewitz the assumption that war fought without restraint tends toward the absolute in destructiveness and borrows from Mao Zedong and Sun Tzu the notion that unconventional warfare can defeat conventional warfare under favorable social, political, and economic conditions.[29] Ironically, unconventional warfare in some ways betters fulfills Clausewitz's observation about the relationship between policy and force than does conventional war. Few who experienced Vietnam would now argue, even if they had prior-to-U.S.-involvement in that conflict, that counterrevolutionary wars are more military than they are political.[30] In revolutionary wars, as Sam C. Sarkesian notes,

> the people of the indigenous area compose the true battleground. Clausewitzian notions and high-tech military capability are usually irrelevant in unconventional conflicts.

Table 8
U.S. Special Operations Command Organization

Headquarters U.S. Special Operations Command (USSOCOM) Macdill AFB, Fla.			
U.S. Army Component HQ Army Special Operations Command, **Ft. Bragg, N.C.**	U.S. Navy Component HQ Naval Special Warfare Command, **Coronado Naval Amphibious Base, Calif.**	U.S. Air Force Component HQ Air Force Special Operations Command, **Hurlburt Field, Fla.**	Joint Special Operations Command, **Ft. Bragg, N.C.**
Special Forces Groups	Naval Special Warfare Dev Groups	Special Operations Wings	
Ranger Units	Naval Special Warfare Groups	Special Operations Groups	
Civil Affairs Units	SEAL Teams	Special Tactics Units	
Psy Ops Units	SEAL Delivery Vehicle Teams	Weather Unit	
Aviation Units	Special Boat Units	Central Flight Training	
Signal and Other Support Units	Special Warfare Units	U.S. Air Force Special Operations School	
John F. Kennedy Special Warfare Center and School	Naval Special Warfare Center		

Note: USSOCOM also has a Washington, D.C. office. SEAL refers to elite navy commando units (SEa, Air Land).
Source: Adapted from Cheney, *Annual Report to the Congress,* 83, and Sarkesian, "Special Operations, Low Intensity Conflict (Unconventional Conflicts), and the Clinton Defense Strategy."

> Conventional military capability and the "largest" battalions
> rarely decide the outcome. The center of gravity is in the
> political-social milieu of the indigenous populace, rather
> than in the armed forces.[31]

The need to fight syncretic wars that are simultaneously conventional
and unconventional drives U.S. military historians and planners back to
the roots of American military practice in our own Revolutionary War.
As historian Russell Weigley has noted, Gen. George Washington preferred to model the Continental Army along the lines of eighteenth-
century European military forces, fearing that irregular forces could
not be counted on against British regular forces.[32] Washington also remained wary of the potential costs to the American social fabric of
guerrilla warfare. Even his postwar efforts to shape the peacetime U.S.
armed forces favored a small regular army supported by a compulsory-
service, federally regulated militia.[33] Still, America's revolutionary war
against Britain also included successful U.S. unconventional campaigns
against British regulars, such as the guerrilla attacks on Burgoyne's lines
of communication and flanks that contributed to his defeat at
Saratoga.[34] U.S. professional military heritage from the War of 1812 was
also a mixed estate. On one side stands the Battle of New Orleans, which
showed that citizen-soldiers could fight with distinction against regular
British forces. On the other side stands the battles of Chippewa and
Lundy's Lane, in which American regulars acquitted themselves well
against their British counterparts in open-field battles without use of
unconventional tactics.[35]

The uniqueness of U.S. civil-military relations has long fueled continuing conflict between the citizen-soldier and professional-regular
traditions for staffing the armed forces. The antitheses of strategies
based on annihilation and those based on exhaustion have long contended for preeminence in U.S. military schools and in the priorities of
military planners.[36] These issues seemed to have been decided during
World War II, in which the United States and its allies successfully
combined *campaigns of annihilation* into a successful *war of exhaustion,* inflicting decisive defeat on Germany and Japan. Because wars
fought for limited aims with limited means pose special constraints on
strategy and force structure, however, the issue of preferred military

doctrine for the U.S. armed forces was called in question again by the Korean and Vietnam Wars. Insurgency was one variation of a strategy of exhaustion, and its protracted nature strained the capacity of democratic societies in both France and the United States.[37] Where local governments were sufficiently astute about maintaining popular support, U.S. support was almost superfluous; where they were not, it was useless.

The Gulf War of 1991 was either the concluding campaign of the Cold War or the first of the post-Cold War era. It was, at the operational-tactical level, a one-sided campaign of annihilation in the model of *Cannae:* crushing blows against Iraqi armed forces, command systems, and military infrastructure from the air, followed by a short ground campaign based on strategic flanking movements.[38] The need for a war of exhaustion, of the kind between Iran and Iraq during most of the 1980s, was avoided. The Gulf War demonstrated that the demise of the Soviet Union had left the United States in a unique position of undisputed conventional and military superpower.[39] No state could threaten the United States with large-scale military defeat, although arms control was still necessary to rid the former Soviet Union of most of its residual nuclear arms. If U.S. nuclear and conventional military power made it all but invulnerable to any campaign of annihilation, its maritime supremacy as of 1991 seemed to ensure against the success of any hostile war of attrition. The odor of unipolarity was indeed in the air as the Bush administration vacated the White House, but Bush initiated an ill-fated intervention in Somalia that brought American self-assessments back to earth.

A large menu of problems remained for U.S. policymakers after the end of the Cold War. Many of these problems will call for military forward presence, peacetime engagement, and other missions not previously undertaken during the Cold War fixation on a one-variant war. The end of the Cold War requires the United States to disestablish a force designed for deterrence of major coalition wars. Post-Cold War U.S. forces will be smaller in size, contingency-oriented rather than scenario-dependent, and arguably committed to peacekeeping and other collective security missions, under United Nations or other auspices.[40] According to RAND defense expert Paul K. Davis, the concept of *environment shaping* now moves to the center of adaptive U.S. defense planning:

The United States is now concerned at least as much with environment shaping (e.g., encouraging regional stability or
peaceful change, and reducing incentives for other nations to
seek superpower status) as with more traditional military
missions. Consistent with that, Cheney [Bush's Secretary of
Defense Dick Cheney] and Aspin [Clinton's first Secretary of
Defense, Les Aspin] reaffirmed the need for significant U.S.
forward presence in critical regions worldwide because of
the unique opportunities and responsibilities the nation now
has and because it is so strongly in the U.S. interest to avoid
the kinds of regional instabilities that might ensue if power
vacuums arose—e.g., a military competition among Japan,
China, and Korea in the Far East, or various worrisome possibilities in Europe.[41]

The concept of environment shaping implies that the United States
should take a combination of political and military proactive measures
to head off crises and wars before they happen. The focus of defense
planning on specific *threats* that the United States might want to *deter*
thus shifts to flexible preparedness for uncertain destabilizing *events*
that policymakers want to *avoid* or *contain*. For example, neither by itself nor in cooperation with its NATO allies could the United States
have *deterred* the outbreak of war among ethno-national communities
in former Yugoslavia in 1991–92. Nor is clear how the United States and
its allies could *deter* expansion of that war, as opposed to employing a
variety of political and military measures to avoid expansion or to contain it.

One problem with environmental shaping is that it does not necessarily require fewer forces than did Cold War preparedness. Environmental shaping presupposes some U.S. forward presence, especially
maritime, in areas of potential instability, and a variety of composite
forces with variable schemes of assembly for rapid insertion and rapid
reaction. Forces of this sort are not necessarily cheap, especially per
unit, a reality complicated by the fact that the size of U.S. forces by fiscal
year 1997, was significantly smaller than that of active duty forces in 1990
(see table 5, above).

The difficulty of using U.S. military force under any circumstances may increase, relative to Cold War precedent. For the remainder of the 1990s and in the early years of the twenty-first century, political leaders may expect to use military force in at least four kinds of situations: regional contingency operations; counterinsurgency; counter-proliferation efforts; and anti-terrorist raids to free hostages, capture terrorist leaders, or destroy identifiable bases of support for terrorist organizations. Of these, the involvement in regional contingencies has the greatest potential for prolonged fighting and high casualties. Historical U.S. experience and recent (1993) events in Somalia suggest that policymakers and military planners can count on little forgiveness from Congress or the American public once U.S. casualties begin to accumulate, especially in wars lacking obvious national interest.

A U.S. military strategy based on regional contingencies may be as controversial as the containment strategy that preceded it; implementation of a contingency-oriented strategy will involve complicated political, economic, and military decisions in the years ahead.[42] Declining U.S. defense budgets will create difficult trade-offs among the desired goals of preserving force size, modernizing weapons and C3 (Command, Control, and Communications), maintaining readiness for crisis response, and preserving sustainability for protracted conflict. Because of constrained U.S. resources, American forces will be dependent upon international coalitions for the conduct of major contingency operations, as they were in Operations Desert Shield and Desert Storm. In addition, as explained by Michael J. Mazarr and his coauthors in their study of Gulf War lessons, "to the extent that deterrent strategies form part of the response to today's threats and challenges, they will increasingly be implemented *multilaterally* and *economically*."[43] Beyond resource constraints, the experience of Desert Storm also suggests a qualitative dilemma for U.S. military planners. Precision-guided munitions, improved communications and command/control, and reconnaissance-strike complexes makes possible, in theory, the selective targeting of enemy military assets while minimizing collateral damage.[44] In practice, though, the economies and social fabrics of Third World states may be so fragile that the "precision" possible in high-technology warfare is of no meaning to those on the receiving end, nor to observers of U.S. and allied efforts. Thus, efforts to maintain specific political and military limitations in war, and to derive from those limitations carefully laid-down strike plans, could fail unavoidably and to the detriment of coalition management.[45]

CONCLUSION

The Cold War enlarged the size of peacetime U.S. armed forces and imposed unprecedented requirements for the support of U.S. policy by coercive military strategy. The United States did possess recent experience of one limited war, in Korea. However, because the Korean War was treated as an exception, no theoretical context or institutional memory for the use of coercive military strategy resulted, and U.S. planners learned few lessons on which to build a model for the fighting of future limited wars. Vietnam compounded the complexities of Korea by adding unconventional warfare, an unstable South Vietnamese government, massive discontent on the U.S. home front, and a resolute opponent. U.S. experience in the Gulf War suggests that successful military coercion requires a different combination of carrots and sticks than had been applied in earlier limited war experiences.

During the Cold War, the nature of the security environment was understood to be that of a global confrontation with the Soviet Union in the context of a bipolar international system. The focus of future U.S. defense planning may shift from threat-based deterrence to the restructuring of security environments. Uncertainty will become the norm rather than an exception in force and budget planning. Future U.S. forces will be called upon to participate in collective security operations more frequently than in the past.

2

Coercive Strategy in the Cuban Missile Crisis

Actions taken by the United States during the Cuban missile crisis were both competitive and cooperative. The United States was *competing* against the Soviet Union to achieve a favorable outcome for U.S. interests, which meant, at the very least, gaining Soviet commitment both to halt shipment of nuclear-capable delivery systems to Cuba and remove those systems already in place. But U.S. and Soviet objectives were also partly cooperative. Subsequent to the discovery of the missiles by U.S. photo-reconnaissance and U.S. President John F. Kennedy's announcement of a "quarantine" or blockade, neither Kennedy nor Soviet Premier Nikita Khrushchev wanted the crisis to escalate to the point of an actual shooting war between American and Soviet forces near Cuba. Nor did they want to risk the potential expansion of such a war into Europe, involving, as it would, both powers' allies on that continent.

In its attempts to resolve the Cuban missile crisis, the United States was forced to draw upon coercive diplomacy and other aspects of coercive military strategy.[1] Coercive military strategy was involved because the United States: (1) mobilized forces for the invasion of Cuba; (2) put its strategic nuclear forces on their largest-ever peacetime alert; and (3) instituted a naval blockade of Cuba that ran a deliberate, if calculated, risk of a confrontation on the high seas between American and Soviet naval forces. Additional components of coercive military strategy were also apparent in both sides' precrisis and crisis maneuvers, as discussed below. The United States could not extricate itself from the crisis without engaging in a degree of nuclear coercion that some crisis participants, then and later, felt unacceptably dangerous for both sides. Shared nuclear danger was like no other.

This chapter begins with a discussion of U.S. efforts to apply coercive diplomacy and coercive military strategy in Cuba, then continues with an examination of U.S. and Soviet perspectives on their own and each others' actions. The chapter concludes with a discussion of the extent to which conventional and nuclear deterrence played a part in the successful resolution of the crisis, presenting arguments and counterarguments laying out the various positions.

I. COERCIVE DIPLOMACY IN CUBA

The U.S. blockade was one aspect of the Kennedy administration's effort to apply coercive diplomacy to the situation in Cuba. According to Alexander L. George, coercive diplomacy can be used in either a less-demanding or more-demanding variant, differentiated in terms of the pressure it places upon one's adversary for compliance.[2] The less-demanding variant uses the "try and see" approach; the more-demanding type issues an ultimatum. Initially, the U.S. blockade was an example of the "try and see" approach. It served to establish Kennedy's resolve in the eyes of Khrushchev and to position the U.S. president to be able to exert additional pressure on the Soviet leader if necessary. It lacked, as is typical of the "try and see" option, two components that Kennedy was later forced to add in order to induce Soviet compliance. The first was a specific time limit for compliance; the second was an equally specific indication of what consequences would follow in the absence of compliance. The subsequent addition of these components turned the "try and see" variant into the harder or "ultimatum" form of coercive diplomacy.[3]

According to Graham T. Allison, the blockade was not sufficient to get Khrushchev to agree to withdraw the missiles until it was coupled with an *explicit* threat of an air strike or invasion on Tuesday, October 30, 1962. Khrushchev's report to the Supreme Soviet after the crisis noted that "we received information from Cuban comrades and from other sources on the morning of October 27th *directly stating* that this attack would be carried out in the next two or three days. We interpreted these cables as an *extremely alarming warning signal*."[4] The "other sources" may have included a warning given to Soviet Ambassador Anatoliy Dobrynin by Robert Kennedy on October 27, combined with a tacit assurance that following the resolution of the crisis (but *not* as an obvious U.S. concession during the crisis) the United States would remove its Jupiter missiles from Turkey.[5] Raymond L. Garthoff emphasizes the impressive size of the U.S. military buildup for possible air strikes and invasion of Cuba, the scale of which must certainly have been noticed in Moscow. The potential invasion force included one marine and five army divisions (with other marine and army reserves if necessary), or more than 100,000 army and 40,000 marine combat troops; 579 air force and navy tactical combat aircraft; and 183 navy ships, including eight aircraft carriers on station. The airborne forces ready to be dropped on the first day of the invasion (14,500) were comparable in size to the forces dropped at Normandy.[6]

The experience of U.S. decision making during the Cuban missile crisis suggests that the requirements for prudent crisis management can be in conflict with those of successful coercive diplomacy.[7] Crisis management emphasizes the need for taking escalatory steps in small stages, with allowance for opponents to reconsider their options at each stage. Successful coercive diplomacy, in contrast, may dictate a firmer and less flexible position, and on occasion a brutal ultimatum, in order to resolve the crisis on satisfactory terms. George states that the difference between the "try and see" and "ultimatum" versions of coercive diplomacy is not the same as the difference between small and large escalation; there are different models of coercion at work.[8] Perhaps so, but I argue that the United States' insistence on an ultimatum and on a knowingly dangerous blockade of Cuba (control of incidents at sea is notoriously beyond the reach of shore commanders and politicians even under the best communication conditions) pushes this encounter beyond George's model of coercive diplomacy and into coercive military strategy. By October 27 the situation (Khrushchev's stalling, the growing impatience of U.S. "hawks" within Kennedy's advisory group, and the continued work on the missiles already in Cuba) called for an ultimatum with a short fuse.

One difference between the "try and see" and "ultimatum" versions of coercive diplomacy is that the "try and see" approach is open ended with regard to available responses. Compliance may be structured as much by the creativity of the one pressured as by the explicit demands of the one who would coerce. There is room for the "bargaining space" between the two sides to be adjusted in the direction of the party being coerced. This approach thus allows for the bilateral influence of *perspective taking,* which has been shown in some research to be an important influence on the probability of reciprocal concessions in bargaining.[9] Perspective taking is the ability to adopt the opposite side's perspective in structuring one's own bargaining strategy. Researchers have found that high perspective-takers are less likely than their opposites to escalate irrelevant demands and more likely to reframe their proposals in positive terms. High perspective-takers are also more likely to have a sense of control over situational factors.[10]

Neither Kennedy nor Khrushchev had demonstrated impressive competency in perspective taking prior to October, 1962. Once the crisis got under way, however, each leader came gradually to grasp the constraints under which the other was forced to operate. Khrushchev began to appreciate more completely the domestic policy constraints under which Kennedy labored, as well as his U.S. alliance commitments to NATO, which limited the array of immediately available policy options. Kennedy, on the other hand, began to appreciate both Khrushchev's embarrassing situation (having been caught while attempting to conceal the missile deployments), and his need for a graceful exit in order to save face.

George defines coercive diplomacy to exclude deterrence. With such a definition, however, it is hard to see how the Cuban missile crisis and its outcome can be explained only as a case of diplomatic coercion. Khrushchev was certainly deterred from further escalation by the plausible threat of a prompt U.S. invasion of Cuba and by the possibility of inadvertent escalation growing out of a Cuban confrontation and leading to a full-scale U.S.-Soviet war. Kennedy's need, finally, to issue an ultimatum with a specific time limit for removal of the missiles clearly demonstrates the presence of coercive military strategy in addition to coercive diplomacy. Other aspects of the crisis, discussed below, also make clear the significance of coercive military strategy on the part of Kennedy and Khrushchev in resolving it.

II. PERSPECTIVE TAKING BEFORE AND AFTER CUBA

The U.S.-Soviet relationship throughout the Cold War years was marked by simplification on each side of the political objectives and military doctrine of the other. As only one example, U.S. policy analysts

and government officials described Soviet military doctrine from the
1960s through the 1980s (including military doctrine for the use of
strategic nuclear weapons) as first-strike-oriented and designed to seek
victory through nuclear war. The Soviet view of deterrence, as described by much of the U.S. defense community, rested on the ability to
fight and win a nuclear war.[11] U.S. analysts who sought to make this case
drew from statements made by party officials, military-technical literature (including important publications in the *Officer's Library Series*),
and some evidence of Soviet research and development on future generations of nuclear offensive and defensive weapons. Officials in the
Carter and Reagan administrations were especially concerned with Soviet ICBM (Intercontinental Ballistic Missiles) capabilities for preemp-
tive attack on U.S. missile silos and command centers, and with Soviet
ballistic missile defenses already deployed and in development.

Had use of this same information been grounded in a larger amount
of U.S. perspective taking of the Soviet strategic view, U.S. assessments
might not have arrived at so ominous a conclusion. Soviet interest in
nuclear offensive and defensive forces could have been interpreted as
components of a strategy emphasizing the deterrence of war and the
limitation of damage, should nuclear war occur. This interpretation
might have been supported by the recognition that Soviet interest in
first-strike strategies waned as their military planners became less dependent on preemption for survivability of their land-based forces.
Then, too, the Soviet force configuration differed from that of the Americans: U.S. capabilities spread over three legs of the strategic "triad"
placed most survivable U.S. striking power in submarines and bombers.
Soviet retaliatory potential as well as first-strike capability resided in the
timely launch of their ICBMs, which carried a disproportionately large
share of their hard-target warheads. The argument that Soviet ICBMs
were targeted against U.S. ICBMs and therefore intended as first-strike
weapons ignored the equally plausible inference that second-strike
counterforce was considered by Soviet military planners, as by U.S. defense officials, as a requirement for credible deterrence.[12]

It is ironic that during the latter 1950s and early 1960s, both the
United States and the Soviet governments were marked by fears of strategic inferiority, based on misperceptions of each others' actual capabilities and military intentions. Khrushchev's atomic diplomacy of the

latter 1950s had sought to exploit U.S. fears that Soviet competency in nuclear rocket weapons greatly exceeded U.S. ability to develop and to deploy those weapons. Khrushchev used extravagant claims of Soviet nuclear superiority to buttress otherwise weak foreign policies and to fend off domestic and foreign critics of his détente policies and military budget cuts.[13] Addressing the Supreme Soviet in January, 1960, Khrushchev (not for the first time) asserted his claim to strategic superiority, argued that world economic trends were moving in favor of socialism, and contended that nuclear war—although certainly devastating for both sides—would result in victory for socialism.[14]

By the fall of 1960, Khrushchev had begun to retreat from some of his more extravagant claims about Soviet nuclear superiority and about the ability of socialism to prevail in nuclear war with comparatively few casualties. His speeches began to emphasize that the consequences of nuclear war for both sides would be highly destructive. This same thematic focus on the mutually destructive effects of nuclear war had appeared in a July, 1960, article in the Communist party theoretical journal, *Kommunist*, by Gen. Nikolai Talenskiy; Talenskiy enlarged his presentation of the same themes in a later article in *Mezhdunarodnaya zhizn'* (*International Affairs*).[15] According to Talenskiy's later article, calculations showed that of an estimated total population of eight hundred million in the main theater of military action (presumably Europe), casualties in a world war would be approximately five-to-six hundred million.[16] One reason for this retreat of Khrushchev and military leaders from previous assertions of nuclear superiority and war-winning capability was the Soviet view that Chinese leaders were far too cavalier about the consequences of nuclear war, challenging the Soviets for leadership of the world communist movement on the basis of ideological claims that disputed Soviet willingness to stand firm in confrontations with the West.

Another reason for a retreat in Soviet nuclear assertiveness was the Soviet leadership's recognition, by 1960, that the United States was beginning to possess a much more realistic picture of the actual state of the strategic nuclear balance of power. Eisenhower's last State of the Union address provided an opportunity for the U.S. president to note that "the 'missile gap' shows every sign of being a fiction."[17] Almost immediately after the Kennedy administration took office, press reports appeared that claimed, on the basis of Pentagon studies, that there actually was no "missile gap."[18] Citing new U.S. intelligence estimates, press reports in September, 1961, acknowledged that actual Soviet ICBM deployments in 1961 would fall far short of the maximum possible number projected in earlier U.S. estimates. Therefore the new intelligence estimates, according to press reports, eliminated completely any notion of a missile gap unfavorable to the United States.[19]

Nor was this all. Beginning in October of that same year, Kennedy administration officials launched an offensive in public diplomacy to dispel any lingering thoughts of a missile gap favorable to the Soviet Union. Indeed, U.S. government officials publicly proclaimed, the United States had attained strategic nuclear superiority over the Soviet Union. The public-relations offensive began with a speech by Deputy Secretary of Defense Roswell Gilpatric on October 21, 1961, and was followed by similar statements from other high Kennedy administration officials. Gilpatric noted that the United States, even after absorbing a Soviet surprise first strike, would probably retain second-strike forces greater than the forces used by the Soviet Union in its attack. "In short," according to Gilpatric, "we have a second-strike capability which is at least as extensive as what the Soviets can deliver by striking first."[20] The actual balance of forces at the time of the Cuban missile crisis (including forces becoming available at the very end of the crisis period, through October 28, 1962) appears in table 9.

As Richard Ned Lebow and Janice Gross Stein have noted, the reaction of Khrushchev and his military advisors to this U.S. public diplomacy was understandably one of concern, even alarm.[21] In order to have determined with such precision that the nuclear strategic balance was so lopsidedly in the favor of the United States, U.S. intelligence had to have mapped correctly the locations of Soviet ICBMs (SS-6s, first generation Soviet ICBM). Therefore, Soviet land-based missile forces might be vulnerable to a U.S. first strike. If so, then U.S. nuclear superiority might mean not only a relative advantage in nuclear striking power, but also the ability to jeopardize the survival of the Soviet deterrent. The Soviets were quick to respond to the Gilpatric speech. Two days later, Soviet Defense Minister Rodion Malinovskiy, addressing the Twenty-Second Party Congress in Moscow, charged that Gilpatric, with the concurrence of President Kennedy, was "brandishing the might of the

Table 9
Strategic Nuclear Forces, U.S.-Soviet Balance,
Cuban Missile Crisis

	Launchers	Warheads/ Launcher	Total Warheads
U.S. ICBMs			
Minute-man 1A	10	1	10
Titan 1	54	1	54
Atlas F	24	1	24
Atlas D	24	1	24
Atlas E	27	1	27
ICBM Totals	139		139
U.S. SLBMs			
Polaris A2	64	1	64
Polaris A1	80	1	80
SLBM Totals	144		144
U.S. Bombers			
B-58	76	2	152
B-47 (y)	338	1	338
B-47 (x)	337	2	674
B-52 (y)	108	3	324
B-52 (x)	447	4	1788
Bomber Total	1306		3276
U.S. Totals	1589		3559

United States" and had "threatened us with force."[22] While Malinovskiy added that "this threat does not frighten us," obviously it did.

Soviet leaders had similarly negative reactions to statements on the subject of nuclear weapons and nuclear war made by U.S. leaders subsequent to the Gilpatric speech, including those by President Kennedy.

Table 9 (Continued)

	Launchers	Warheads/ Launcher	Total Warheads
Soviet ICBMs			
SS-7	40	1	40
SS-6	4	1	4
IRBM	16	1	16
MRBM	24	1	24
ICBM Totals	84		
Soviet SLBMs			
SSN5	6	1	6
SSN4	66	1	66
SLBM Totals	72		72
Soviet Bombers			
Bear-A	75	2	150
MYA-4	58	4	232
Bomber Totals	133		382
Soviet Totals[a]	289		538

Source: Author's estimates from sources listed in notes.
[a]Totals include Soviet MRBMs and IRBMs scheduled for initial deployment in Cuba but not Soviet MRBMs or IRBMs deployed in the Soviet Union.

A spring, 1962, interview with Kennedy published in the *Saturday Evening Post* was interpreted in the Soviet press as an attempt to intimidate the Soviet leadership by threatening the possibility of a U.S. nuclear first strike.[23] Taking note of the assertively optimistic trends in U.S. official statements on the nuclear balance of power in July, 1962, Khrushchev described the new U.S. appraisals as meaningless, arguing that the real military balance of power could only be determined in the course of an actual war.[24] This was obvious backing and filling. The general trend in Soviet statements about the strategic balance after mid-

1961 was one of acknowledgment and acceptance of parity as the basis for political relations between the two powers.[25]

Khrushchev's rocket rattling of the immediate post-Sputnik period had set the stage for his own humiliation when the facts were revealed about the true nature of the nuclear-strategic balance in 1961. His strategy of nuclear bluff annoyed the United States and helped to provoke a U.S. response that appeared to the Soviet Union to be based on nuclear bullying. The result of Soviet nuclear bluffing followed by U.S. nuclear bullying was that both sides moved further from a shared understanding the security dilemma created by their military competition, and especially by their strategic forces.

Perspective taking might have suggested to the Americans in 1962 that the Soviets were less concerned with the "bean count" of U.S. versus Soviet nuclear weapons, and more concerned with the broader correlation of social and political forces. At least until Gorbachev, the role of nuclear weapons and other forces in Soviet military strategy was to support Soviet policy, including the spread of revolutionary Marxism-Leninism to states outside of the Soviet bloc. This could hardly be accomplished by nuclear adventurism against an opponent with superior forces, as the Politburo reminded Khrushchev when it decided it no longer required his services. It was not a given that Soviet political strategy would always select the most risky or assertive military strategy, as the superpower's willingness to adhere to the SALT I and SALT II agreements, including the ABM Treaty, attested.

Soviet perspective taking of the American standpoint might have helped to avoid the misjudgment that the United States would accept Soviet missile deployments in Cuba. Although U.S. observers still do not know as much as we would like to know about the Soviet interpretation of the United States' failure at the Bay of Pigs, it seems safe to infer that the episode could not have impressed the Soviet Union favorably with U.S. determination and sagacity. Khrushchev must have wondered why Kennedy authorized the expedition and then failed to rescue the situation in extremis. It was reasonable of Khrushchev to doubt Kennedy's resolve; many Americans doubted it too. Kennedy's reluctance to follow through in the Bay of Pigs might have seemed to Khrushchev as a characteristic propensity for hesitation in crises, instead of a singular uncertainty on the part of a new president facing an unexpected debacle.

Khrushchev also seems to have erred in assuming that Kennedy perceived only a domestic policy problem with regard to possible Soviet
missile deployments in Cuba. Soviet assurances to U.S. officials in September, 1962, made a point of suggesting that no offensive missiles or
other objectionable weapons would be deployed in Cuba that might
complicate matters for the U.S. president during an election campaign.

Kennedy and his advisors, in turn, were insufficiently sensitive to the
problem of how the Soviets might (wrongfully) interpret U.S. domestic
policy debates. Kennedy's reassurances to members of Congress that
there were no "offensive" Soviet weapons in Cuba and that he would not
accept the deployment of offensive weapons in the future drew a fine and
legalistic line between offense and defense. Soviet leaders might well
have interpreted this distinction as a loophole that could be exploited to
justify the deployment of nuclear weapons in Cuba. After all, whether
weapons are defined as offensive or defensive is an issue of purpose as
much as it is an issue of technology. If, from the Soviet perspective, the
purpose of the missile deployments was to contribute to the deterrence
of an attack on Cuba, or to the defense of Cuba if attacked, then the
weapons could, from that perspective, be described as defensive.

Some U.S. students of the Cuban missile crisis have concluded that
only the U.S. ultimatum and threat of an immediate air strike or invasion forced Khrushchev to agree to remove the missiles. An equally plausible argument could be made that the game was up for Khrushchev
once the United States obtained unambiguous photographic evidence
of the Soviet deployments. From then on, Khrushchev's agenda was to
save as much political face as possible and to withdrew the missiles
without drawing a U.S. attack on Cuba. Obviously, from the standpoint
of sheer military power, there was little the Soviet Union could do to
prevent the United States from using its conventional force superiority
to overthrow Castro. Because the United States was not eager to repeat
the Bay of Pigs fiasco, any U.S. invasion decision would have had to commit major forces against a significant Soviet and Cuban conventional
defense. Khrushchev's missile deployments almost gave the United
States a rationale for such an invasion—a difficult and costly military
undertaking that Kennedy would have been hard pressed to justify without the symbolism of Soviet nuclear power deployed in the Caribbean.
Thus Khrushchev turned a conventional force potentially dissuasive

against all but massive invasion into a lightning rod that could justify exactly that kind of U.S. attack on Cuba.

III. DETERRENCE AND THE CUBAN MISSILE CRISIS

The significance of deterrence in the Cuban missile crisis and the United States' ability to exploit deterrence to its advantage are markers for the presence of coercive military strategy in addition to coercive diplomacy. Once the Soviet missiles had been discovered in Cuba and the U.S. president determined to have them removed, the United States was able to use deterrence to its advantage. Specifically nuclear deterrence entered into the picture only as a backdrop to the successful application of conventional deterrence and the willingness to engage in crisis bargaining based on the appearance of reciprocal concession. The credible threat to destroy Soviet offensive missile emplacements in Cuba by air strike and land invasion, and the corollary threat to remove the Castro regime from power, could be accomplished with conventional forces alone. The burden of geographical war-widening or nuclear escalation would be Khrushchev's, not Kennedy's.

The Cuban missile crisis's favorable outcome as a result of U.S. crisis management should not obscure the fact that both nuclear and conventional deterrence had failed prior to the crisis. On the basis of what he must have known about the military balance in nuclear and conventional forces, Khrushchev was taking an extreme risk when he placed Soviet missiles into Cuba. The explanation that he did so in order to adjust an unfavorable strategic balance is consistent with U.S. deterrence theory only up to a point.

A strategic nuclear balance-of-power ratio tilted seventeen to one in favor of the United States should have deterred Khrushchev from his Cuban initiative, according to *both* orthodox and heterodox schools of nuclear deterrence strategy. The orthodox school argues that mutual vulnerability and second-strike capability are necessary and sufficient conditions for the preservation of deterrence stability. The heterodox school contends that mutual second-strike capability is not enough for credible deterrence when push comes to shove. In this second model of credible deterrence, the United States would also require for crisis management a significant relative advantage in nuclear striking power or, in what amounts to the same thing, in capability to limit damage.[26]

Neither the orthodox nor the heterodox model of deterrence predicts the kind of challenge Khrushchev made in the face of overwhelming U.S. conventional and nuclear superiority. According to orthodox logic, the United States in 1962 possessed a second-strike capability against the Soviet Union; the Soviet Union did not have a similar capability against the United States. According to heterodox logic, the United States had significant advantages in nuclear striking power and in the ability to impose a relatively favorable war outcome (if not an absolutely acceptable one). Making reasonable assumptions about the performance parameters of Soviet and U.S. weapons, table 10 shows the plausible outcome of any nuclear exchange in the last days of the Cuban missile crisis.

One can argue that Khrushchev was "irrational" according to the logic of U.S. deterrence theory, but the observation eludes the central issue whether deterrence logic has any explanatory power. Deterrence nomenclature is pervasive in the literature; demonstrating the explanatory or predictive power of a deterrence model is more difficult. However, deterrence supported by the credible ability to prevail in battle at an acceptable cost to the threatener is another matter entirely. The United States was in this position in Cuba, unless nuclear weapons were brought into the picture by the Soviet Union in the Caribbean or elsewhere. The United States had established conventional "escalation dominance" in that it could remove the missiles forcibly if it chose without nuclear escalation or geographical war-widening. The burden of further escalation was placed upon Khrushchev, but no step that Khrushchev could have taken, subsequent to a U.S. invasion of Cuba, could have saved Soviet missile sites from destruction or, in all likelihood, the Castro regime from military defeat.

Khrushchev attempted to implement his own model of "extended deterrence," but it was more of a political than a military model. The ties between Cuba—standard bearer of socialist community deep within the U.S. sphere of influence—and its Soviet benefactor were not those of a military guarantee. When Castro sought an explicit Soviet defense guarantee and wanted to go public with the news of Soviet missile deployments in Cuba, Soviet leadership demurred on both counts. Cuba was a prize worth keeping in the Soviet camp so long as the risks of doing so fell well short of actual military conflict with the United States.

Table 10
U.S. and Soviet Survivable and Deliverable Forces, October, 1962

Summary	Numbers
Total Soviet deliverable warheads	41
Total Soviet deliverable EMT (Equivalent Megatons)	109
Deliverable Soviet reserve warheads	26
Deliverable Soviet reserve EMT	33
Percent deliverable Soviet reserve warheads	0.63
Percent deliverable Soviet reserve EMT	0.31
Total U.S. deliverable warheads	659
Total U.S. deliverable EMT	655
Deliverable U.S. reserve warheads	591
Deliverable U.S. reserve EMT	587
Percent deliverable U.S. reserve warheads	0.90
Percent deliverable U.S. reserve EMT	0.90
Correlation of deliverable warheads	16.03
Correlation of deliverable EMT	6.02
Correlation of reserve warheads	6.00
Correlation of reserve EMT	17.5

Source: Author
Note: This table compares U.S. survivors (warheads not destroyed) of a Soviet first strike and Soviet survivors of a U.S. first strike. It is not therefore an example of a classical "exchange model" but a statistical comparison derived from an exchange model. Information about the exact model used is available from the author.

Khrushchev was not prepared to give Castro a blank check in the form of excessive leverage over Soviet decisions for war and peace in the Caribbean.

Evidence for this interpretation comes from Soviet behavior before and during the Cuban crisis; some of the most interesting recent evidence appears in crisis correspondence between Khrushchev and Castro recently published in the December 2, 1990, issue of *Granma*. In a message to Khrushchev on October 26, 1962 (two days before the crisis was resolved), Castro tells Khrushchev that "aggression is almost imminent within the next 24 or 72 hours" in the form of a U.S. air attack or invasion.[27] Castro then conveys his "personal opinion" that if "the imperialists invade Cuba with the goal of occupying it, the danger that that aggressive policy poses for humanity is so great that following that event *the Soviet Union must never allow the circumstances in which the imperialists could launch the first nuclear strike against it*."[28] Castro added in this message that if the United States actually invaded Cuba, then "that would be the moment *to eliminate such danger forever* through an act of clear legitimate defense, however harsh and terrible the solution would be, for there is no other."[29]

Khrushchev's response to this request for a Soviet nuclear first strike on the United States following any U.S. invasion of Cuba (sent October 28, 1962, the day that the Soviet Union agreed to remove the missiles in return for a U.S. pledge not to invade Cuba) was to urge Castro "not to be carried away by sentiment and to show firmness."[30] Khrushchev argued that the Soviet Union had settled the issue in Castro's favor by obtaining a noninvasion pledge from the United States and by preventing war from breaking out. Khrushchev also offered the argument that Pentagon "militarists" were now trying to frustrate the agreement that he and Kennedy had reached. This was why, according to Khrushchev's response to Castro, the "provocative flights" of U.S. reconnaissance planes continued. Khrushchev then scolded Castro for shooting down a U.S. reconnaissance plane on October 27: "Yesterday you shot down one of these, while earlier you didn't shoot them down when they overflew your territory."[31] The Soviet leader implied that such trigger-happiness would play into the hands of those in U.S. government circles who wanted war: "The aggressors will take advantage of such a step for their own purposes."[32]

The United States, despite its apparent military superiority at the nuclear and conventional levels, was as ready to terminate the crisis without war as was the Soviet Union. The U.S. objective was not to sever completely the "extended deterrence" connection between the Soviet Union and Cuba. U.S. crisis management objectives did emphasize, nonetheless, two aspects of the U.S. view of the Soviet-Cuban connection. The first was that, from Washington's standpoint, the Cuban-Soviet relationship was perceived as one of client and patron, or dependency.

This was emphasized in U.S. insistence upon dealing only with Khrushchev on the conditions for removing the Soviet missiles. Second, the United States and the Soviet Union resolved the crisis on terms which called for United Nations inspection and verification of the Soviet missile withdrawal. Fidel Castro objected on both counts. He disliked the willingness of Khrushchev to arrange for crisis termination without having consulted Cuba first. And he refused to permit United Nations or other on-site inspection of missile launcher dismantling and removal. The United States and the Soviet Union worked around this obstacle by arranging for the removal and shipment of the missiles in such a way that the process could be verified by U.S. aircraft surveillance and by other means. Castro objected to the terms on which the crisis was ended on the grounds that they implied a relationship between Havana and Moscow of one-way dependency, instead of two-way exchange.

IV. COUNTERARGUMENTS

There are several counterarguments to my contention that the results of the Cuban missile crisis of 1962 can be viewed as an escape from inadvertent mutual disaster and, at the same time, an instance of successful, but risky, coercive military strategy. I assume that Khrushchev's Cuba gambit was not based on the actual desire for a military showdown with the United States, but on the reasoning that the United States would choose political démarches rather than military threats to get the missiles out. My argument pushes the U.S.-Soviet nuclear deterrence relationship into the background of the crisis, and ignores the possibility that calculations about nuclear victory or defeat would have mattered to policymakers.

But nuclear deterrence may indeed have been a primary consideration in the crisis; and so the first counterargument to my position, and the strongest argument in favor of the importance of extended nuclear deterrence in the Cuban missile crisis was the possibility of a trade of U.S. Jupiter missiles in Turkey for Soviet MRBMs (Medium Range Ballistic Missile) in Cuba. U.S. Jupiter intermediate-range ballistic missiles were deployed in Turkey and Italy during the Eisenhower administration. Decisions for U.S. IRBM (Intermediate Range Ballistic Missile) deployment in Europe were taken in the aftermath of the Suez crisis of

1956, which shook allied NATO confidence in American guarantees of European security, and in the context of post-Sputnik American concerns about the viability of the U.S. nuclear deterrent.[33] Some arguments used by U.S. proponents of the Thor (in Great Britain) and Jupiter IRBMs were not too dissimilar from those used by the Soviets on behalf of Cuban MRBM deployments (and planned IRBM deployments) in 1962. U.S. leaders feared after the initial test launches of Soviet ICBMs in 1957 that they needed an interim fix for a perceived status of missile inferiority (although not overall-force inferiority, given the size of U.S. bomber forces in the latter 1950s). The Jupiter missiles deployed in Turkey were liquid fueled and used "soft" (above ground) launchers, which made them vulnerable to first strikes or prompt retaliatory launches.

U.S. leaders saw the Jupiter missile deployments as a concession to the requirements for NATO alliance unity. The host European nation would "own" the missiles and launchers, but the United States would maintain control over warhead dispersal and launch decisions (presumably in consultation with the host state). For the Turkish government, this meant that they had accepted a share of the U.S. nuclear deterrent despite the obvious provocation this would provide for Moscow. The strategic rationale for the Thor and Jupiter deployments was vitiated both by technology that made possible sea-based missile deployments and by ICBMs based in North America that could cover the same target base in the Soviet Union or Eastern Europe. The Kennedy administration recognized that the Jupiters in Turkey constituted a technological dinosaur and a potential political provocation. Kennedy had decided in principle to order the removal of the Jupiter missiles from Turkey prior to the development of the 1962 Cuban crisis, but he had not pressed the issue assertively after initial approaches to Turkey were rebuffed by that government.

The Cuban missile crisis thus caught the Kennedy administration with obsolete nuclear missiles deployed in a forward, exposed position, obviously vulnerable to Soviet conventional as well as nuclear attacks. Moreover, Soviet attacks against U.S. missiles in Turkey, in response to any U.S. attack on Cuba, could draw the entire NATO alliance into a war with Moscow. Kennedy and Secretary of Defense Robert McNamara, during deliberations of the ExComm (Executive Committee of the U.S.

National Security Council, President Kennedy's ad hoc high level advisory group for the Cuban Missile Crisis), recognized the political irony that obsolete missiles deployed in Turkey were now potential hostages to Soviet horizontal and vertical escalation. In addition, McNamara was especially conscious of the danger of escalation once a U.S. NATO ally was attacked in the aftermath of fighting in Cuba.

McGeorge Bundy, Kennedy's Special Assistant to the President for National Security, and James G. Blight transcribed and edited tapes of the October 27, 1962, meetings of the ExComm, portions of which appeared in the Winter 1987/88 issue of the journal *International Security*.[34] In these meetings, Kennedy continually returns to the theme that insistence on removing the Jupiter missiles offered Khrushchev an attractive way out of his predicament that Kennedy might not be able to refuse. Khrushchev's "second" letter of October 27 toughened the terms suggested in his "first" letter of October 26, wherein he agreed to remove Soviet offensive missiles from Cuba in return for a U.S. pledge of noninvasion. The October 27 letter (which may, for reasons still not fully understood, have been composed and sent first) insisted upon a trade of U.S. Jupiter missiles in Turkey for Soviet missiles in Cuba. Kennedy was bothered by the apparent symmetry of the trade, and the way it was likely to appear in the eyes of world, allied NATO, and U.S. opinion.

The president's principal advisors, on the other hand, emphasized the potential damage to NATO solidarity, to U.S.-Turkish relations, and to future credibility of extended deterrence in Europe if the United States made an obvious missile trade under the pressure of the Cuban crisis. As the president kept returning to the possibility of such a trade, his advisors sharpened their cautionary notes about the impact on NATO and future deterrence. One example of such cautions occurred during ExComm discussions on how to respond to Khrushchev's two apparently contradictory letters:

> **KENNEDY:** How much negotiation have we had with the Turks?

> **DEAN RUSK, SECRETARY OF STATE:** We haven't talked with the Turks. The Turks have talked with us—the Turks have talked with us in—uh—NATO.

KENNEDY: Well, have we gone to the Turkish government before this came out this week? I've talked about it now for a week. Have we had any conversation in Turkey, with the Turks?

RUSK: . . . We've not actually talked to the Turks.

GEORGE W. BALL, UNDERSECRETARY OF STATE: We did it on a basis where if we talked to the Turks, I mean this would be an extremely unsettling business.

KENNEDY: Well, *this* is unsettling *now* George, because he's got us in a pretty good spot here, because most people will regard this not as an unreasonable proposal, I'll just tell you that. In fact, in many ways—

BUNDY: But *what* most people, Mr. President?

KENNEDY: I think you're going to find it very difficult to explain why we are going to take hostile military action in Cuba, against these sites—what we've been thinking about— the thing that he's saying is, "If you'll get yours out of Turkey, we'll get ours out of Cuba." I think we've got a very tough one here.[35]

Kennedy's advisors continued to express hostility to the idea of a missile trade throughout the remainder of this discussion. Rusk commented that "the Cuba thing is a Western Hemisphere problem, an intrusion into the Western Hemisphere." Paul Nitze, Assistant Secretary of Defense and arms control expert, argued that the president should try to get the missiles out of Cuba "pursuant to the private negotiation" (the terms of the first Khrushchev letter). Bundy cautioned that a missile trade, if accepted at this stage of the crisis, would mean that "our position would come apart very fast." Ball noted that if the United States talked to the Turks about an immediate missile deal, they would take it up with NATO and "our position would have been undermined." He added that the United States "persuaded them (the Turks) that this *was* an essential requirement" and that Turkey now felt that a matter of prestige was involved. Bundy then argued that a missile trade would create the impression of trying to sell out U.S. allies for

American interests, adding that "that would be the view in all of NATO."[36]

Despite the consensus of his advisors against the concept of a missile trade, Kennedy held the possibility open until the very end of the crisis. He approved a backchannel initiative from Dean Rusk to the Secretary General of the United Nations that would have resulted in a "United Nations" proposal for a missile trade as the basis for resolving the crisis. The Rusk initiative was developed as an option; the president had not made up his mind at the time whether he would accept a missile trade if Khrushchev refused to deal on the basis of the latter's first letter.[37]

The second counterargument to my assertion that nuclear deterrence remained secondary to conventional deterrence in the Cuban missile crisis is the importance of the perceived role of escalation in bringing the crisis to a conclusion. Pressure to end the crisis in a timely manner came not only from fear of a limited war in the Caribbean, but also from the possible expansion of fighting into a general U.S.-Soviet conflict. Absent nuclear weapons, the crisis may have been much more prolonged, and the terms on which it was resolved, much more ambiguous.

All of these counterarguments that nuclear deterrence, in addition to conventional deterrence, made a difference in the Cuban missile crisis assume a connection between nuclear *weapons* and nuclear *deterrence* that is not necessarily proven. Whereas conventional deterrence may have operated asymmetrically to support crisis management in favor of U.S. policy objectives, the impact of nuclear weapons on decision making may have been symmetrical. The Soviet and U.S. leaderships might equally have feared loss of control more than either feared a deliberate first strike by the opponent. This type of deterrence is different from conventional deterrence, in which leaders' hopes and fears are almost directly correlated with expected battlefield outcomes. Leaders planning a conventional war may still guess incorrectly, with disastrous results. Nevertheless, expected battlefield outcomes in conventional war can be projected with more reliability than they can for nuclear war scenarios, however subject to error the former are necessarily going to be. The disconnection between nuclear deterrence and military victory makes the effort to control crisis a military as much as a political objective.

Support for this counter-counter argument would be provided by evidence showing that a side with a great deal of nuclear "superiority" in terms of number of second-strike weapons feared, despite this superiority, that loss of control would result in nuclear war with unacceptable outcomes for the superior power. Members of the U.S. ExComm decision-making group, including the president and his leading Cabinet officers, did show this perceptual inclination to fear loss of control leading to nuclear escalation despite apparent U.S. strategic nuclear superiority. McNamara, estimating the U.S. numerical advantage in strategic nuclear weapons at a seventeen to one ratio in October, 1962, nevertheless doubted that this relatively advantageous position was meaningfully related to the attainment of U.S. crisis-management objectives without war. In his interview with James G. Blight in May, 1987, McNamara explained his earlier reasoning in terms that indicate the irrelevance of relative advantage for a cost-benefit calculus in which unknown risks of absolute destruction are involved:

> Look, in my judgment, in fundamental terms, the so-called strategic balance hasn't shifted since 1962. The significant question isn't: How many weapons did we have then and now, relative to the Soviets? The question you should ask is: What did each side have in its arsenal then and now that was, or is, militarily useful? Let me put it another way: What is the likelihood then and now that either side might initiate the use of nuclear weapons and come away with a net gain? The answer to both questions is: Zero! Then and now, for both the U.S. and the Soviet Union, there are no militarily useful nuclear weapons in their arsenals and thus there is no advantage in using them.[38]

Others on the ExComm did not agree with McNamara's pessimism about the irrelevancy of the nuclear balance of power. C. Douglas Dillon, Secretary of the Treasury under Presidents Kennedy and Johnson and a member of the ExComm, shared the view of Nitze and other "hawks" that U.S. nuclear superiority was decisive in forcing Khrushchev to back down. Dillon recalled in 1987 that as the crisis wore on he became progressively less worried, in contrast to other ExComm participants who became more nervous about possible war and nuclear escalation. Dillon noted that because he was working in the Treasury Department for several years before the crisis, he had not been current on the details of U.S. force structure when the crisis began:

> I was not, when I first heard about it, fully aware of the extent of the nuclear superiority that we had. And, when I became aware of that, then I changed my view entirely and, of course, I agree totally with Nitze and think the McNamara thesis that our nuclear superiority made little or no difference is dead wrong. Our nuclear preponderance was essential. That's what made the Russians back off, plus the fact of our total conventional superiority in the region.[39]

Dillon's reasoning here exhibits transference of the logics of nuclear deterrence and conventional dissuasion; as the interview continued he advanced supporting points to explain why others, including McNamara, discounted U.S. nuclear superiority.

Of particular interest was Dillon's contention that the more experienced policymakers on the ExComm were hawkish because they had been through crisis-management and decision-making situations before. As he explained, "I think simple inexperience led to an inordinate fear of nuclear damage, the fear of what might happen. McNamara, in particular, felt that way, I guess, although I wasn't so conscious at the time that that was his reason." (p. 153)

One reason for the greater concern on the part of McNamara and other ExComm "doves" about the risks of escalation was undoubtedly the higher sensitivity of the Defense and State Departments to the implications for Europe and NATO of a failure in crisis containment. An example of this sensitivity to the European implications of risk assessment occurred on October 27 when McNamara pushed his ExComm colleagues to consider the aftermath of a U.S. air strike and invasion of Cuba. McNamara persisted in raising the troubling issue of what U.S. responses would be if the Soviets struck at Jupiter missile bases in Turkey.[40] Most other ExComm members did not see the point, so McNamara drove home the danger of nuclear escalation by sketching a plausible scenario. The "minimum" military response by NATO to a Soviet attack on the Jupiter missiles in Turkey, according to McNamara, would involve fighting a conventional war in and near Turkey, including strikes by Turkish and U.S. aircraft against Soviet warships and/or naval bases in the Black Sea area. McNamara emphasized that such exchanges would be "damned dangerous" and insisted that the implication of imminent escalation to nuclear war was obvious.[41] He then argued that the United States should defuse the Turkish missiles before any invasion of Cuba (presumably making this public) so that the missiles would be useless as hostages.

In making this argument about the risks of escalation in an alliance context, McNamara was not necessarily breaking faith with his earlier emphasis on the priority of shared nuclear risk and the irrelevance of putative nuclear superiority. Rather, his acknowledgment of the hostage status of the Jupiters in Turkey and their potentially catalytic role in crisis or wartime escalation was an acknowledgment of the mistake made in deploying those missiles. They were deployed, among other reasons, in order to create deterrence "coupling" between theater forces and strategic nuclear forces. The assumption was that coupling would make *extended* deterrence more credible than it would otherwise be, by adding additional levels of U.S. force deployments in Europe between conventional and all-out nuclear war. The same assumption would help to drive U.S. and allied NATO rationales in 1979 for deploying Pershing II missiles and GLCMs (Ground-Launched Cruise Missile) in Western Europe (begun in 1983, and disbanded as a result of the INF (Intermediate Nuclear Forces) Treaty of December, 1987).

As the Jupiter missiles in Turkey in 1962 became nuclear crisis-management hostages and potential catalysts of escalation, so, too, would the NATO "572" (464 GLCMs plus 108 Pershing II Ballistic Missiles equal NATO's 1983 Theater Nuclear Modernization Plan) deployments become hostages slowing the momentum of arms control and détente in Europe during the 1970s. The reason for the irrelevance of Jupiters in 1962, as for the Pershing II and GLCMs in the 1980s, had little to do with their technical characteristics (such as the Jupiters' vulnerability and long launch preparation, or the Pershings' range). The issue is political: Because nuclear dissuasion cannot be substituted for nuclear deterrence, "intermediate" nuclear weapons do not necessarily support the successful management of crisis and the control of escalation. Instead, such weapons deployments can contribute to the deterioration of crisis and to the loss of control over escalation. They can do this, as the Jupiters did, by commingling horizontal escalation, i.e., geographical war-widening, with vertical escalation, i.e., the expansion of conventional into nuclear war fighting. An attack by Khrushchev on Jupiter missiles in Turkey would have constituted a "nuclear" war even if the Soviets had used only conventional weapons: nuclear weapons would be destroyed in the attack, and perhaps fired back at the Soviet Union if its conventional first strike were unsuccessful. (The same potential problem faced U.S. air-strike planners once Soviet MRBMs in Cuba were thought to be operational.) This "vertical" expansion of the fighting could have been compounded in 1962 by "horizontal" extension of combat to Berlin or Turkey.

Against my arguments here, it might be contended that the issue of intermediate nuclear weapons deployed in Europe was actually irrelevant to the resolution of the Cuban missile crisis. One could take the strict position that the missiles in Turkey were not a clandestine U.S. deployment but a publicly acknowledged agreement under NATO auspices, that the Turkish missiles were a red herring introduced into the Cuban missile crisis by a Khrushchev seeking face-saving exit.

I concede that this argument has some validity, but it misses the distinction between precision of policy objective (getting the missiles out of Cuba without introducing irrelevant issues) and the potential for U.S. nuclear weapons deployed abroad to contribute to inadvertent escalation. Kennedy was right to keep the policy focus on the removal of Soviet missiles from Cuba without a *publicly acknowledged* linkage to subsequent removal of Jupiter missiles from Turkey.[42] On the other hand, transcripts of ExComm deliberations and other evidence suggest that Kennedy also recognized that the presence of vulnerable, nuclear-capable missiles deployed so close to Soviet borders created complications for his management of the Cuban crisis. And indeed, the Turkish missiles had served as part of Khrushchev's justification for deploying Soviet MRBMs and IRBMs to Cuba: He would pose to the Americans a threat similar in scope and in geographical proximity to that presented by U.S. IRBMs in Turkey and in other European countries.[43]

The irrelevance of Turkish missiles can be asserted only on the assumption that what mattered in the resolution of the Cuban missile crisis, and perhaps in the instigation of it also, was the strategic nuclear balance of power. Although some members of the ExComm do assert that this balance was of primary importance, other key policymakers, including the U.S. president and Secretary of Defense, did not assume so direct a connection between nuclear superiority and ability to prevail in a crisis. The successful resolution of the Cuban missile crisis in 1962 may suggest that nuclear deterrence is only loosely coupled to crisis management even in a two-sided U.S.-Soviet confrontation, and so is perhaps even less relevant in multisided crises among nuclear-armed states with less experience in conflict resolution and intracrisis communication.[44]

CONCLUSION

While it is true to say that coercive military strategy was used successfully by the United States to compel the Soviet Union to withdraw its offensive missiles from Cuba in October, 1962, this simple statement conceals a great deal. Policymakers "living through" the crisis did not have the same sense of destined success that some later historians or political scientists would ascribe to it. The United States had nuclear and conventional forces superior to those of the Soviets. The Soviet missile challenge took place despite the apparent salience in U.S. politics of the Monroe Doctrine against outside interference in the Western Hemisphere. The United States was defending a vital interest and the Soviets were not. Granted these asymmetries in capabilities and motivation, it should have been a cakewalk for President Kennedy to reverse Khrushchev's scheme. Nuclear deterrence, according to this logic of force and motivational asymmetries favoring Kennedy, would have forestalled any escalation by Moscow in Berlin or Europe. Meanwhile, the United States could have pulverized Castro and finished the Bay of Pigs, ensuring Kennedy's place in history and eventual reelection.

But Kennedy and his advisors did not see the Cuban missile crisis in these terms. Their intent was to achieve the objective of removing the Soviet missiles from Cuba while controlling the risks attendant to that objective. Toward that end, they chose a coercive military strategy that involved a combination of bargaining and demonstrative military action. The strategy allowed for mutual perspective taking on the part of Kennedy and Khrushchev, with regard to each other's motives for settlement and fears of escalation. The coercive strategy allowed Khrushchev a face-saving retreat from a course that could only have moved

3

Coercive Military Strategy and Desert Storm

Limitation without Restraint

The Gulf crisis and war in 1990–91 may seem an inappropriate venue for demonstrating the military relevancy of coercive strategy. Iraq's President Saddam Hussein was held to be the very prototype of the undeterrable leader, capable of being dissuaded only by being bludgeoned into submission; otherwise, it is believed, he would have held onto Kuwait, and possibly have advanced further, at any apparent risk.[1] In addition, the "Powell doctrine"[2] of an all-or-nothing force commitment was thought to dominate the U.S. approach to the use of force once committed to war; in contrast to the frustration experienced by the U.S. military in Vietnam, planners and military analysts expected that no political constraints imposed from Washington would tie the hands of military commanders in the Persian Gulf.[3]

This chapter argues, nevertheless, that the United States successfully employed coercive military strategy in the Gulf War, as dictated by both political and military constraints on the United States and its allies in the anti-Iraq coalition. Politically, U.S. President George Bush and his military advisors recognized that the total destruction of Iraq's armed forces was neither attainable at an acceptable political cost, nor desirable from the standpoint of U.S. postwar policy for the region.[4] In military terms, the U.S. air war employed a targeting strategy designed to rapidly eliminate much of Iraq's command and control and air power—setting the stage for the collapse of Iraqi armed forces in and near Kuwait—without initiating a protracted ground war.

During the Gulf War, the United States and its allies used massive force within the assigned theater of operations to execute the mission assigned by President Bush and allied heads of state. Operation Desert Storm and its aftermath illustrate that neither the goal of limited war nor the use of a coercive military strategy necessarily requires a nation to dribble out force in small doses. Massive and comprehensive attacks on appropriate target sets at the outset of a campaign may be successful in influencing enemy intent both by denying the opponent significant military means with which to continue fighting at acceptable cost and by credibly promising further destruction unless peace terms are met.[5]

This chapter begins by presenting the decisions made by the Bush administration in deciding to go to war with Iraq, as well as the strategic context within which those decisions were made. The chapter then examines the ways in which allied forces used coercive diplomacy to target their actions for maximum coercion. finally, the chapter discusses the strategy involved in the U.S.-led coalition decision to escalate its activity from coercive diplomacy to coercive war.

I. THE BACKGROUND TO DECISION

Iraq's decision to invade Kuwait was based on reasoning that drastically misjudged the international climate for that action. The Bush administration's swift response was partly an exercise in attempted deterrence through coercive diplomacy. Having succeeded in deterring Iraq from further incursions, the United States then expanded its objective to that of compelling Iraq to leave Kuwait.

A. The View from Baghdad

In the early morning of August 2, 1990, Iraqi armed forces invaded Kuwait without provocation. Within hours the invasion force subdued resisting Kuwaiti defenders. Within a week the invasion force swelled to some 100,000 troops armed with modern equipment, including surface-to-surface missiles. The Emir of Kuwait and his retinue fled ahead of Iraqi tanks; Saddam Hussein announced that the government of Kuwait had been deposed and that a new regime would be installed that was more consistent with his definition of Islamic polity.

The 1990 Iraqi invasion of Kuwait placed the Bush administration in a situation similar to that faced by President Harry S Truman and his advisors in June, 1950, when North Korean forces crossed the 38th parallel and overran South Korea. Prior to the North Korean attack, many leading U.S. military experts and political figures had been uncertain whether South Korea lay within the United States' "defense perimeter."[6] Once the attack was actually under way, however, Truman and his advisors quickly recognized the area's strategic importance. The loss of all of Korea to the North Korean regime would be a catastrophic setback for U.S. policy and an immediate strategic threat to Japan, America's principal ally in the Far East. As Robert Jervis has noted with regard to presidential perceptions of U.S. interests in Korea in 1950 and the Gulf in 1990: "Events and decision makers' instinctive reactions often shape definitions of vital interests, rather than preexisting definitions shaping behavior."[7]

To say that the North Koreans and the Soviets were disappointed by Truman's reaction to the North Korean attack would be a considerable understatement. The two communist regimes had miscalculated badly, forgetting that great powers do not necessarily define in advance all the interests for which they will fight. War, or the imminent prospect of it, changes calculations dramatically.[8] The North Koreans and the Soviets were disappointed in a way that most students of American foreign policy find quite reassuring. Not all disappointments are of this sort, however. In 1956, after Egyptian President Gamal Abdel Nasser had nationalized the Suez Canal and the British, French, and Israelis had mounted an invasion against him, the United States chose to define its strategic interest quite unexpectedly: siding with Nasser, and against its own NATO and Israeli allies. In the face of U.S. opposition, the attack was called off and Nasser emerged from the crisis as a hero. The all-too-public advertisement of the limitations of France and Britain's global reach, compared to that of the United States, would have long-term effects in the region.

Saddam Hussein calculated, as had North Korean Premier Kim Il Sung in 1950, that he could bring about a fait accompli in the form of a complete and total military conquest of Kuwait and the replacement of its regime by an Iraqi puppet. His essential political and military objectives would be accomplished while the United States, its NATO allies, and the other states in the Persian Gulf/Southwest Asia cauldron

dithered about what to do. This was a reasonable supposition on the part
of the Iraqi ruler. NATO allies of the United States were preoccupied
with the winding down of the Cold War in Europe and with the rapid
changes convulsing the Soviet Union. The Soviet Union itself—which
had for many years built up the Iraqi armed forces through military aid,
equipment, and training—would at worst, Saddam Hussein reasoned,
turn a deaf ear to American or United Nations entreaties. And the Arab
states of the Gulf, Southwest Asia, and North Africa would no doubt live
up to their well-deserved reputations for finding excuses not to oppose
his version of Arab imperialism.

The common perception that Saddam Hussein's reasoning is almost
always flawed confuses after-the-fact knowledge about Iraqi military
losses with what the Iraqi leader could have estimated about the military
capabilities and political will of his probable opponents.[9] One could
argue that the invasion was a "reasonable" decision given Iraq's economic constraints, Kuwait's heedless twisting of Saddam Hussein's tail
on oil prices, and confusing U.S. signals with regard to American vital
interests.[10] Nor were Saddam Hussein's decisions *subsequent* to the invasion consistently off the mark. He expected that the United States
would not be willing to wage war, or, if it were, that it would not have
much toleration for high casualties and protracted ground warfare. Even
if his air forces lost, Saddam Hussein thought, his army, still intact,
would be capable of inflicting a political defeat on the United States and
its allies by extracting from them unbearable domestic political costs.
(This chain of reasoning would prove false to fact, as we now know, because the coalition's air campaign would prove more destructive and
more demoralizing to Iraqi *ground forces* than Saddam Hussein had expected.)[11] He was correct in projecting that air power alone could not
compel his forces to leave Kuwait. Satisfying that objective would require
a ground offensive—the beginning of which caused the Iraqi leadership
to recognize for the first time that its strategy had totally failed.

Indeed, the Iraqi dictator might "reasonably" expect that the United
States would take no action at all. During in 1980s, the United States had
shown more official and unofficial sympathy toward Iraq than Iran in
the two countries' war, which lasted most of the decade.[12] And U.S.
public diplomacy during the period of Iraq's military buildup and diplomatic posturing against Kuwait was not very deterring.[13] In addition to

the much-disputed meeting between U.S. Ambassador April Glaspie and Saddam Hussein in late July, 1990, high officials in the U.S. government provided little reassurance that the United States would come to Kuwait's defense should Iraq attack. For example, in Congressional testimony before the House Foreign Affairs Committee on July 31, 1990, John Kelly, an assistant secretary of state, declined to be pinned down on the issue:

> **REP. HAMILTON (D.-Ind.):** What is precisely the nature of our commitment to supporting our friends in the Gulf? I read a statement—I guess an indirect quotation in the press that Secretary [Dick] Cheney said that the United States' commitment was to come to Kuwaiti—to Kuwait's defense if it is attacked. . . . Perhaps you could clarify. . . ?

> **MR. KELLY:** I'm happy to. . . . I'm not familiar with the quotation. . . . We have no defense treaty relationship with any Gulf country. That is clear. We support the security and independence of friendly states in the region. . . .

> **REP. HAMILTON:** If there—if Iraq, for example, charged across the border into Kuwait . . . what would be our position with regard to the use of U.S. forces?

> **MR. KELLY:** That . . . is a hypothetical or contingency question, the kind of which I can't get into. Suffice it to say we would be extremely concerned, but I cannot get into the realm of "what if" answers.[14]

An additional factor leading to Saddam Hussein's optimism about the unlikelihood of any U.S. military response was his misperception of the influence of "Vietnam syndrome" on the willingness of the United States to employ force. Saddam Hussein's conjecture, that any prewar expectation of high casualties would deter an American military response, confused U.S. domestic politics in the face of a conflict of uncertain purpose with its politics in an entirely different circumstance—that of undoubted vital interest.[15]

The Iraqi leadership's reading of U.S. intentions may not have been illogical from Iraq's perspective, but Iraq's fatal vision combined bad history with what is called *mirror imaging*—a decision pathology in which the motives of one's opponent are assumed to be analogous to one's own.[16] The Iraqi leadership was thus astonished by the unequivocal U.S. reaction as expressed by President Bush in his address to the nation on August 8, 1990. Bush laid down the general thrust of U.S. policy, outlining four policy objectives that would have to be met to resolve the crisis on terms that would be judged satisfactory to American interests. first was the "immediate, unconditional, and complete withdrawal" of all Iraqi forces from Kuwait.[17] Second was restoration of the legitimate government of Kuwait. Third, Bush explicitly defined the stability and security of the Persian Gulf as vital to U.S. interests (as had more than one of his predecessors). And fourth, Bush indicated that he would be concerned about the lives of American citizens living abroad, including those in Kuwait and Iraq.[18]

In addition, Bush ordered an immediate embargo of all trade with Iraq and, with allied cooperation, froze all Iraqi and Kuwaiti financial assets in the United States and elsewhere. U.S. diplomacy sought to isolate Iraq as an aggressor state and to mobilize international opinion against it. Toward that end, U.S. leaders succeeded, on August 6, in getting the UN Security Council to approve—for the first time in twenty-three years—mandatory sanctions under Chapter VII of the UN Charter. These sanctions gave international blessing to the United States' effort to ostracize Iraq from other military, economic, and political support. Further to the discomfiture of Iraq, Mikhail Gorbachev's Soviet Union did not even make sympathetic noises in the direction of Baghdad. Instead, Gorbachev sided with Bush and with the United Nations in declaring the Iraqi aggression illegal and calling for a restoration of the *status quo ante*. This was the first post-Cold War crisis in which the superpowers acted in diplomatic concert, and it gave the Americans a virtual carte blanche for a military response of the most unambiguous sort.

That response was not long in coming. Bush immediately authorized the deployment of elements of the 82nd Airborne Division to Saudi Arabia. By the middle of September, 1990, the United States had some 150,000 troops in the region, including air force and naval personnel. Twenty-six countries also committed forces and support, including Egypt, Morocco, and Syria. Many more U.S. forces were to follow in

October and November, with increasing controversy over the political objectives motivating the deployments.

B. Coercive Deterrence

The United States first poured this sizable contingency force into the Gulf and its environs as an exercise in deterrence. The particular form of deterrence chosen was coercive diplomacy, the combined use of arms and diplomacy—stopping short of an actual war—in order to induce an opponent to behave in a preferred way.[19] The objective was not to get into a shooting war with Iraq, but to discourage further Iraqi aggression, primarily the threat of attack on Saudi Arabia. Because it partakes of coercion rather than force, coercive diplomacy is intellectually demanding on the resources of military planners and policymakers alike.

It is customary for analysts to define the problem of having prevented Iraq's attack on Kuwait as one of deterrence, and the subsequent mission of getting Iraq to withdraw from Kuwait as what is called *compellence.* Whereas deterrence aims at prevention, compellence seeks the undoing of an action already taken or in progress.[20] One can overstate the difference between deterrence and compellence, implying that deterrence is always passive and compellence always active. This is far from the case. It is sometimes impossible to make a deterrent threat credible by words or military preparedness without an actual demonstration in battle. At this point, defense and deterrence may be commingled. One can respond to an attack with forcible defense per se, which is simply designed to defeat the attack, destroy the attacking forces, and eliminate their combat power. Or one can use defense as a way of making a statement relative to intrawar deterrence: defense, once in progress, makes more apparent the willingness of the defender to pay actual costs in lives lost and resources expended in battle. What was previously a hypothetical possibility—that the defender would resist—becomes a certainty.[21]

The idea of intrawar deterrence is not as self-contradictory as it might sound. Fighting can have a twofold purpose: to force the attacker to use up combat power, and to send the message that there is a potentially higher risk in the continuation of combat for the attacker than the defender. The United Nations sought to achieve both purposes during the Korean War, putting the North Koreans on notice that the conventional defenses of the United States, South Korea, and other allies would deny North Korea an inexpensive victory, or, once the fighting had stabilized in 1951, any victory at all. North Korea was also led to believe, as was China, that continued fighting might expand in directions that were not simple extensions of the ground and tactical air warfare previously fought to a standstill. In 1953, the Eisenhower administration warned the Chinese and the North Koreans through intermediaries that the United States would not necessarily confine future fighting to the Korean peninsula unless more progress was made toward the conclusion of an armistice. The deterrent threat against additional North Korean or Chinese escalation was posed in part by the availability of American and other forces that were prepared to continue fighting, and in part by the possible expansion of the war into other theaters of operations and by the United States' potential use of tactical nuclear weapons.[22]

President Bush and his advisors decided that the ability to exclude Iraq from meaningful allied support was a necessary condition for the establishment of escalation dominance in the crisis. The United States moved rapidly and successfully on the diplomatic front to obtain military and other support from NATO allies; troop commitments were obtained from Egypt, Syria, and Morocco for deployments in support of U.S. forces in Saudi Arabia. The Soviet Union was also engaged in support of the U.S. aim to reverse the results of the attack on Kuwait. The UN Security Council supported the embargo of trade with Iraq in goods other than foodstuffs and medicine. As the diplomatic noose closed around Saddam Hussein as a result of effective U.S. international politicking and a globally shared dependency on oil, Iraq's options became more limited. Its further diplomatic isolation was brought about by its own incompetence: The sacking of the French embassy in Kuwait, for example, prompted a French decision in September, 1990, to dispatch an additional 4,000 troops to the region.[23] (France had previously declined to join in the active naval quarantine against Iraq, on the grounds that doing so would make it a cobelligerent.) Divested even of Soviet support for its war effort, Iraq in desperation turned to its former enemy, Iran, offering attractive terms to Iran for terminating their conflict, including the repatriation of Iranian prisoners of war.

The diplomatic aspects of crisis management were supported by an extensive military buildup that would place some 430,000 U.S. forces in the Persian Gulf region by the end of January, 1991. Having inserted the trip-wire force (a force of limited capability designed to stand in place and deter aggression by symbolizing commitment) to establish U.S. commitment, the Bush administration built it into a formidable air-, ground-, and sea-based force supported by allied deployments that were more than ceremonial. The commitment of other Arab forces to the defense of Saudi Arabia testified to the isolation that Saddam's diplomacy had brought about. The difference between the United States' ability to mobilize international support for its position and Iraq's inability to do so created military alternatives for the Americans and limited the military options available to Iraq. As the U.S. and allied military buildup proceeded, Saddam's window of opportunity for a blitzkrieg against Saudi Arabia—of the kind he had imposed on Kuwait—rapidly closed.

By mid-September of 1990, the United States had successfully prevented Iraq from accomplishing further aggressive aims in the region by employing the "try and see" rather than the "ultimatum"[24] variant of coercive diplomacy.[25] Having deployed a blocking and deterring force into Saudi Arabia and the Gulf region, the United States was in a position analogous to that of President Kennedy after having imposed a quarantine against Soviet missile shipments into Cuba in October, 1962. The United States established a line that Saddam Hussein could not cross without raising the risks of escalation, as Khrushchev could not have repeatedly violated the U.S. quarantine without risking at least conventional war between the superpowers. The analogy is one of approach to decision making, and of the character of the relationship between force and policy. The United States was in a superior military position relative to that of its antagonists in 1962 as in 1990. In 1962, the United States would have won a conventional war in the Caribbean; given this fact, the Soviet Union faced unpleasant options of nuclear escalation in the Caribbean or conventional war in Europe with a very high probability of nuclear escalation there. In similar fashion, the United States' superiority in force relative to that of Iraq was very important to the calculations being made both in Baghdad and in Washington. An all-out war in the Gulf would be costly, but the eventual expulsion of Iraq from Kuwait and the destruction of Saddam's regime seemed to be highly probable, if not inevitable, outcomes.

C. From Deterrence to Compellence

The deterrent objectives of the U.S. deployments seemed easier to accomplish than the compellent ones, however. It would not suffice, according to U.S. policy, merely to deter Saddam from attack on Saudi
Arabia. As previously noted, U.S. political objectives included the withdrawal of Iraqi forces from Kuwait and the restoration of the preinvasion
emirate government. This compellent mission was more complicated
than the deterrent one, in both political and military terms. Politically,
the allied and UN support that had signed onto the United States' deterrent mission now complicated U.S. planning for use of military force
for the purpose of compellence. The Soviet Union was not eager to go
beyond its commitment to the slow squeeze on Iraq by blockade and
embargo. Nine European states proposed a further refinement of the
"try and see" variant of coercive diplomacy to the UN Security Council
on September 18, suggesting a tightening of the blockade by means of
an interdiction of air traffic to and from Iraq—a plan that would be
complicated to administer and posed the risk of inadvertently strafing
or forcing down a civilian jetliner.

The United States now sought to compel Iraqi leadership to reverse
a course of action previously undertaken, as opposed to the simpler task
of deterring further aggression Saddam might contemplate. But an un-
provoked attack on Iraq launched by U.S. forces without UN approval
would lack broad international, allied NATO, or Gulf Cooperation
Council support. To achieve its objectives, the United States needed a
compellent option that supported the diplomacy of slow squeeze while
chiseling away at the Iraqi military position. Instead, during September
Iraq progressed quickly toward termination of its war with Iran, immediately transferring its forces from that front into Kuwait. In August,
1990, U.S. planners anticipated an Iraqi force in Kuwait of some 250,000
troops; now they faced the prospect that by the end of December as
many as 600,000 Iraqi forces might be deployed in forward defensive
positions or in operational reserves of high readiness stationed behind
the covering forces. However inferior they were in *offensive* professional
competency to the crack U.S. divisions being deployed in Saudi Arabia,
Iraqi forces in Kuwait presented a significant defensive capability
against any ground invasion.

On November 8, 1990, President Bush announced a virtual doubling of U.S. military deployments to the Gulf, a move interpreted by many in Congress and in the news media as a shift from a defensive to an offensive strategy. Although Congress had recessed following the national elections two days earlier, congressional leaders indicated their concern and demanded to know whether the Bush administration had abandoned its blockade for a course of action leading to war. The official response was that the addition of some 200,000 combat forces to the estimated 230,000 U.S. forces already deployed in Persian Gulf area did not constitute a transition from a defensive to an offensive military strategy. Instead, it amounted to a tightening of the screw, an increase in compellent pressure by a demonstrative show of force that might, or might not, be used. As explained by a "senior official" of the Bush administration in early November, 1990, "what we are trying to do is tell Saddam Hussein, 'Look, we are serious.'"[26]

The administration was not yet prepared to issue an ultimatum demanding Saddam's withdrawal, although the ground was being prepared for that next step as the compellent pressure on Iraq was being tightened. U.S. Secretary of State James Baker sought and received approval from the Soviet leadership for a conditional use of force if other options were to no avail. And U.S. officials—working to deadline because the United States' term as chair of the UN Security Council would expire on December 1—worked with other UN delegations throughout November on draft resolutions authorizing the use of force against Iraq. The "senior official" cited above noted—in contrast to some other Bush administration policymakers—that the new U.S. military deployments were not related to any assumed failure of economic sanctions. Speaking in early November, the official told reporters that it was too soon to draw any conclusions about how well sanctions might ultimately work.[27]

The new forces were designed to support sanctions by conveying to Saddam a sense that his time for compliance was not unlimited; they represented an ultimatum of a sort, although specifying no time line for compliance.[28] This relatively passive form of compellence failed to move Iraq; in response, Saddam Hussein mobilized another 150,000 to 200,000 forces for deployment into or near Kuwait, raising his expected total to over 600,000 by January, 1991. It therefore became clear to U.S. officials that a stricter form of coercive diplomacy would be necessary, one of the more active forms of compellence.

In the last week of November, 1990, the United States worked at a hectic pace to establish a consensus among the permanent members of the UN Security Council in favor of an ultimatum. On November 29, the Security Council voted twelve to two (with one abstention) to authorize the use of force against Iraq if Iraq did not withdraw from Kuwait by January 15, 1991. During the forty-seven-day period between that deadline and passage of the resolution authorizing members to use "all necessary means" to enforce UN resolutions on Kuwait, the Security Council announced a "pause of good will" to concentrate on diplomatic approaches to resolve the crisis.[29] This made little immediate impression on Iraq, which vowed defiance immediately prior to the expected Security Council resolution authorizing force if necessary.

U.S. officials indicated that they sought the deadline not as a guarantee that American and allied forces would take offensive action immediately after that date, but as an "open door" through which subsequent attacks could be launched at any time. Although the resolution seemed to allow the United States the upper hand in the competition of coercive bargaining, the use of this variant of coercive military strategy was not without risk. Iraqi planners now had an outside date to use as a guideline for military preparedness and allied planners could not preclude a possible first-strike by Iraq in the intervening "pause." Iraq also had the option of making coercive "reprisal" attacks in response to the UN-imposed deadline, attacks that would be short of all-out war but nevertheless stress the coalition supporting U.S. and UN objectives.

One obvious question to which no answer was known at the time of the passage of the UN resolution authorizing force against Iraq was how the U.S. Congress would figure into the equation of U.S. compellence. A Congress strongly in support of the president would add to the credibility of compellent threats, but an attempt to force Congress to stand up and be counted on this issue risked defeat for the administration, which lacked a Congressional majority. Both Houses of Congress did eventually vote to authorize U.S. use of force against Iraq in January; armed with these resolutions and those of the United Nations, Bush was legally and politically protected against charges of "presidential war."[30] In the weeks ahead this would prove to be a considerable asset for him with regard to the support of the international community, Congress, and the U.S. public.

By waiting to virtually double the size of the force deployed in the Persian Gulf until immediately after the fall elections, Bush circumvented a congressional and public debate over the shift in mission for U.S. forces from deterrence to compellence. A force of roughly 200,000 troops could be maintained in Saudi Arabia almost indefinitely without significant strain on U.S. resources and patience; a force of 400,000 or more (and ultimately more than 500,000) was too large for such an extended, constabulary mission. Pressures would surely build within the armed forces and within the administration for a resolution of the crisis by war or by Iraq's voluntary withdrawal from Kuwait. While Bush administration officials publicly scorned the idea of "saving face" for Saddam and viewed his aggression against Kuwait as criminal and inadmissible, they understood that the avoidance of war would require some kind of bargaining over minor aspects of the crisis, even if they were not willing to compromise on the major stakes. The other option was to fight, and the Bush coercive strategy had more credibility on that subject following the UN resolution of late November that authorized the use of force if necessary.

Even should the guns speak, however, military persuasion would not be silent. The United States would still be fighting for political objectives, holding together a diverse multinational coalition, including Arab states of heterogeneous ideological persuasions and regimes. "Economy of violence" (as recommended by Machiavelli) would call for a rapid and decisive campaign against Iraqi forces in Kuwait, but it was not clear how much further the United States and its allies ought to go. Military forces commonly find it hard to resist targets of opportunity, and hints from high places in Washington suggested to Saddam Hussein that his regime's days, and perhaps his own, would be numbered should war begin.

II. TARGETING FOR COERCION

The uppermost question in the minds of U.S. and allied strategists planning for the outbreak of war should compellence fail was the decision of whether Saddam Hussein should be permitted to survive in power. Wartime operations might give the U.S. coalition an opportunity to depose him, but not necessarily at an acceptable cost in battlefield casualties and allied disunity. Saddam's strategy for the conduct of war could be assumed to include a postwar world in which he maintained effective control over Iraq's armed forces and security services, allowing for his later return to the Middle East and Persian Gulf stage of major players. If Bush's objectives for war against Iraq included the dethronement of Saddam and the end of his political and military power over Iraq, then U.S. and allied military operations fell short of the commitment necessary to attain those objectives.

Variations of what was called the "Instant Thunder" air-war plan, developed in the Pentagon and modified in Riyadh, called for a variety of strikes against military and other targets and set ambitious objectives for battle damage. The eighty-four targets shown in table 11 are enumerated by target class, together with expectations for target destruction conveyed in early Distant Thunder briefings.

The U.S. Joint Chiefs of Staff (JCS) concluded that only massive use of air power against a wide variety of targets could force Iraq out of Kuwait and bring the war to an acceptable conclusion.[31] Air force planners interviewed academics, journalists, "ex-military types," and Iraqi defectors to determine "what is unique about Iraqi culture that they put a very high value on? What is it that psychologically would make an impact on the population and regime of Iraq?"[32] Israeli sources allegedly advised that the best way to hurt Saddam Hussein was to target his family, his personal guard, and his mistress.[33] The expectation that the air war alone could either loosen Saddam's grip on Kuwait or cause the destruction and capitulation of Iraq's forces in the Kuwaiti Theater of Operations (KTO) was to be disappointed, despite one of history's most one-sided bombing campaigns over a period of thirty-nine days preceding the outbreak of a 100-hour ground war.

Planners frequently approach the problem of targeting as a question of destroying so many physical things: bridges, air defenses, depots, and so forth. This is a legitimate concern, but from the point of the relationship between force and policy, it is not the most important issue. Targeting can also be treated as the effort to disrupt or to destroy the coherence of an enemy organization. The opponents' command system is its "brain," without which its "body" is susceptible to paralysis or disintegration. Targeting the command and control system of an opponent, including its leadership, is thought by some analysts to be an

Table 11
**Instant Thunder Air-War Plan Early Target Categories
and Damage Expectancies**

Category of Target	Number of Targets	Objectives
Strategic air defense	10	Destroy
Strategic chemical	8	Long-term setback
National leadership	5	Incapacitate
Telecommunications	19	Disrupt/Degrade
Electricity	10	Destroy 60 percent in Baghdad, 35 percent in rest of country
Oil (internal consumption)	6	Destroy 70 percent
Railroads	3	Disrupt/Degrade
Airfields	7	Disrupt/Degrade
Ports	1	Disrupt
Military production and storage depots[a]	15	Disrupt/Degrade

Source: Adapted from Gordon and Trainor, *The Generals' War,* 86, 89.

[a]This list presumably includes known nuclear, biological, and chemical weapons production and storage facilities ("NBC" targets).

economical approach to victory as compared to a prolonged war of attrition. The counter-command approach commends itself especially when political power and enemy leadership are concentrated in one or a few hands. Undoubtedly this was one reason why the headquarters of dictator Muammar Quaddafi were specifically targeted in 1986 during the U.S. raids against Libya.

However, targeting for coercion, as opposed to targeting for destruction, is more complicated than the killing of one individual or the elimination of a few persons in a leadership group. Targeting for coercion is an influence process directed at a reactive military organization.[34] Military organizations react and adapt to changed conditions, according to repertoires of procedures and professional expectations. The U.S. and allied bombing offensives against Germany in World War II, for example, proved to be less effective than the most optimistic proponents of strategic air power had assumed because German civil and military organizations were able to adjust previously established routines and priorities. As another example, although prewar planners and futurists had predicted a decisive, air-delivered knockout blow against the British isles, that situation did not materialize, and the bombs that did fall in 1940 failed to coerce Britain into surrender.[35] In the latter case, Luftwaffe misjudgments in setting targeting priorities shifted the thrust of German attacks away from potentially crippling strikes against British airdromes toward terror raids against cities.

Warfare in the age of information equips commanders with more numerous and more diverse media of observation, communication, and assessment. This may increase or decrease vulnerabilities, as Kenneth Allard has argued with unusual emphasis:

> The command structure is the one part of a military organization that, more than any other, must function as a weapon of war. It must either be a lethal, predatory weapon, capable of preying upon and killing other command structures—or else it runs the risk of becoming a bizarre, expensive techno-gaggle more likely to generate friction than to reduce it.[36]

The relationship between the coercive and attritive uses of air power is therefore one of subtlety and reciprocity. The persuasive force of air power is linked to its decisive use in either of two ways against command and control or other target sets. First, devastating attacks against a small but highly important target set may be indicated, especially if striking or destroying that target set might bring the entire system to a halt or render it confused and paralyzed. Second, prompt and massive strikes against a variety of military and economic assets must be of sufficient strength to convince the enemy that further destruction is both possible and potentially ruinous. As Eliot A. Cohen has noted, "to use air power in penny packets is to disregard the importance of a menacing and even mysterious military reputation."[37] The two-faced potential of air power for coercion and for attrition may require a willingness on the part of policymakers to take immediate and dramatic escalation *now,* in order to quicken the decision in the enemy's capital to avoid further punishment and denial later. (Punishment-oriented deterrence rests upon the credible threat of unacceptable consequences. Deterrence by denial depends on the ability to deny enemy objectives.)

The history of command and control systems shows that there is no one right way to organize a defense establishment or a fighting force. It follows that there is no all-purpose magician's trick that will destroy any given system's cohesion.[38] Coercive diplomacy in war or crisis cannot be based on *optimistic* assumptions about toppling the opponent's command system. In some cases the "system" will consist of one dominant leader and his or her immediate coterie of retainers. Destruction of this group of persons might change short-term war aims, but little historical evidence suggests that the change would be for the better. Hawks are as likely as doves to emerge from the rubble when the top leadership group is eliminated by internal coup or external attack.[39] As Fred Charles Ikle noted in his definitive study of conflict termination, it is arguable whether those who favor continuation of fighting or those who are prepared to surrender an unfavorable position are truly "patriots" or "traitors." It frequently happens that a "peace of betrayal" can be brought about only by a military hero from an earlier era.[40]

The original Instant Thunder plan was modified considerably by air force planners in the Riyadh "Black Hole" planning cell under the direction of Lt. Gen. Charles Horner and Brig. Gen. "Buster" Glosson. The resulting plan retained from Instant Thunder the concept of working from the "inside out" in order to destroy or incapacitate highly valued target classes. But it rested on no single theory or approach to command-and-control disruption. In addition, it called for attrition of Iraqi capabilities in order both to impair the Iraqi war machine and to cause Iraq to rethink its continued occupation of Kuwait. The adapted air campaign plan resulted both from modifications by planners in Riyadh and revisions suggested by exigency once the campaign got under way.

III. FROM COERCIVE DIPLOMACY TO COERCIVE WAR

On January 16, 1991, the United States and its allies launched a massive air campaign against Iraq. The objective of the campaign was to induce

Saddam's compliance with the demands of President Bush and the United Nations for a prompt withdrawal of Iraqi forces from Kuwait. The U.S. and allied air campaign was unprecedented in its scope. More than two thousand U.S. and other coalition aircraft flew as many as three thousand sorties per day. The setting for the application of air power was ideal. Bombing targets were not obscured by jungle, woods, or other natural interference or camouflage. And Iraq's air force was no match for the combined air power of the allies. As former U.S. Air Force Chief of Staff Gen. Michael Dugan noted, "If there ever was a scenario where air power could be effective, this was it."[41]

From an operational standpoint, the U.S. air campaign against Iraq had three overlapping phases. The first phase was designed to involve air attacks on Iraqi command and control targets; on Iraqi nuclear, chemical, and biological warfare manufacturing facilities; and on other components of the Iraqi military infrastructure. In preparation for this phase of the attack, and in order to clear the skyways for the operation of coalition aircraft throughout Iraqi battle space, U.S. planners emphasized the suppression of Iraqi air defenses. In the second phase, an interdiction campaign was designed to isolate Saddam Hussein's crack Republican Guard and other forces from reinforcement and resupply of forward deployed elements in the KTO. In the final phase, air support would be provided to the ground forces of the coalition as they moved against the Iraqi forces remaining in Kuwait.[42]

The Iraqi air force, including its air defenses, was caught by surprise on January 16, a fact that might seem monumentally absurd, given the pervasive public knowledge that President Bush had received UN authorization to use force against Iraq as of that date. But the expectation that the United States would eventually attack had not transferred into an accurate prediction by Iraqi intelligence about the specific timing of the attack. In a classical case of "signal to noise" confusion, the flurry of last-minute diplomatic exchanges and proposals in search of a peaceful resolution to the Gulf crisis by various world leaders probably obscured from Iraq the resolve and immediate preparation for war by U.S. and allied air forces. The initial attacks on January 16 were devastating, clobbering Iraqi air defenses and command and control targets with such effectiveness that the Iraqi Air Force was essentially out of the picture of air superiority combat.

These initial successes in the strategic air war cleared the way for accomplishment of the missions of interdiction and close air support for the ground phase of the war. The interdiction campaign against a "target-rich" environment included Iraq's entire military infrastructure, not omitting its stationary defensive forces in Kuwait and its mobile armored and mechanized forces in Kuwait and in Iraq. The objectives of the interdiction campaign were to weaken further the command and control of the Iraqi armed forces, so that they would be forced to fight in disaggregated globules; to reduce the combat power of Saddam's crack Republican Guard forces so that they could not intervene decisively to rescue other Iraqi forces later cut off and destroyed in Kuwait; and to continue the destruction of other military- and defense-related targets in order to increase the price that Iraq would have to pay to keep fighting.

The third point is most pertinent to the discussion here. The U.S. and allied air campaign was designed not only to destroy a complex of targets in Iraq and thus deny those capabilities to Saddam Hussein but also to punish the Iraqi leadership by influencing its expectation of further damage to come. The air campaign was therefore as much a war of coercion as it was a war of destruction. The hope in some quarters of the U.S. and allied governments was that the bombing campaign by itself might induce the Iraqis to withdraw from Kuwait, without the necessity for a major ground offensive.

It was also the case that a mainly coercive air campaign could not avoid inflicting significant numbers of enemy casualties and causing some unplanned collateral damage. As Eliot A. Cohen noted in his assessment of the U.S. and allied air war against Iraq, there is no getting round the point that force "works" by causing destruction or death or by presenting the enemy with the fear of destruction and death.[43] And making fear believable in the enemy's mind requires that you actually have both the capability and the will to carry out the necessary punishment and denial missions.

A distinction must be made between the operational-tactical and the strategic level of warfare, relative to the political objectives of President Bush and U.S. allies, in order to assess the limits of coercive air war in the Gulf.[44] Air power can neither hold ground nor forcibly disarm soldiers in their defensive redoubts. Even under the most optimistic assumptions about the effectiveness of air power, then, ground operations would be necessary in order to "mop up" those Iraqi forces remaining in Kuwait unless Iraq chose to withdraw them voluntarily. Although these limitations of air power are clear on a tactical level, they are incidental to the question of whether air power alone could accomplish the strategic objectives of the United States in Iraq. The theory that it *could* do so rested on assumptions about the coercive effectiveness of air power in both punishment and denial roles.

Western strategists generally accept that the punishment capabilities of nuclear weapons are more meaningful for deterrence than are their denial capabilities. Most U.S. strategists also generally assume that, for conventional forces, the reverse is true: conventional denial capabilities are more important than conventional deterrence based on the threat of retaliatory punishment. Thus, many strategists would argue that a coercive air campaign with conventional forces should be *counterforce* (targeting emphasizes the destruction of enemy forces and supporting military capability) rather than *countervalue* (targeting emphasizes the destruction of social and economic values). Its objective would be to destroy the instruments of military power of the opponent, in order to induce the opponent to see the futility of further fighting.[45] In addition to avoiding gratuitous attacks on civilians, a counterforce-oriented campaign reduces the competency of the enemy force, thereby influencing the decision calculus of the enemy leadership against continued fighting.

Although these arguments are widely held in the U.S. defense community, they must be qualified in several ways. In conventional war, the decision calculus of an opponent may not be amenable to influence based on subjective estimates of future losses, until the point at which the opponent's entire war machine's back is broken. Rather than experiencing a gradual shift in will to fight from "yes" to "no," the opponent may meet air and other attacks with stiff resistance until suffering a "catastrophic fold" in ability to fight back. Sudden collapse of an opponent's fighting power may shift the decision calculus overnight from extreme optimism to extreme pessimism. Hitler insisted that wonder weapons, including newer versions of V-2 rockets, would come to his rescue even as his leading generals saw their forces collapse on the eastern and western fronts. During the last months and weeks of war Hitler issued orders affecting imaginary or mostly destroyed forces. Only the virtual collapse of the city of Berlin on his head finally persuaded the Führer that all was lost.

A second qualification is that air power, especially in the massive doses administered by the allied coalition against Iraq in January and February of 1991, is not a surgical instrument. The precision of bombing has improved dramatically since World War II, and even since Vietnam. Nonetheless, the colocation of civil and military installations combined with inevitable bombing errors ensure that massive numbers of sorties against "military" targets will also include significant amounts of "collateral damage." There is no such thing as a purely counterforce air war, except on a very small, and therefore insignificant, scale. This argument, if correct, implies that not only the denial aspects of counterforce campaigns, but also the inadvertent punishment that inevitably accompanies them, are important in inducing the opponent to "cooperate" by negotiating for war termination.

Third, coercion of an enemy government that is losing a military campaign is more likely to be successful if that government is divided into various factions. The "outs" can exploit the losses already sustained by the armed forces and by the civilian population to bring policy judgments to bear against the prior decisions of the "ins." If, on the other hand, the enemy leadership is united in its pursuit of war aims, or if dissenters lack powerful and influential voices compared to those in favor of continued war, the potential for coercive influence is diminished.[46] One of the factors that limited the effectiveness of U.S. air power in Vietnam was the lack of any "peace party" within the political leadership of North Vietnam. Although they emphasized tactical flexibility in their use of diplomacy and fighting tempo, North Vietnam's strategic compass never deviated from the objective of taking over South Vietnam. In similar fashion, Saddam brooked no opposition to his decisions, reducing the opportunity for any dissident faction to organize in favor of early war termination. In cases such as these, the coercive influence of air power may be as dependent upon the expectations of an undivided enemy leadership about future punishment, including their own survival, as it is dependent upon the diminished future competency of their armed forces. Conventional deterrence, unlike nuclear deterrence, depends upon punishment and denial capabilities that are based in the same military forces.

The U.S. air war against Iraq is but one case among many that demonstrates that the coercive and attritional aspects of the use of force cannot easily be separated in many actual cases. Policymakers may adopt a "try and see" variant of coercive punishment just as they have adopted "try and see" variations of crisis diplomacy.[47] In the first stages of the Gulf crisis, the Bush administration clearly *preferred* to attempt to induce Saddam Hussein to withdraw his forces from Kuwait voluntarily, just as President Kennedy had preferred to induce Khrushchev to voluntarily withdraw his missiles from Cuba. Kennedy avoided actual war, and Bush did not, although the military balance in both cases overwhelmingly favored the United States. Nevertheless, the initial phase of the U.S. war against Iraq was not just a campaign designed to bring about the destruction of Iraqi military capabilities. President Bush indicated repeatedly that the destruction would stop if Saddam would withdraw from Kuwait, and that the destruction would continue if Iraq did not withdraw. Given the declared U.S. objective of compelling Iraqi withdrawal from Kuwait and nothing more, the coalition air war against Iraq fit the paradigm of coercive bargaining.[48] As shown in table 12, the authoritative *Gulf War Air Power Survey* summary of objectives and accomplishments in the air war against Iraq supports the argument for the interdependency of coercive and attritional air warfare.

Subsequent to the Gulf War of 1991, however, some expert analysis was deliberately cautious in attributing to air power the keys to strategic victory against Iraq. The *Gulf War Air Power Survey* noted that precision attacks against Iraqi leadership and command/control/communications (CCC; C3) "clearly fell short of fulfilling the ambitious hope entertained by at least some airmen that bombing leadership and C3 targets might put enough pressure on the regime to bring about its overthrow. . . ."[49] The same study noted that "bombing alone therefore, failed to achieve the objective of eliminating the existing Iraqi nuclear weapons program" and that attacks on oil refineries and storage in Iraq "bore no significant results."[50] Coalition targeting of Iraqi nuclear assets fell short of expectations because prewar intelligence about Iraq's nuclear program was misleading.

Air Vice Marshal Tony Mason's centennial assessment of air power noted that "after 100 years there is still no incontrovertible evidence that strategic bombardment has been decisive in breaking the determination

Table 12
Summary of Air Campaign against Selected Target Sets,
Operation Desert Storm

Target Sets	Intended Objectives/Effects	Actual Results
Integrated air defense system (IADS), Strategic air defense (SAD), and airfields	Early air superiority: • suppress medium- and high-altitude air defenses throughout Iraq • contain/destroy Iraqi air force (AF)	IADS blinded and suppressed, or in some cases intimidated: • low-altitude anti-aircraft artillery (AAA) and Iraqi strategic air missiles (SAMs) remained • Iraqi AF bottled up on bases • possible two air-to-surface Iraqi sorties • 375 of 594 hardened air bases (HABs) destroyed/damaged • Iraqi AF fled to Iran beginning Jan. 25, 1991
Naval	Attain sea control: • permit naval operations in northern Persian Gulf	All Iraqi naval combatants neutralized or sunk: • other vessels sunk • Silkworm missiles remain active throughout war

Table 12 (Continued)

Target Sets	Intended Objectives/Effects	Actual Results
Leadership & Telecommunications	Disrupt government, destroy key gov't. control facilities Isolate Iraqi leadership from forces in Kuwaiti Theater of Operations (KTO) and weaken leadership control over people	Some disruption, to uncertain degree: • Saddam remains in power • no decapitation of politico-military high command Telecommunications reduced substantially: • links to KTO are never completely cut • international communications cut
Electricity & Oil	Shut down national grid: • minimize long-term damage to civilian economy Cut flow of fuel and lubricants to Iraqi forces: • avoid lasting damage to oil production	Rapid shutdown of grid: • electric grid down 55 percent by Jan. 17; down 88 percent by Feb. 9 • lights out in Baghdad • some unintended damage to generators Refining capacity down 93 percent by Day 34: • destruction of about 20 percent of the fuel and lubricants at refineries and major depots • 43-day war precluded long-term effects

Table 12 (Continued)

Target Sets	Intended Objectives/Effects	Actual Results
Nuclear, biological, and chemical weapons (NBC)	Destroy chemical and biological weapons: • prevent use against coalition • destroy production capability Destroy nuclear program	Some chemical weapons destroyed: • most survived • chemical use by Iraq deterred No biological weapons found by UN Nuclear program "inconvenienced" (UN): • most program elements survive
&		
Short-range, surface-to surface missile (SCUDs)	Prevent/suppress use: • destroy production and infrastructure • keep Israel out of war	Firings somewhat suppressed, not salvos: • SCUD operations pressured • aircraft destroy few (if any) MELs/TELs (mobile SCUDs)
Railroads/Bridges	Cut supply lines to KTO: • prevent retreat of Iraqi forces	All important bridges destroyed: • many workarounds by Iraqis • short duration of war limits effects
Republican Guard (RG)	Destroy the RG	• attrition by G-day (start of the ground war) is less than 50 percent
&		• some RG units and 800+ tanks escape

Table 12 (Continued)

Target Sets	Intended Objectives/Effects	Actual Results
Other Ground Forces in KTO	Reduce combat effectiveness 50 percent (armor and artillery) by G-day RG immobilized:	Front-line forces are destroyed in place or waiting to surrender • attrition by G-day is greater than 50 percent • morale destroyed by air bombardment

Source: Keaney and Cohen, *A Revolution in Warfare,* 102–103, as adapted by author.

of any opponent to carry on fighting."[51] This cautious appraisal of air power's centrality to victory in the Gulf or in any previous war would no doubt be contested by air enthusiasts in and out of uniform. My concern is not to resolve that debate, but to call the reader's intention to the yardstick by which critics are evaluating the performance of air power in Desert Storm and elsewhere. The *Gulf War Air Power Survey* claims that air power did not create enough pressure to induce regime overthrow; Mason claims that strategic bombardment is not incontestably able to break wills.

Both statements are noteworthy for what they assume about the *object* of air power in the Gulf War: not only to destroy target sets in order to forcibly prevent Iraqi action, but also to *induce* Iraqi compliance with behavior desired by the coalition. The goalposts are rooted firmly in coercive evaluative criteria: Air power is judged for its effectiveness as a persuader, albeit a persuader by means of coercive destruction. Indeed, one of the valuable lessons of Desert Storm is that the coercive use of air power against military and war-supporting infrastructure targets may be *more dissuasive* than the comprehensive attack on populations or other target sets envisioned by air power's founding fathers.[52] "Coercive," in this case does not imply "limited" in the sense that operational and tactical decisions are muddled by policy "adhocracy."[53]

One argument for a strong fit between the U.S. and allied air war against Iraq and a coercive bargaining model was that the choice of continued suffering was left up to Saddam Hussein. Bush would have been under great pressure from the U.S. Congress and from members of the allied coalition, especially Arab members, if Saddam Hussein had taken up the challenge of conciliation and begun to remove his troops from Kuwait in January or early February, 1991, even at a slow pace. But Saddam would not play this diplomatic card until later, after coalition air attacks had caused significant, if not decisive, losses to his ground forces deployed in Kuwait and in Iraq. Only the imminent expectation of total military defeat for his forces in Kuwait changed his decision calculus for or against continued war. He surely realized by the middle of February that this defeat might also be accompanied by the destruction of the remainder of his offensive military power, and perhaps by his own political disestablishment.[54]

Saddam's "strategic" objectives, once crisis management faded into combat, were apparently threefold. First, he sought to create a war of attrition, including an extended phase of ground fighting, which would make the war unpopular with the U.S. public, Congress, and media. Extended ground fighting with high casualties would also alienate allied members from the U.S. coalition.[55] Saddam's second objective was to expand the war geographically (horizontal escalation) by bringing in Israel, a move that would also, in his view, divide some Arab members of the coalition from the United States. A third Iraqi objective—which became clear only in February, as Saddam entertained visits from Soviet officials offering to mediate the conflict—was to hold the United States to its declared objective only, of expelling Iraqi forces from Kuwait, and to deter or otherwise prevent the expansion of U.S. and allied war aims to the destruction of all of Iraq's military power and the removal of Saddam as a player in the postwar world.

The problem for Iraq was that each of these objectives required that elements of a coercive strategy, that of bargaining while fighting, had to be amalgamated with elements of traditional fighting in order to succeed. But Iraq was unable to impose any unacceptable costs on the United States and its coalition partners. As the coalition proceeded to destroy Saddam's air and ground forces, his bargaining leverage for the postwar world progressively diminished. When the effectiveness of his armed forces reached the point of "catastrophic" failure, his future influence rested solely on his potential to prolong an already-lost military campaign. Having missed the opportunity to negotiate for war termination while he still had the means to apply a coercive strategy, Saddam Hussein ensured that the final terms of armistice would be that much more unfavorable for his country.

CONCLUSION

The Gulf War was a successful use of coercive military strategy in the context of a limited war within a single theater of strategic military action. It was a military-technical overture to the revolution in military affairs that has made precision strike weapons and "C4ISR" (Command, Control, Communications, Computers, Intelligence, Surveillance, and Reconnaissance) the trump cards of future war. It was also successful in meeting the challenges of an unusual context for coalition management. The most unusual group of odd fellows ever assembled for battle went to war against Iraq in 1991. One nonmember of the coalition, Israel, even "participated" by not officially jumping into battle. The United States was aided by a large force structure remaining from the Cold War, by a theater of operations conducive to air mastery and isolation of the battlefield, and by Saddam's fortuitous strategic incompetence.

Although these conclusions about the Gulf War and Desert Storm are not new, their use in this chapter results in another conclusion: The Gulf War showed that limited war can, and sometimes should, be fought without restraint. The phrase "without restraint" does not imply the repeal of Clausewitz; war still serves the requirements of policy. But in the Gulf War the United States demonstrated that a war that *remains subordinate to policy* objectives can be concluded more quickly and more successfully if *force application* to the assigned mission is not hobbled by *self-imposed and arbitrary* limitations. The air war against Iraq was both an exercise in coercive bargaining and a campaign of attrition to reduce Iraq's wartime and postwar military capabilities. The coercive aspects were most apparent in the early destruction of Iraq's air defenses, command and control, and offensive air power. A calculating adversary might have quit right there, but Saddam Hussein was not using the decision calculus of Western deterrence theory.

4

Vietnam and Coercive Strategy

Of all limited wars fought by the United States in the Cold War years, none remains as controversial as the war in Vietnam. Some critics of U.S. strategy in Vietnam contend that the Johnson administration erred in choosing a strategy of coercion rather than a traditional military strategy for victory in combat, charging former Defense Secretary Robert S. McNamara with responsibility for this flawed strategy of coercion.[1] But was it indeed a mistake to apply a coercive form of military strategy in Vietnam? Was it this flawed strategy that led to the eventual U.S. withdrawal and South Vietnamese defeat?

This chapter argues that the failure of U.S. policy and strategy in Vietnam was not a necessary consequence of the United States' attempt to employ coercive military strategy.[2] Vietnam was not Europe; no U.S. commitment to fight in Southeast Asia, however expansive, could have been permitted to escalate into a direct military confrontation with China or Russia, the outside sources of military and diplomatic succor to North Vietnam. International politics thus dictated, from the outset, a war of limited aims and means. U.S. domestic politics also dictated limited war, especially after both strategy and policy had apparently failed.

The chain of assumptions that led to a dead end for the United States in Vietnam can best be seen in microcosm: the perspectives held by Robert McNamara and shared widely within the highest circles of Kennedy-Johnson policymakers.[3] To use McNamara as a conceptual pivot is appropriate not only because of his Cabinet responsibility for the U.S. war effort but for two other reasons, examined in more depth below. First, McNamara was the product of a civilian culture that was, and mostly remains, innocent of serious tutelage in the art of war. Second, McNamara's ideas were partly crafted by a hubris about war that proved, in the event, deficient both in theory and in application. In Vietnam, the United States unsuccessfully and unwittingly coerced itself.

I. GOVERNMENT IS LIKE BUSINESS

The first assumption widely shared by elites who made U.S. policy in Vietnam, and one that still resonates in the halls of Congress and throughout the body politic, is that the way to improve government is to run it like a business. The business of America, we are told, *is* business; or, as former Defense Secretary and General Motors head Charles Wilson once said, what's good for General Motors is good for the country. This shibboleth dies hard; today's Congress is every bit as vocal as that in the 1960s about "eliminating waste" and running the government in a "more businesslike" manner.

McNamara, who had been an automobile executive and operations analyst, brought this perspective to the Pentagon and applied it to management and strategic decision making. His Planning, Programming, and Budgeting System (PPBS) had a profound effect on the Pentagon and spread like a bacillus to other departments throughout the federal government. (This was before the day of sophisticated desktop computers and their statistical program packages.) McNamara and his "whiz kids" imported from think tanks and universities felt that they had discovered something new.

It should be said, in fairness to McNamara, that whatever the justice of his claims as a strategist, his methods keep reappearing from boardroom to seminar in protean guises: management by objective, quality control management, total quality management, and so forth. Because much of this paradigm now emanates from the private sector and because most of the young tyros who run businesses today would not know McNamara's Pentagon from McNamara's band, the source of this legacy has largely been forgotten. Whether McNamara improved Pentagon management itself is debatable; what he did accomplish— beyond doubt—was to improve the publicity surrounding Pentagon management.

McNamara accomplished this feat by the use of adroit jargon and by bringing into the Pentagon economists and systems analysts to assist him in centralizing control of resource allocation. The assumption made by

McNamara and his statisticians was that they could seize the strategic initiative by controlling the division of the resource pie among the various army, navy, and air force claimants. Having put the military on the defensive about resource allocation, they believed, they could control it through its need to justify future weapons and missions in terms suited to the PPBS process.[4] The U.S. armed forces' leadership quickly learned that the "how" of justification was now as important as the "what." Once they adjusted, they fed back to the Office of the Secretary of Defense (OSD) those indicators and categories that OSD was anxious to hear.[5]

That this approach to resource allocation seemed to work is deceptive. It "worked" only because the defense budget grew rapidly in the Kennedy-Johnson years. The members of the Joint Chiefs of Staff and other military leaders would have been far more resistant to the new methods of decision making, and their implications for the autonomy of their individual services, had McNamara's management revolution taken place during a period of fiscal belt-tightening in defense. As it was, military leaders decided to play along, up to a point: They gave way on resource allocation, but demanded and largely received autonomy on strategy making.

In the world of business, resources do drive strategy, but McNamara's business-like assumption that control of military resources was equivalent to control of military strategy was wrong.[6] In the military, much more is involved in the strategy-making process than the surges and declines in available resources. Military strategy is a process of concept formation dominated by the ideas in the minds of today's generals about the kinds of wars that the United States might have to fight tomorrow.[7] It is therefore abstract rather than concrete, and prospective instead of retrospective. It cannot be pinned down to a balance sheet. Clausewitz derided the mistaken idea that war can be reduced to numbers as war by "algebra."[8] The term is not meant as a compliment.

McNamara's management methods told the military that the way to impress the Secretary of Defense, in discussions of strategy as in all else, was to quantify everything. The more quantification, the better.[9] But whereas the logistics and technological aspects of war are problems amenable to mathematical solutions, the will of an enemy is not. The systems analysts of the McNamara Pentagon made some contributions to the improvement of weapons procurement and budget forecasting, but when their zealotry ranged into military operations and strategy making the results were less impressive. According to two U.S. military historians,

> McNamara's "revolution" in the Pentagon gave "flexible response" a life that outlived Kennedy, for it brought such disarray to the armed forces and Congress that it took another war and a decade of learning and political infighting to devalue its assumptions. The very success of PPBS and systems analysis as defense management techniques—a success dependent upon Presidential support and Congressional confusion—extended the power of its practitioners from the development of military forces to the employment of those forces.[10]

It is possible to acknowledge a difference between war and business without isolating the study of war from that of other social disciplines. War is, after all, a social phenomenon: It takes place at a specific time and within a given social setting. The observation that war is not business does not exclude the possibility that strategic thinking is important in business as well as war. It is nevertheless the case that business strategy and war strategy have different *politics*. The politics of business strategy usually take place within a more or less consensual legal and social context. Even international business is highly regulated by custom and law, to the advantage of the competitors who would otherwise be cast adrift in an unpredictable world. The fate of U.S. savings and loan associations in the 1980s and of risky investments in derivatives in the 1990s show that business, however competitive it might be, recognizes "strategy" as appropriate only within a normative and legal framework that makes predictable the outcomes of that competition. Otherwise, business gives way to anarchy, and investment in the future is relegated to the past.

War, in contrast, assumes no mutually agreed-upon legal or normative framework between combatants. Although international law does provide some markers for "just war" and for other restraints upon the ferocity with which war can be fought, no enforcement exists apart from the voluntary willingness of the combatants to observe the various protocols of good behavior. The record in this regard is mixed. It is no small achievement that Geneva conventions and other agreements on the treatment of prisoners of war have helped to avoid gratuitous abuse of captives and to save lives in the largest wars of this century. But the record also shows that, whenever a state has chosen to violate the prevailing international norms against mistreatment of prisoners of war or of civilians, the state was not prevented from doing so unless and until it was defeated in battle. From Hitler's death camps to massacres in Rwanda, states have paid contextual attention to human rights of combatants and noncombatants, and usually when there was a reciprocal advantage in doing so.

Strategic thinking means defining objectives and identifying appropriate means to attain those objectives. In that general sense, individuals, corporations, and other entities engage in strategic thinking on a daily basis.[11] Strategy for war is set apart from this common-sense application in the business world as in other peacetime pursuits. Strategy for war is fundamentally political; its purview is the issues about which political leaders, representing the collective aspirations and hatreds of their followers, disagree—for example, the distribution of territory, the control of economic resources, and the balance of power or other values for which supply is inadequate to demand. Most fundamentally, the legal anarchy of the system of sovereign states places leaders in a permanent condition of possible or potential war, as the great English philosopher Thomas Hobbes explained. Survival of the political system as an independent unit, or of the culture and society, requires the ability not to lose in war against those who would destroy that state, society, or culture.

Because war is so political, it is a realm of absolute as well as relative losses. Or, in what amounts to the same thing, it is the realm of perceived absolute losses. The idea of national honor may not impress cynics as something worth fighting for, but history records that national honor rides into battle along with soldiers, sailors, and bombardiers whether invited or not. National honor is not divisible. It cannot be apportioned in percentages, some to the enemy and some to us. In a democratic society, public psychology places national honor at risk every time troops are sent into harm's way. The fighting forces of the United States carry this public psychology into battle as surely as they carry flags and division banners.

In the case of U.S. democracy, *America* goes to war, not just American armed forces. Standing behind U.S. armed forces are the hopes and fears of Americans not at the front. Although Americans despise politicians as a class and distrust peacetime military display, they will nevertheless agonize or exult over every news report of American failure or success in combat. American fighting forces lofted by public support for the stated objective of a war will more easily endure greater risk, and for a longer duration, than those uncertain of public sympathy. When American public opinion turns against a war's ends or means, American fighting forces feel stranded by failed policy and strategy, isolated from the culture that sustains them, and separated from the community that legitimizes their waging of battle.

The differences between war strategy and business strategy, including the heavier leavening of war strategy with "soft," value-laden variables that leaders neglect at their peril, are important in another respect. In military strategy above all, the strategist must comprehend the essence of the enemy. Commanders must know not only data points about the numbers of enemy effectives or combat forces, but also the more intangible enemy "otherness." Knowledge of the otherness of the enemy includes knowledge of cultural folkways and social mores, for they provide the keys to *anticipating* the enemy's next move. As Eliot A. Cohen and John Gooch note in their discussion of military failures to anticipate, "When military organizations look at future war they must think as hard and realistically about the politico-military conditions under which it will occur as about the tactics each side will adopt, and they must attempt to see how the one level of warfare will shape or direct the other."[12]

Had U.S. leaders ascertained correctly the politico-military context for the commitment of U.S. combat forces to the war in Vietnam, they would not have underestimated the determination of their North Vietnamese foes. The mind of the enemy was assumed amenable to military persuasion of the Western, high-technology style *and*, simultaneously, to diplomatic suasion in the form of bombing pauses and peace overtures. McNamara's apologia of 1995 acknowledges that the "otherness" of the opponent was never correctly grasped: "The CIA felt that the North Vietnamese had much greater staying power than the administration (and Westy) believed. It turned out the CIA was correct."[13]

II. NOT-SO-LIMITED WAR

The Kennedy administration was faced with the task of fleshing out a theory of competition against revolutionary wars of national liberation and providing the means for competing. Kennedy and his advisors, including McNamara, went about doing so with zest and optimism about a U.S. democratic counterrevolution that could offer an alternative to communist-inspired or -directed revolution. The idea of democratic counterrevolution was in keeping with the theories of limited war that had developed in the 1950s and trickled into the Kennedy administration by the time he assumed office. Limited war was more political than military in its means, as well as in its ends. Not fully understood then or now is the fact that limited war also has a *moral* dimension. Waging a limited war creates the expectation that force can be used in a discriminating and humane manner, an expectation not always shared by combatants or possible to accomplish in the fog of war.[14]

However, the limited wars imagined by the U.S. explicators of limited war theory in the 1950s were conventional, not unconventional, wars.[15] The theory had explained why wars had to be limited to something below the threshold of global war, but not how the concept of limited war applied to a state torn by civil strife and alternate factions competing for the sole prerogative of rightful governmental rule.[16] In addition, the theories of limited war and coercive diplomacy told leaders more about how to manage crises between nuclear-armed Americans and Soviets than it did about how to conciliate two opposed sides in a feral, primordial, life-and-death struggle for survival and control. In a nuclear crisis-management situation, the graduated application of force is possible because a win-win solution exists: the avoidance of any outbreak of nuclear war, no matter what else happens.

Civil war, in contrast, is about as close to a zero-sum game in politics as one can imagine: any gain for one side amounts to a loss for the other. Even the act of slowing down the pace of events in order to forestall unintended violence—an obvious component of any nuclear crisis management—is contradicted by the logic of internal war: if the insurgent opponents of the government in power do not lose, they win. Unless and until they have abandoned their quest or lost their ability to depose the existing regime, insurgents represent a political alternative that gives hope to the discontented and frustrated. That hope is the touchstone of revolution, now or later.[17]

Because of this strategically zero-sum character of revolutionary civil war in Vietnam, U.S. coercive air war between 1965 and 1968 (Operation Rolling Thunder) proved unable to pressure North Vietnam to the conference table, nor to halt its support for its allied National Liberation Front (NLF) activities within South Vietnam.[18] Rolling Thunder was conducted in four phases. The objective of the first phase, during the spring and summer of 1965, was to gradually increase the tempo of operations against a variety of military, transportation, and industrial targets, while engaging in diplomatic signaling. In the second phase, from the summer of 1965 through the winter of 1966–67, U.S. bombing emphasized air interdiction in order to disrupt the flow of troops and supplies from North into South Vietnam. In phase three, from the spring to fall of 1967, President Johnson removed previously imposed political constraints against bombing certain targets by authorizing attacks against the majority of industrial and transportation targets in and near Hanoi, Haiphong, and the buffer zone between North Vietnam and China. During the fourth, and final, phase of Rolling Thunder, from April to November, 1968, bombing was gradually de-escalated in the aftermath of the Tet Offensive, Johnson's decision not to seek reelection, and rising public opposition to the war.[19] A summary of these phases and their rationales appears in table 13.

The failure of Operation Rolling Thunder was twofold. First, the mix of strategic concepts or influence models by which the campaign was directed almost ensured that it would be inconsistent in its results. Although the imagery of "phases" can indeed be applied to the changes over time in U.S. target lists, the United States was in fact trying to accomplish all three goals at once and the contrasting and competing images of strategic *effect* were never resolved within the administration.[20] Second, the United States' varying coercive air strategies were mostly irrelevant to the enemy's strategy, which from 1965 to 1968 relied mainly on unconventional warfare immune to coercion by conventional military power. (In contrast, the United States would have some success in using coercive air power against Hanoi in 1972 [Linebacker I and II massive bombing campaigns intended to force North Vietnam to confer-

Table 13
Phases of Operation Rolling Thunder, 1965–68

	Model	Timing	Targeting Emphasis
Phase 1	"Lenient" Schelling model (civilians in Johnson administration)	Spring-Summer, 1965	Subject North Vietnam's economy, especially industry, to gradually increasing risk Emphasis on military, transportation, and industrial targets, gradually moving northward
Phase 2	Denial by air interdiction (U.S. Army leadership)	Summer, 1965, through Winter, 1966–67	Disrupt North's ability to send troops and supplies to South Armed reconnaissance against infiltration targets throughout most of North
Phase 3	"Genteel" Douhet (U.S. Air Force leadership)	Spring-Fall, 1967	Sudden escalation in intensity of attacks against majority of industrial and transportation targets previously withheld from target lists Targets included electric power, chemical and steel plants, and key rail bridges
Phase 4	President and advisors, feeling various pressures	Apr.–Nov., 1968	Gradual deescalation Bombing rolled back from Hanoi-Haiphong area, first to 20th parallel, then to 19th

Source: Pape, *Bombing to Win,* 181–88.

ence table] because North Vietnam had by then begun to employ a conventional offensive strategy vulnerable to air interdiction.)[21]

U.S. military strategy in Vietnam was further handicapped by the army's institutional professional biases in favor of large-scale conventional warfare based on firepower and attrition. This conceptual rigidity on the part of the army was not shared by the marines and the CIA, which were successful in adapting to the requirements of counterinsurgency warfare. Counterinsurgency strategy emphasized getting close to the rural population and providing them training and support for the securing of villages. This involved the local population in their own security and denied the North Vietnamese and Viet Cong access to vital sources of supply, intelligence, and other supports. Civilian Irregular Defense Groups (CIDG), trained by the Green Berets under CIA direction, and Combined Action Platoons (CAPs), organized by the marines, showed that U.S. civil and military agencies could apply counterinsurgency doctrine with success in Vietnam. Counterinsurgency did not fit the army concept of warfare, however. At most, the army acknowledged that counterguerrilla training might be useful for special operations *within a conventional war*. The Kennedy and Johnson administrations' civilian-leadership interest in counterinsurgency doctrine was deflected by army leadership. Gen. George H. Decker, U.S. Army chief of staff from 1960 to 1962, was of the opinion that "any good soldier can handle guerrillas," and Gen. Maxwell D. Taylor judged that counterinsurgency was "just a small form of war," adding that "all this cloud of dust that's coming out of the White House really isn't necessary."[22]

III. ESCALATION OBSESSION

One of the reasons why the United States was unwilling to take more direct military action against North Vietnam was the assumption that if it did so, the Chinese and possibly the Soviets would become active combatants on the North Vietnamese side, thus expanding a regional conflict into a general conventional war among great powers, and possibly touching off a nuclear war. The U.S. assumption that the Soviet Union would have been willing to act as North Vietnam's security guarantor in the face of an escalated U.S. war effort in the North was driven by an emphasis in U.S. diplomacy on the consanguinity, if not political identity, of all communist states in the region. It was also driven by the "domino effect" assumption with regard to the military vulnerability of noncommunist states in South Asia: if one fell, according to this reasoning, the rest would follow.

These assumptions set the stage for an out-of-context U.S. military strategy in which the North became a de facto military sanctuary except for air attacks on a target list that, although progressively expanded, could not inflict decisive pain. Thus North Vietnam could not be coerced to come to the table and negotiate peace terms that were acceptable both to South Vietnam and to the United States. Rather than use the United States' position of nuclear parity with Moscow to isolate the theater of operations between 1965 and 1968 and apply decisive force within that theater against Hanoi, U.S. leaders allowed Hanoi to define the battlefield and confine it to South Vietnam, where they and their NLF allies had the advantages of a supportive social and political milieu for counterinsurgency and later, after the United States departed, for conventional war.

The United States' fear of escalation based on a possible nuclear confrontation with Moscow was misplaced. The Soviet Union was risk-averse, not risk-acceptant, about involvement in any war with the United States during this period, including nuclear war. In the aftermath of Khrushchev's ouster, the Soviet leadership under Leonid Brezhnev had just embarked on a nuclear buildup designed to correct an assumed nuclear inferiority in survivable and deliverable strategic or intercontinental nuclear weapons. One reason for this buildup was the Cuban missile crisis and the revelations preceding that crisis about the asymmetrical relationship between U.S. and Soviet strategic nuclear capabilities. One prominent Soviet diplomat told his U.S. counterparts immediately after the denouement of the Cuban missile crisis that "you will never do this to us again," meaning that the United States would never again be able to extract concessions from Moscow by nuclear coercion based on a significant difference in second-strike capability. This buildup—which actually began under Khrushchev before the Cuban missile crisis but accelerated under his successors—was designed to establish strategic nuclear parity by the end of the decade, and it effectively did so with regard to at least one category of delivery systems: land-based strategic missiles, also known as intercontinental ballistic missiles, or ICBMs.

However, achieving missile parity was not the same as attaining overall strategic nuclear equivalence with the United States, and the Soviets knew it. The United States maintained effective advantages in the deployment and capabilities of two other elements of the strategic nuclear triad: submarine- and bomber-delivered weapons. The Soviet long-range bomber force of the 1960s was grossly inferior to the American in numbers and in capabilities, and remained so throughout the Cold War. Even more significant was U.S. supremacy in capacity to wage strategic nuclear warfare from the sea by means of submarine-launched ballistic missiles. Although the Soviets eventually built larger numbers of ballistic missile submarines and had more generations of SSBNs (Submarine-Launched Ballistic Missile) deployed at any one time, the United States had a crucial advantage in the competition over sea-based delivery systems. In the 1960s and throughout the Cold War, the United States was unsurpassed in its ability to conduct open ocean anti-submarine warfare (ASW), mainly through its fleet of nuclear-armed attack submarines (SSNs) supported by advanced systems of communications, control, and underwater sound detection. In addition, the United States' surface naval fleet would have (for most of the Cold War) been able to dominate its Soviet counterpart almost anywhere on the open oceans apart from the littoral regions of the Soviet Union.

This overall leadership in sea-based warfare, including the potential to conduct nuclear war from beneath the oceans, was significant because sea-based nuclear weapons were the most *survivable* against any surprise attack. U.S. and eventually Soviet sea-based systems ensured that neither side could contemplate—even under the most "optimistic" (or fatalistic) assumptions—a first strike against the other side with a good chance of denying its opponent the ability to inflict an historically unprecedented, and socially unacceptable, retaliation. The sea-based deterrent locked the nuclear genie into the bottle until and unless one side or the other could come up with credible defenses against massive nuclear attack. Both tried, but neither could. In effect, although the United States and the Soviet Union of the 1960s and early 1970s could make credible nuclear threats against the allies of one another, they could not make credible nuclear threats to attack each others' homelands.

McNamara, who coined the term "mutual assured destruction" (MAD) as the United States' declared nuclear policy (although the term had little or nothing to do with actual targeting doctrine), was a major proponent of the argument that defenses were bad, and offenses good, for deterrence. He argued in 1967, to the consternation of then-Soviet Premier Alexei Kosygin, that the deployment of Soviet anti-ballistic missiles (ABMs, now called "BMDs" for ballistic missile defenses) would destabilize the arms race by forcing the United States to react with a compensatory buildup of its own offensive forces. In other words, the United States would maintain a certain target coverage no matter what the Soviets did. If the Soviets sought to protect their cities against an American retaliatory strike, U.S. leaders would interpret that activity as indicating Soviet leaders' willingness in a crisis to risk a massive and disarming first strike against U.S. nuclear forces.[23]

The assumption that the Soviet leadership would risk their entire political system or society on the fractional advantage of relative numbers of megatons or warheads was an assumption that could appeal only to a technologist like McNamara. With or without defenses, no sane Soviet leader would deliberately start a war involving tens of millions instant fatalities, let alone those that would soon follow.[24] Improved defenses would not make a general nuclear war—involving thousands of nuclear missiles and warheads on each side—any more fightable or winnable than no nuclear defenses at all. Defenses did have two more practical and modest purposes: First, they might be used to protect national command centers in order to maintain political control or accountability, including political control over the commanders of nuclear weapons, during the early stages of a limited nuclear war that politicians had some hope of stopping. Second, defenses might be used to protect the most vulnerable portions of each side's second-strike force, thereby both complicating any attacker's strategy and reassuring the defender that forces need not be placed on permanent hair-trigger alert to avoid prompt destruction.

Using the second of these rationales, the Nixon administration succeeded for a time in getting Congress to support missile defenses for the United States, but the commitment was mostly a symbolic bargaining chip for the START (Strategic Arms Reduction Talks) negotiations as leverage to limit Soviet missile defenses. Neither the U.S. Congress nor the Department of Defense, then or later, expected that defenses could play a serious part in deterrence or in protecting important national values during a limited nuclear war. Even during the Reagan administration, after the President's 1983 "Star Wars" speech calling for research into a comprehensive missile defense program, most of the Pentagon simply dismissed the idea of anti-missile defense as a strategic pipe dream. The Gulf War of 1991 and the use of Patriot theater missile defenses against Iraqi SCUDs (Soviet-designed surface-to-surface missile of tactical range) has temporarily revived interest in missile defense for tactical missions, and several research and development projects toward that end are now in progress in the United States and elsewhere. Theater missile defenses against attacks on U.S. or allied forward-deployed forces may be feasible by the turn of the century, as well as limited, national missile defenses against accidental or rogue-state attacks. But the prospect of nuclear defenses effectively destabilizing the long-standing balance based on offensive retaliation is not within reach even after a half century of the nuclear age.

McNamara himself, early in his tenure of office, attempted to set out a doctrine for graduated nuclear deterrence that emphasized prompt attacks on military targets and the withholding of attacks against cities.[25] It soon became clear to him that gradual nuclear deterrence could not be implemented without a quantity of U.S. weapons, relative to Soviet ones, sufficient to create a perception of U.S. nuclear counterforce superiority. The secretary of defense thereafter became more interested in the firebreak between conventional and nuclear war, an interest that led him to insist that U.S. European allies in NATO collaborate on a buildup of forces sufficient to fight a conventional war in Europe against Soviet and allied forces without recourse to nuclear weapons. It also led him to see the war in Vietnam through the conceptual lenses of possible nuclear escalation to a war with China and/or the Soviet Union if the United States were to strike directly to overthrow the regime in Hanoi. McNamara's memoirs give direct evidence of the linkage between his view of nuclear strategy and his insistence that the war in Vietnam had to be limited, both in political objectives sought and in military means used.[26]

Ironically, McNamara's fear of nuclear escalation was based in part on the fear of an aggressive Soviet Union that never was. The actual Soviet Cold War strategy was not one in which the Red Army was poised for a conventional military attack on Western Europe, backed by the intimidation of Soviet nuclear power to deter U.S. and allied NATO escalation. In fact, Soviet Cold War strategy emphasized a "defense of the Fatherland" complex in which preparedness for any and all forms of war was the only reliable preventive for war. Rejecting the U.S. notion of deterrence as intimidation (*ustrashenie*), Kremlin military planners focused on avoiding a replay of June 22, 1941, when they were caught inadequately prepared to conduct a strategic defensive preparatory to a counteroffensive.[27] Stalin's insistence upon ritualistic observance of the nonaggression pact with Hitler signed in 1939, and Stalin's purges of his own military high command from 1937–39, left Soviet defenders neither politically nor militarily ready for the German surprise attack. Gorbachev's military revisionism was less real than apparent: he built on a trend already in existence among Soviet defense intellectuals by the early 1980s. Even officially authorized Soviet military publications designed for internal consumption emphasized after 1977 that nuclear war could not be won and that Moscow would never be the first to initiate the use of any nuclear weapons. Gorbachev's "defensive sufficiency" was a new rhetoric to express a widely perceived military reality: Neither a nuclear nor a conventional offensive against NATO would leave Moscow with an acceptable outcome.

U.S. leaders' image of the Soviet Union—based on the U.S.-Soviet nuclear deterrent relationship but colored by an arms-race-driven assessment of Soviet motives—placed constraints on their development of a contextually appropriate strategy for victory in Vietnam. Nuclear weapons tied the hands of both Moscow and Washington, but U.S. leaders were more attentive to the risks of escalation. Soviet support for the North Vietnamese continued throughout the war but at a level of aid and assistance short of Soviet combat involvement. In Afghanistan during the 1980s, the United States would turn the tables and apply the same indirect support strategy against Soviet military power, to the same kind of effect.

The preceding argument does not propose that an *unlimited* war against North Vietnam would have been a preferred U.S. strategy for the use of ground, air, or maritime forces between 1965 and 1968. It contends, instead, that the context for military decision making in Vietnam precluded an effective strategy for victory in South Vietnam, instead turning North Vietnam into a virtual sanctuary, and assuring it against any jeopardy to its national self-defense capability or to its regime. So assured, North Vietnam could wage war without restraint, albeit in stages and in relation to its changing assumptions about U.S. and South Vietnamese staying power.

CONCLUSION

The United States never found an appropriate coercive military strategy for winning the Vietnam war at an acceptable cost. Given the determination of the North Vietnamese and their NLF allies, it is conceivable that such a strategy did not exist. A successful strategy requires that the coercer have available and be willing to use decisive means for influencing the subject's calculation of cost and benefit. It also requires that the coercer understand correctly its own mix of costs and benefits and how that calculus can be influenced by domestic politics. The United States did not have nor use decisive means to influence the decisions of the South Vietnamese National Liberation Front, nor those of Hanoi.[28] And even if it had, the question "to what end" never really received a serious answer from U.S. policymakers who occupied themselves with falling dominoes, deterrence theories, world communism, and other abstractions far removed from the realities of counterinsurgency in Vietnam, while military art collapsed in the mud.

5

Collective Security
and Coercion

The idea of collective action among states to preserve peace or punish aggression is as old as the state system itself. Some attempts at collective security have been formalized as interstate alliances; others have been ad hoc coalitions. It can be prudent to fight with allies, despite the increased difficulty of coordinating military plans and policy guidance among multiple players. The United States' war in Vietnam suffered for lack of moral influence in part because important American allies shunned, or opposed, the effort. In contrast, U.S. efforts against Iraq in 1990 and 1991 acquired additional legitimacy due to UN and allied support, including the support of key Arab and Islamic countries.

This chapter discusses the relationship between collective security and coercive military strategy. It begins by explaining the theory of collective security; continues with a consideration of crisis management and collective security; and concludes with an examination of collective security and conflict limitation or termination. At each stage of the discussion, this chapter focuses on the ways in which past concepts of collective security have become irrelevant or endangered by dimensional changes in the principal sources of conflict since 1945. International institutions and great powers have long designed their peace-support mechanisms for a world in which most wars are between states, and the most important wars are among great powers. That assumption became less and less tenable as the Cold War grew older; in the post-Cold War world, it has been deflated entirely. Further, new technology for warfare may make possible the instigation and termination of "virtual" or real conflicts at nearly the speed of light.

I. COLLECTIVE SECURITY THEORY AND CONFLICT LIMITATION

The theory and practice of collective security are prone to widespread misunderstanding.[1] As John J. Mearsheimer has noted, "It is difficult to find scholarly work that makes the case for collective security without simultaneously expressing major reservations about the theory, and without expressing grave doubts that collective security could ever be realized in practice."[2] Collective security is not an alternative to a system of states based on self-help. It does not obviate the requirement for states to maintain credible deterrent and defensive forces. In essence, collective security is a form of balancing against aggression. It calls upon those members of the international community who are willing and able to commit their forces against aggressors or disturbers of the peace. Collective security is thus one of a number of possible strategies for coping with, not for transcending, the interstate balance of power. As Charles A. Kupchan and Clifford A. Kupchan have noted,

> Fully aware of the war-causing features of the international system, collective security seeks to provide a more effective mechanism for balancing against aggressors when they emerge, as well as to make aggression less likely by ameliorating the competitive nature of international relations.[3]

Collective security theory assumes that in most interstate conflict situations, one can determine with reasonable clarity the identities of both the aggressor and the defender.[4] The identity of the aggressor having been established, it follows that member states of the world community will permit their forces to be used to reestablish international order according to the status quo ante. No judgment is required about the correctness of the cause for which any of the combatants may be fighting. The assumption is that a state that disturbs the international status quo by military means has defined itself as an aggressor under international law. The legal obligation of other states is to resist that aggression. Collective security is therefore, in practice if not explicitly in theory, a formula which favors the international status quo. It also is theoretically biased in favor of interstate, as opposed to intrastate or nonstatist conflicts; of this, more below.

Little is said in the literature on collective security about the problem of crisis management. The assumption is that the overwhelming force of the majority of states arrayed against the possible aggressor will deter the aggressor state from actual resort to violence. The assumption that superior force will naturally deter aggression is one that seems to meet standards of common sense; regrettably, historical evidence does not always support the assumption. States have gone to war against other states or coalitions with actual or potential power far superior to their own. Examples of this behavior include Argentina's attack on the Falkland Islands in 1982 and Hitler's willingness to take on the United States, Britain, and the Soviet Union simultaneously during World War II. In neither of these cases did the entire world community attempt to deter the aggressor *before* the fact, so neither case really falsifies collective security theory as stated.

Cases in which the entire international community acts in crisis management or war against a potential or actual aggressor are so rare as to defy inference by means of sampling. Usually one or several of the great powers acts as representative of the world community or of international organization on behalf of the world community. In those instances, it is not actually the world community which is doing the deterrence or fighting, but one or more great powers on its behalf. For example, in 1991, when the United Nations authorized a U.S.-led coalition to take military action to expel Iraq from Kuwait, approximately thirty states participated in the victorious coalition, but U.S. military power was the basis of the operation and the justification for U.S. President George Bush's attempts at prewar compellence through diplomacy.

The fact that one or more of the great powers generally exercises deterrence or crisis management on behalf of the world community does not necessarily invalidate collective security as an approach to peace. But it does introduce asymmetries into the process of conflict termination, either by crisis management or by war. In the autumn of 1990, when Iraqi President Saddam Hussein deliberated about whether to stay in Kuwait or make a face-saving retreat, his decision was based primarily on what he thought President Bush would accept in the way of Iraqi behavior.[5] The acceptability of Iraq's actions to other heads of state was less significant to Saddam because only U.S. military power could, if necessary, guarantee to drive him out of Kuwait at an acceptable cost to the victors.

Different approaches to the calculation of costs and benefits by the members of a collective security coalition is an important matter in itself, for it bears on the probability that the coalition will hold together under the duress of later crisis states and war. Governments may share the political aim of deterring or compelling an aggressor, but they and their publics are rarely willing and able to pay equal shares of the cost of deterrence and compellence. The fate of various coalitions against Napoleon, for example, shows the problem of coalition management in the face of alliance burdens that are judged to have been unequally distributed. Even its contribution to the Peninsula War fought against Napoleon in Spain did not relieve Britain of the international stigma that it had been little involved in chewing up French forces and pushing them out of allied territory, in comparison to the sacrifices made by Austria, Russia, and Prussia. Stalin's resentment at the Allied delay until 1944 of a second front against Germany was based in the same feeling of relative deprivation within an ultimately victorious coalition.

Deterrence, however, is an unequal game. The credibility of deterrence, at least by means of conventional forces without any prospect of nuclear escalation, depends very much on the actual war-fighting or denial capabilities of the states that are attempting to deter.[6] Those with the greater capabilities will almost certainly be expected to take the lead in military operations and to accept higher costs in blood and treasure, compared to secondary and tertiary members of the coalition. The UN Security Council format, with five permanent members having ultimate responsibility for peace and security, assumes that peacekeeping as well as war-fighting on behalf of internationally sanctioned causes is not an equal business. Depending on the stronger nations in order to deter those that are weaker, but dissatisfied, is not a "defect" of collective security theory or practice, but an international fact of life. Even a failed collective security system may be no worse than a decaying international status quo unsupported by institutions of coalition management. As Kupchan and Kupchan remark,

> Collective security at its worst (that is, when all member states other than those directly threatened renege on their commitment to resist aggression) is roughly equivalent to balancing under anarchy at its best. Should non-threatened

states opt out of collective action, the remaining coalition would consist of the same directly threatened states as the alliance that would form through balancing under anarchy.[7]

It is also the case that the dominant issues involving the possibility of multilateral intervention change from one historical period to another. A comparison of the frequency of issues leading to wars in four international systems from the end of the Thirty Years War to the end of the Cold War shows that the growing significance of issues related to the internal unity of the state, and of the struggle over who shall rule among contestants for power within states, dates to well before the end of Cold War (see table 14).

The frequency of causes for war is related to the kinds of solutions available to the disputants or to outside mediators. In a comprehensive study of how wars ended between 1800 and 1980, Paul Pillar classified the possible endings of wars as absorption; extermination/expulsion; withdrawal; negotiation before armistice; negotiation after armistice; proposal by international organization or other third party of settlement acceptable to combatant sides; and capitulation.[8] In a case of *absorption,* the immediate conflict of interest is absorbed into a larger war before being terminated, as in the July, 1914, conflict between Austria and Serbia. When one side stops fighting without having decided to stop, its opponent has rendered it incapable of continuing to fight, either through *extermination* or *expulsion* from the theater of operations. If a war ends as the result of decisions made by both parties, it may occur without any explicit agreement, as in a *withdrawal,* or by acceptance of an explicit agreement. If the parties reach an explicit agreement by negotiation, the agreement may precede or follow an armistice. If the parties to war cannot reach agreement themselves, they may accept a solution offered by a third party or one side may *capitulate,* with or without conditions, to the superior strength of the other.[9] Using a threefold typology of wars developed by J. David Singer and Melvin Small, Pillar classified patterns of war termination for the three types of conflicts fought between 1800 and 1980: interstate wars, extrasystemic wars, and civil wars (see table 15).[10]

Two findings from this table have striking implications for collective security after the Cold War. First, civil wars are not usually terminated

Table 14
Issues Causing Wars in Four International System Periods, 1648–1989

Issue	1715–1814	1815–1914	1918–41	1945–89
Territory	67	42	47	24
Balance of power	1	3	3	-
National liberation/state creation	8	29	13	28
Protect ethnic kin	-	16	7	9
Ethnic/religious unification, irredenta	-	6	17	12
Government composition	14	13	17	28
Maintain integrity of state/empire	8	55	30	28

Source: K. J. Holsti, *Peace and War: Armed Conflicts and International Order 1648–1989, 308,* excerpted and adapted by the author.
Note: Cell entries in percent. Percentages do not total to 100 because only selected columns and rows are excerpted for purposes here.

by mutual agreement.[11] As many civil wars are ended by one side's capitulation to the other as are terminated by negotiation before or after armistice. In addition, the number of civil wars ended by extermination or expulsion of one side exceeds the number of conflicts ended by explicit mutual agreement. A second, and related finding, is that the category "international organization" is marked by a dearth of cell entries: no tabulated extrasystemic wars (colonial or imperial wars during this period) and only a single civil war were terminated as a result of third party/international organization proposals acceptable to both sides.

Taken together, these two findings suggest that civil wars are especially hard to terminate, and that international organizations through 1980 had not garnered an impressive track record in terminating any kinds of wars.[12] This is not altogether surprising given evident trends in

Table 15
Types of War Termination

Outcomes	Asorption or Extermination/ Expulsion	Wthdrawal or Capitulation	Proprosal by International Organization	Negotiation Before or After Armistice	Total (row)
Interstate war	8	15	8	38	69
Extrasystemic war	17	22	0	13	52
Civil War	7	7	1	6	21
Total (column)	32	44	9	57	142

Source: Adapted from Pillar, *Negotiating Peace: War Termination as a Bargaining Process*, 22, 25.

the form and nature of warfare. Most wars since 1945 have been about the nature of the state and the fate of various communities within states, rather than being conflicts between states. Institutionalized war, following the concepts of Clausewitz and the forms of eighteenth- and nineteenth-century conflicts, is no longer the norm. In place of interstate wars fought by accountable governments in control of legalized armed forces, as Kalevi Holsti writes, most wars now are "wars of the third kind," or people's wars, in which there are "no fronts, no campaigns, no bases, no uniforms, no publicly displayed honors, no *points d'appui*, and no respect for the territorial limits of states."[13]

These "wars of the third kind" are sometimes waged by ethnic, linguistic, or religious groups, but they are not necessarily *about* primordial values as much as they are about the fate of communities within states. Some communities seek a state of their own; others, a more equitable distribution of value within an existing state. Deterrence of the kind practiced by major powers in the Cold War years, or in earlier years among the great powers in a balance-of-power system, is almost irrelevant. The very concept of sovereignty is at bay as "failed states" or dissolving states break apart. In the international system of the near future, the principal problem for conflict management and termination will become that of preventing state breakups or repairing broken states. However, existing international institutions are perhaps not constitutionally well-endowed to achieve this. As Holsti notes, with regard to the United Nations,

> The United Nations Charter is a Westphalian document *par excellence*. Only states can become members of the organization. Membership requirements are only two: a commitment to the principles of the Charter, which sustains the territorial sovereignty principle, and a declaration of being "peace-loving." There are no entrance requirements that refer to the internal arrangements of states. The Charter prohibits actions dealing with members' domestic politics. The major purpose of the organization is thus to protect the territorial integrity, sovereignty, and independence of its members.[14]

Despite this constitutional framework, the United Nations has had to respond to failed states, humanitarian disasters, irredentist claims, ethnic and religious warfare, and other fissiparous tendencies of the new world disorder. The UN Security Council has attempted the following responses in order to deal with the problems of weak or failed states since the end of the Cold War, despite the contravention of the institutional norm against interference in the internal affairs of sovereign states:

(1) organized a military intervention to guarantee secure delivery of food and medicine to victims of starvation and war in Somalia, in the absence of local government approval or consent;

(2) created no-fly zones within sovereign states (Iraq and Bosnia), without the consent of their governments, in order to establish a safe haven from government attack (by Iraqi Kurds) or deny use of air power to those who might subvert efforts to arrange a peace settlement (in Bosnia);

(3) established six safe havens for civilians caught up in cross fire among warring factions in towns in Bosnia;

(4) deployed an armed force in Macedonia to act as a plate-glass window in order to symbolize deterrence of any Serbian military attack against Albanians in Kosovo and Macedonia; and

(5) authorized the U.S. removal of the military regime in control of

Haiti and the restoration of an elected government (under Jean Bertrand Aristide), previously deposed by the military.[15]

If these examples are illustrative of what is becoming "normative" UN behavior, it appears that international organizations (universal or regional in membership) will be called upon with increased frequency to rebuild Humpty Dumpty within savage internecine conflicts *about* the state and about the status of its constituent political communities, be they divided along ethnic, linguistic, religious, or other lines. Whether militaries of the great powers and their political masters are prepared for the kinds of stressful environments typical of this peaceful war making within states is another story for another chapter. The present point is that a set of tools crafted by international organizations for the settlement of interstate conflicts must now be adapted or redesigned for crisis management or conflict termination in failed or failing states. The ability of international organizations to develop better tools for intrastate conflict resolution matters because in some instances states cannot, or will not, do the job, and in other cases states can gain moral influence by acting under the international imprimatur of the United Nations or a regional organization.

II. CRISIS MANAGEMENT AND COLLECTIVE SECURITY

The need for crisis management arises because states have both common and opposed interests. An absence of common interests provides no basis for negotiations; an absence of opposed interests makes conflict unnecessary. While this point may seem trite, its application to crisis management is more complex. Crisis management involves *interstate* interests that are both common and conflictual: this fact brings into the picture issues of basic state security. Because crisis management involves reason of state, crises involving states are much more complicated and less amenable to rational decision rules than are crises involving individuals. Some otherwise compelling analyses of rational conflict resolution procedures extrapolate from techniques that work in resolving interpersonal conflicts to the attempt to resolve interstate conflicts. This is not an innocent assumption; the jump from interpersonal to interstate crisis management involves a paradigm shift.

International or interstate crisis management involves both political and military objectives and instruments. The onset of a crisis changes the behavior patterns of political and of military leaders, who become much more aware of the signals sent by their behavior. Political leaders attempt to signal their resolve to adversaries and their determination for audiences on the home front at the same time as they attempt to send to potential opponents signals of intent to negotiate, provided that no unacceptable concessions are demanded by the other party. The start of a crisis also points toward a new regimen for military leaders. The war machine that was previously maintained in a status of partial readiness must now be lurched into high gear. To fail to make the state's defense establishment ready for war is to invite surprise attack before proper readiness has been attained, the worst nightmare for military planners.

As previously noted, the objectives of political and military leaders may be at cross purposes during crisis management, not only because advance military plans may be uncomfortable for political leaders to implement, but also because those leaders may not have taken the time and trouble to familiarize themselves with military planning in peacetime. The lack of knowledge on the part of U.S. civilian political leaders, including presidents, about Cold War plans for nuclear war has been well documented.[16] Most Cold War presidents facing nuclear crisis would have been forced to choose among options with which they were unfamiliar or would have insisted upon improvisation that would bring the military machine to a halt (as was the case when the Kaiser asked Gen. Helmuth von Moltke, chief of the general staff, to attack Russia first instead of Germany in early August, 1914). Military command, control, and communications systems are not necessarily as fault tolerant as civilians are apt to assume.

Organizational complexity makes the problem of coalition warfare or crisis management through collective security that much harder. NATO military strategy during the Cold War was hobbled by the problem of planning for coalition war among sixteen member states and for the use of nuclear and conventional weapons on land-based, sea-based, and airborne launchers. Had NATO ever actually had to go to war, the problems of coalition management and alliance command and control might have torn apart the military fabric of its resistance to Soviet aggression. Fortunately NATO's very existence acted as a deterrent and its fighting power was never tested. Assessments of Warsaw Pact military competence as the Soviet Union dissolved and withdrew its forces from Eastern Europe have colored the entire picture of Soviet Cold War capabilities, which in retrospect seem less imposing than Department of Defense estimates had depicted. Allowing for this U.S. government propensity for military oversell in threat assessment, an even less-than-perfect Soviet war machine from the mid-1960s to the mid-1980s could still have played havoc with NATO's comparatively disaggregated command and control system.

Of course, NATO is a collective *defense*—not security—organization.[17] UN authorization of the use of force against Iraq in 1991 by the United States and its coalition allies was an experiment in collective security, and by most judgments a successful one. However, the success was more apparent in the use of U.S. war-fighting capabilities than it was in the ability of the United States or the United Nations to avoid an outbreak of war through crisis management. The U.S. task in crisis management from August 2, 1990, until the outbreak of war on January 16, 1991, was *compellence,* a more active form of deterrence that seeks to force an adversary to undo an undesired action already taken, to reverse a commitment for which material and psychological investments have already been made (see chapter three for an expanded discussion of coercive strategy in Desert Storm).[18]

The failure of collective security in crisis management against Iraq prior to the outbreak of Desert Storm in January, 1991, is a qualified one. Success in crisis management involves a certain degree of shared political values between potential adversaries. They must speak at least some of the same political and cultural language. The Ba'athist regime in charge of Iraq in 1990 and 1991 was apparently not operating out of any sense of accountability for its deeds to domestic or foreign bodies. Political legitimacy within Iraq was defined according to Saddam Hussein's personal wishes; foreign policy objectives were those declared into existence by the Iraqi leader himself. Iraq thus represented less of a *state* in conflict with other states than it did a personal fiefdom autocratically imposed on a state, and in conflict with other states. Crisis management practice, let alone theory, as understood in the West, apparently meant little or nothing to desperate Iraqi leaders who wanted immediate and rapid rises in oil revenues and political hegemony over the Gulf region.

It is difficult for a single country, and even more difficult for a coalition, to employ coercive diplomacy or other crisis management instruments against a nonstate actor masquerading as a state.

Whether nonstates can be coerced by collective security organizations in the name of interstate stability is not a new issue. The Concert of Europe that followed the end of the wars against Napoleon was in part built on the assumption that the postwar coalition would prevent nationalist and democratic revolutions from disturbing the post-Napoleonic peace. The difficulty was that the powers (Britain, France, Austria, Russia, and Prussia) differed on the connection between revolution and international instability. British Foreign Secretary Castlereagh argued that threats to peace were inherent in only those revolutions with the potential to spread irredentist nationalism beyond the borders of the revolutionary state, as in the aftermath of the Napoleonic wars. French Foreign Minister Talleyrand and Austrian Chancellor Metternich, on the other hand, argued that revolutions anywhere constituted a de facto threat to international peace. The reasoning of Metternich and Talleyrand was based in part on the assumption that there was no clear dividing line between the pathogens of internal revolution and foreign aggression based on revolutionary ideology. The Napoleonic outcomes of the revolution in France seemed to confirm this more pessimistic appraisal.

The tactic of military interposition in support of preventive diplomacy was used repeatedly by the United Nations to prevent the resumption of interstate or intrastate wars during the past three decades or so. Preventive diplomacy by military interposition might be regarded as a technique of anticipatory crisis management. The presence of a UN force in a particular region, say Cyprus or Lebanon, gives the Security Council a rationale for meddling into the affair without seeming precipitous. During the Cold War years this technique had to be used with care, and preferably with the active collaboration of the Americans and the Soviets. The United Nations' involvement in the Congo during the early 1960s showed that the commitment of UN forces to a situation of domestic political turmoil might involve the United Nations despite itself as the arbiter of a state's domestic political fortunes. The continuation of the operation after strong objections from the Soviets and their supporters almost caused a financial disaster for the United Nations, and it turned Khrushchev against the United Nations at a time of rising Cold War tensions between the Americans the Soviets.

III. COLLECTIVE SECURITY AND CONFLICT LIMITATION OR TERMINATION

Future collective security activities, including peace operations, will take place within a very different technological and political environment than that from 1945 to 1990. Two aspects of this new environment for collective security are discussed in more detail below. First, the vast majority of conflicts will occur within, not between, states, taking the form of "wars of the third kind" instead of institutional war.[19] Second, the revolution in computers and electronics has already brought about a global society of information intensity that has several important implications for the conduct of collective security and other military operations.

A. Collective Security and Peace Operations
UN peacekeeping in Bosnia from 1992 through 1995 demonstrated that insufficient force and a lack of willingness to escalate may cripple the effectiveness of a peace operation. Eventually the United Nations was required to move its blue-helmeted troops to the background and invite NATO into the foreground of military action in Bosnia.

Prior to taking over the military aspects of implementing the Bosnian peace agreement of December, 1995, NATO had sent clear signals of its interest in peace operations even as it acknowledged that the operation was not without significant risks. A military operation of this kind is only as good as the political consensus that lay behind it. NATO's own consensus might hold, but what of the non-NATO participants, including Russia. Bosnian Serbs reluctantly accepted the Dayton agreement but were obviously less than pleased with many of its provisions, which had been negotiated over their heads, more or less, by Serbia. NATO's lead in firepower over any potential adversary in Bosnia was not doubted; no force could challenge NATO's command of the air nor match its impressive logistics, command-control, and intelligence systems. Still, much of the problem in Bosnia between 1992 and 1995 was more political, social, and cultural than it was military. NATO's presence provided about a twelve-month breathing space for the combatant parties. It also provided a shield behind which the Bosnian-Croat federation, accorded fifty-one per cent of the territory of Bosnia-Herzegovina by the Dayton agreement, could rebuild its armed forces toward parity with Serbian forces in Bosnia.

In September, 1996, the NATO military chain of command was tasked by SACEUR (Surface Allied Commander, Europe) to begin planning for the possibility of a continued presence in Bosnia. Later that autumn, NATO's political leadership decided to extend its implementation force (IFOR) into a stabilization force (SFOR) of about half its size and to maintain a military presence in Bosnia into 1998. SFOR, which built upon the breathing space created by IFOR, was tasked to provide military security for the conduct of ordinary politics and to signal NATO's determination and ability to respond to escalated violence. The transition from IFOR to SFOR signaled NATO's confidence in the success of its first-phase mission in Bosnia. Whether these decisions set a precedent for military intervention elsewhere was not clear.

NATO could argue with some merit that Operation Joint Endeavour (NATO's multinational military operation in Bosnia) had established its competence as a collective security organization, in addition to its traditional mission of collective defense. Those—including this author—who had been skeptical when the intervention was first proposed had to concede NATO's first-round success in dampening conflict. This success was conditional, however; even NATO could not guarantee the transition from military to political and social stability among suspicious and antagonistic political communities. Military stability in Bosnia was the necessary, but less than sufficient, condition for enduring peace among previously warring factions.

Joint Endeavour was the first of a kind of collective security operation short of war that may become normative for the remainder of this century. U.S. government nomenclature suggests "peace operations" as a more inclusive term for a variety of activities designed to assist in peacemaking, e.g., restoring a broken peace, imposing a peace, and so forth. The even more inclusive term "operations other than war" also appears in U.S. government publications and U.S. Army manuals. Operations other than war (inevitably, OOTW) include peace operations as well as activities designed to shore up civil governments, including disaster relief, humanitarian aid, security assistance, police training, and other measures not calling for combat except in self-defense.[20] Although not every collective security operation short of war would involve the United States or NATO, the expectation is reasonable that military forces of the great powers will be used to isolate trouble spots and provide the opportunity for political mediation and conciliation. As one scholarly assessment has recently noted:

> Regional conflict is not only a humanitarian crisis but also a serious threat to world stability. The problem is not merely that hopes for a new harmony have proven false, but that without some sort of management by the global powers the international system could as easily disintegrate as did the USSR and Yugoslavia themselves. This could lead to a global catastrophe that would eventually damage the American and European economies, which have become highly interdependent with the outside world. The specter of a new world war through the "Sarajevo scenario" of escalating foreign involvement sucked into a disintegrating state is no longer dismissed as irrelevant or fantastic.[21]

Another scholar has suggested the even more inclusive and less emotive term "stability support" for peacekeeping and other operations involving both political and military missions. In offering this terminology, Lawrence Freedman makes an important distinction between "wars of survival" and "wars of choice."[22] Wars of survival are those undertaken against a rising hegemon that threatens an entire region or larger area with conquest and who poses an obvious threat to vital interests. Wars of choice are created by the internal problems of weak states, including civil war and communal violence. Publics understand the necessity for costs, including possible high casualties and economic privations, in undertaking wars of survival. But they do not readily understand or accept the rationale for wars of choice, and the level of sensitivity for even moderate casualties and other costs is apt to be extremely high.[23]

Before an entity undertakes stability support operations in wars of choice, it should be clearly understood that progress will be slow, hard to measure, and not necessarily denoted in military increments. Outside powers will have to use coercive military strategy both to intimidate the worst sources of internal disorder and to create incentives for cooperation in rebuilding civil authority on the part of those sitting on the political fence. In Somalia in 1993 and 1994, and in Bosnia during 1992–95, when the UN Protection Force in Bosnia (UNPROFOR) held responsibility for peace operations, there was insufficient force to intimidate the diehard opponents of stability as defined by the outside powers. Both Gen. Mohammed Farah Aideed's forces in Mogadishu and Gen. Ratko Mladic's forces in Bosnia openly defied UN and U.S. declared policy aims and sought to outlast the willingness of the American public and Congress to involve U.S. forces in "wars of choice." The United States was unsuccessful in Somalia and the verdict in Bosnia for NATO is still unknown. But as Freedman notes, one lesson pertinent to this study about stability support operations has already been made clear:

> The risks of stabilizing missions are increased, the more half-hearted the response. It is as difficult to have a marginal intervention as it is to have a marginal pregnancy. Just putting in a few troops as a token force leaves them vulnerable and at best will provide local relief while diverting the fighting elsewhere. . . . The paradoxical lesson of recent conflicts is that that costs over the long-term can be minimized the more that they are accepted in the short-term.[24]

B. Collective Security and the Revolution in Military Affairs

Futurists Alvin Toffler and Heidi Toffler have argued that "third wave" postindustrial economies will cause a fundamental change in military art: The way in which a state makes wealth is, sooner or later, going to change the way in which it makes war.[25] The Tofflers envision a third-wave war form, evolving from the U.S. concept of AirLand battle and evident in the use of high-technology conventional weapons during the Gulf War of 1991. The Tofflers and others envision future war as more dependent upon the use of space, computers, robotics, and other developments related to improved exploitation of information in all its forms.[26] Studies of advanced military concepts (supported by the U.S. National Defense University) have contended that "dominant battle-space knowledge" can be available to the state that most effectively exploits the spectrum of present and foreseeable technologies related to information warfare.[27] As Adm. William A. Owens, USN, then-vice chairman of the Joint Chiefs of Staff, has argued,

What is happening, driven in part by broad conceptual architectures, in part by serendipity, is the creation of a new *system of systems*. Merging our increasing capacity to gather real-time, all-weather information continuously with our increasing capacity to process and make sense of this voluminous data builds the realm of dominant battlespace knowledge (DBK).[28]

Michael G. Sovereign of the U.S. Naval Postgraduate School notes that the principal benefits of DBK are: (1) that it removes much of the uncertainty as to whether an enemy attack is actually under way: (2) that it provides essential information about the composition, status, and location of attacking forces; and, (3) that it provides sufficient knowledge about friendly forces.[29] He cautions, however, that DBK is limited by the constraints of enemy decision and reaction as well as by other realities of the future battlefield:

DBK is the upper limit of what intelligence systems 10 years hence can be expected to do. It entails the precise location of enemy units and their general status, but not the status and location of each platform. The location of mobile units can be known intermittently but they do move over time. Not all this data will be known instantly by all units, nor is it equally available from difficult environments or in the face of countermeasures. There would remain a gap between DBK and actual targeting that may require additional local information, man-in-the-loop, or very intelligent weapons with terminal guidance capability.[30]

The competition to exploit dominant battlespace knowledge is only part of a broader Revolution in Military Affairs (RMA), according to U.S. military planners and widely cited expert analysts. This "revolution" involves a transformation of the entire relationship between armies and technology, and it may have broad institutional and cultural impacts on the future of U.S. and other armed forces.[31] According to one RAND study, the basic features of an emerging form of "strategic information warfare" (IW) include: (1) a low entry cost for those wishing to attack information networks; (2) expanded opportunities for deception, image-manipulation, and other forms of "perceptions management"; (3) "formidable" problems of warning and attack assessment against strategic IW attacks; and (4) vulnerability of the U.S. homeland due to the increased dependency of the American economy and society on a highly networked information infrastructure.[32]

David S. Alberts warns that we cannot stop or slow down the information explosion. Therefore, the United States must design a strategy for using information technology that anticipates the negative repercussions of these technologies, takes advantage of unexpected opportunities to exploit technology, and somehow balances the costs and risks of disaster avoidance and successful use.[33] This task will not be easy to accomplish despite the apparent U.S. lead in advanced information technology related to military applications. War is fought against a reactive and intelligent opponent. The Gulf War of 1991 advertised the significance of conventional, advanced-technology weapons and thus alerted potential future U.S. adversaries to the importance of information warfare. Future Saddam Husseins may not be so cooperative in permitting one-sided dominance of the information and decision-making spectrum.

Sorting out all the significance of the Revolution in Military Affairs and information warfare is beyond the scope of this discussion. The immediate and near-term technologies with the greatest demonstrated potential to change the battlefield are, on the evidence: (1) intelligence, surveillance, and reconnaissance (ISR) technologies that permit better real-time, all-weather awareness of enemy and friendly activities on land, at sea, and in aerospace; (2) command, control, communications, computers, and intelligence (C4I) systems for making sense of the all-source awareness in order to assign missions and allocate forces; and (3) precision force, including precision-guided weapons and the ability to deliver those weapons over greater distances and at greater speeds than hitherto. Most significant is the *interdependency* and *interaction* among these parts of the puzzle: ISR and C4I make possible the combination of speed and lethality that give precision weapons their potential and that allow the user to circumvent enemy countermeasures.[34]

One danger lies in the assumption that the revolution in computers and communications will affect only "high-tech" wars waged among major state actors. On the contrary, information technology will also empower revolutionaries, narco-terrorists, and other nonstate actors who have scores to settle with their governments or who wish to spread terrorism across international borders. State and nonstate actors can undertake at least two kinds of activities that will make collective security harder. First, they can engage directly in "information warfare" against individual, corporate, or government target sets.[35] Second, they can use the availability of information for intelligence and deception in order to conceal their true identities; deceive foes about their intentions; and create interdependent links among various terrorists, insurgents, and others opposed to existing state governments and boundaries.[36]

Gen. Wayne A. Downing notes one paradox for military planners in a world of states under siege: Both war and military operations other than war will be conducted under equally demanding, but opposite, conditions. One condition is "third generation" or "Information Age" warfare among modern, high-technology states, in which knowledge dominance of the enemy will be the key to victory. The opposite, but equally taxing, prospect is "fourth generation" or "Niche" warfare, including transnational terrorism, extortion, and psychological operations.[37] This polarized-threat paradox is married to another: Information and communication technologies that cross state borders and push people together in "McWorld" are also available to anti-government forces, including ideological revolutionaries, criminal cartels, and ethnonational or religious dissidents. The tools of economic and technological integration thereby ignite the incendiaries beneath political orders, putting high-tech goods in the service of primordial redemption or criminal consumption. Consider, for example, the following illustration:

> The command and control structure of drug cartels sited in Third World countries, and even remote jungle backwaters, watch CNN via generators and satellite communications, use computers which have been programmed with multiple viruses to protect their databases, encrypted fax machines, cellular phones, global positioning navigational systems (GPS), and have automatic arms, even ground-to-air missiles, just as the legitimate authoritative decision-making command and control structures of modern nation states do.[38]

Those seeking to break up existing states into new communities based on ethnicity, religion, or redefined political affinity will now have the tools to track the movements of government forces, to ascertain in advance the intentions of government policymakers, and to expedite the transfer of information, arms, and intelligence across borders through cyberspace. A knowledge-intensive form of "low intensity conflict" or unconventional warfare in the next century will challenge states and international organizations with a collective sense of information insecurity. Those opposed to existing states or to international peacekeeping efforts will not necessarily need to destroy their armed forces; it may suffice only to disrupt and impede their economic, political, or military information networks.

CONCLUSION

Collective security depends upon coercive military strategy. It is hard enough to make coercive military strategy effective without allies. With coalition partners becoming more the rule than the exception in collective security operations, the coercive aspects of military strategy become even trickier. The use of UN forces for peacekeeping, for example, depends upon the collaboration of former adversaries mutually agreeing not to fire at one another, nor at the intervening UN force. Peace enforcement imposes a cease-fire and demilitarization, but the imposed solution cannot last without the at-least-tacit consent of the formerly belligerent parties. Thus those who would apply coercive strategy to collective security must engage in perspective taking and perceptions management, not only between local enemies but also between each of them and the international force sent to put out the fire. In Bosnia, for example, evolution of Bosnian Serb perspectives toward a recognition of shared favorable stakes in the peaceful coexistence of a Serb Republic and Muslim-Croat Federation within former Bosnia-Herzegovina was crucial for any successful outcome to NATO's Operation Joint Endeavour in 1996.

Collective security systems do not necessarily make crisis management and war termination easier than they are without such systems. The relationship between collective security and crisis management or conflict termination is very context dependent. States were bringing wars to a conclusion and managing crises long before theories were developed to account for either set of behaviors. Historical precedent and contemporary experience suggest that Europe's potential for collective security *between* states is high, but *within* states is another matter. It is quite conceivable that an expanded version of the Western European Union (WEU) combined with Conference on Security and Cooperation in Europe (CSCE), now Organization for Security and Cooperation in Europe (OSCE), can effectively contain military adventurism in Eurasia, given a continuation of favorable evolutionary trends in Russian politics and in other states of East Central Europe.[39] Meanwhile NATO and coalitions of the willing and able will have to shoulder the burden of collective security, as the French say, "condemned to succeed."

Wars within states will defy existing tools for crisis management and conflict termination by means of collective security, including peace enforcement as now practiced. NATO's experience in Bosnia is atypical, not prototypical. The state-strength dilemma ensures that more states will swallow themselves despite the best efforts of international mediators or those who would impose peace from outside to find remedies. No brief is offered here that the effort is not worth making: The United Nations and the major powers must do what they can to provide succor for those states capable of being salvaged. But not all will make it; international political "triage" will rule the new world order.

6

Operations "Not War" and Coercive Military Strategy

The end of the Cold War has removed the threat of global war, and in the near future, a large-scale conventional war in the developed and democratic parts of Eurasia seems a remote possibility. But the spread of ethnic, religious, and other conflicts of identity within and across territorial state borders has only increased since Soviet communism became an historical anachronism. The United States, other powers, and the United Nations have all been invited or tempted into involvement in peace promotion and stability restoration within failing or failed states.

This chapter considers the problem of using operations apart from war or nonwar actions as components of a coercive military strategy. The chapter proceeds in three steps: First, it attempts to identify the size and shape of the animal itself—no small task—surveying some representative definitions of operations apart from war or "other than war" for what they reveal about the length and breadth of the topic. Second, the chapter considers the specific problem of U.S. adaptation to a world in which operations apart from war may become normative instead of atypical for the armed forces of developed countries. Third is a discussion of possible challenges to security in the new international order, broadly defined, and their implications for the ability of the United States or others to engage successfully in military operations apart from war.

I. UNDERSTANDING THE PROBLEM: WHAT IS THE REAL SHAPE OF THE ELEPHANT?

The U.S. Department of Defense recognizes that its responsibilities now include preparedness for so-called "unconventional" conflicts including revolutionary and counterrevolutionary warfare, terrorism, anti-drug operations, and peace operations, among others. This recognition is beginning to find its way into manuals and other publications giving the accepted version of military doctrine and practice. For example, specific kinds of Operations Other Than War (OOTW) included in a recent version of army doctrine were: (1) support to domestic civil authorities; (2) humanitarian assistance and disaster relief; (3) security assistance; (4) noncombat evacuation operations; (5) arms-control monitoring and verification; (6) nation assistance; (7) support to counterdrug operations; (8) combating terrorism; (9) peacekeeping and peace-enforcement operations; (10) show of force; (11) support for insurgency or counterinsurgency; and (12) attacks and raids.[1]

Operations other than war constitute an elastic category. As such, they invite controversy about the boundary line between "war" and "other than war." When, for example, does U.S. support for the counterinsurgency or counterterror operations spill over from NW into de facto involvement in a war? The object of insurgents is to blur the line between peace and war until such a time as they are ready to wage open, conventional warfare to their advantage. This question is more than merely a problem of terminology. Confusion about whether the United States is actually at war invites disjunction between policy objectives and military operations. A working solution to the boundary problem in one version of the conflict spectrum is depicted in table 16.

James B. Motley, a retired colonel in the U.S. Army and expert on terrorism and unconventional conflicts, divides "noncombat operations" into three categories: peacekeeping, humanitarian assistance, and security assistance.[2] *Peacekeeping* implies the noncombatant deployment of armed forces to separate hostile parties, with their consent. *Humanitarian assistance* involves several agencies of the U.S. government whose role is to meet disasters caused by famine, civil war, weather, or other causes of massive dislocation and disruption. *Security assistance* includes a variety of programs that use funds and legal assistance to support governments against internal threats, including both those that are entirely indigenous and those that are externally supported.

The requirement for constrained force and political-social sensitivity to local cultures on the part of U.S. or UN forces may encourage the deployment of U.S. special operations forces (SOF) on behalf of peace

Table 16
The Spectrum of Conflict; Operations not War

Non-Combat[a]	Unconventional Conflicts[b]	Conventional Conflicts	Nuclear Conflicts
-	Special operations[c] Revolution/Counterre volution[d]	Limited war Major war	

Source: Adapted from Sarkesian and Connor, "Conclusion: The Twenty-First-Century Military," in their *America's Armed Forces: A Handbook of Current and Future Capabilities,* 423.

[a]Noncombat activities include shows of force, military and economic assistance, peacekeeping, humanitarian, and related contingency operations.

[b]The line between noncombat operations and unconventional conflicts is indistinct. Peacekeeping and humanitarian operations, for example, may lead to involvement in unconventional conflicts.

[c]"Special operations" include counterterror, surgical strikes, hostage rescues, and raids, sometimes in support of conventional military operations.

[d]Revolutions and counterrevolutions occur in various phases, the first of which shades into Operations Other than War: Phase 1 includes economic and nonmilitary assistance, weapons or police training, military training cadre; Phase 2 extends Phase 1 support with Special Forces A Teams; Phase 3 adds Special Forces Headquarters (Teams B and C) and additional A Teams to Phase 1 and 2 support; Phase 4 adds light infantry forces in defensive role to Phase 1–3 support; and Phase 5 adds to Phase 1–4 support light infantry forces in active combat, administrative and logistical base established for expanded role, air and sea support, U.S. assumption of major responsibility for conflict.

operations and other NW missions. Special operations forces have certain obvious advantages for NW missions: they can be deployed rapidly, have exceptional training and versatility, and do not risk large numbers of casualties should things go unexpectedly wrong. On the other hand, special operations forces (U.S. or others) are not a "silver bullet" that can redeem failed conventional operations or incompetent strategy.[3]

Special operations forces have unique strategic value for the conduct of small-scale, high-risk, potentially high-payoff, and unorthodox operations for which conventional forces are not trained. They can also support a variety of missions across the spectrum of possible threats. Table 17 depicts five categories of possible future threats to U.S. security and indicates whether the missions performed by special operations forces are relevant to each.

Table 17
Relevancy of Special Operations Force Missions by Threat or Problem

	Foreign internal defense	Special reconnaissance	Direct Option	Counter terrorism	Unconventional warfare	Psychological operations	Civil affairs	Collateral areas
Balance of Power	x	x	x	x	x	x	x	x
Regional Rogue	x	x	x	x	x	x	x	x
Local Disorder	x	x	x	x	x	x	x	x
Nontraditional Threat[a]	x	x	x	x		x		x
"911" Emergencies[b]							x	x

Source: Gray, Explorations in Strategy, 213.

[a] Nontraditional missions include dealing with transnational drug trafficking, terrorist organizations, international criminal organizations of various types, and industrial and scientific espionage.

[b] "911" emergencies can include humanitarian rescue prompted by natural or other disasters as well as military search and rescue.

One can see from this variety of SOF capabilities cross-matched with possible missions a dangerous temptation for future U.S. and other policymakers. As the number of nonwar missions suitable for specially trained (including but not limited to SOF) forces grows, the propensity to "do something" with available forces may increase. Another temptation might be to increase the size of SOF forces to the point at which they are no longer so elite or specially trained. And, although special operations forces can be committed without the visibility of larger, regular, conventional battalions and divisions, casualties among these forces are not necessarily less problematical for democratic leaders. U.S. experience in Grenada and in Somalia, separated by a decade, shows that public, media, and Congressional reaction to U.S. casualties has little if any correlation with branch of service or assignment.

Military planners and scholars have been frustrated by the lack of a conceptual framework for understanding how the internal wars of the post-Cold War era are different from the revolutionary wars of the Cold War. Donald M. Snow outlines some of the important ways in which contemporary internal wars differ from traditional insurgencies.[4] First, traditional insurgencies are fought with the object of capturing control over the political system; for many of the new internal wars, this object is absent, or secondary. Criminal organizations and narco-terrorists, for example, prefer a weak state, not a strong one, and are comparatively indifferent to who rules it as long as they can escape effective control. Second, Cold War insurgencies were fought with comparatively more restraint than contemporary internal wars. Insurgent tactics emphasize winning over the "hearts and minds" of a politically ambivalent population. But the internal wars of the 1990s, for example in Bosnia and Rwanda, were marked by "ethnic cleansing" and other massacres with no apparent object other than the killing itself.

A third apparent difference between Cold War insurgencies and post-Cold War internal wars, according to Snow and others, is that many internal wars are concentrated in the economically least-developed states or in politically failed states. Failed states are those in which the government has suffered a terminal loss of both legitimacy and effectiveness. Loss of *legitimacy* means that the state is no longer regarded as authoritative, i.e., as entitled to rightful rule. Lack of *effectiveness* in a failed state is often apparent in the shift of control to local centers of real power and resistance: warlords, clans, criminal syndicates, ethno-national rebels, and others from a list difficult to exhaust.[5] Although a weak or failing state may give the appearance of sovereignty and strength, its durability rests solely on coercion. As the weak state increases its level of coercion, seeking in vain to substitute for lost legitimacy and effectiveness, resistance to coercion also increases. Eventually the state fails of its own apparent incompetence as even its coercive powers dissolve or are overthrown by its enemies.[6]

This discussion has not resolved all matters of definitional controversy, but it has established some baselines from which the participation of U.S. and other developed armed forces in operations apart from war might be evaluated. First, it is judicious to retain the term "peacekeeping" only for operations that take place with the *consent* of the host government and/or previously belligerent parties. Activities beyond the realm of consent are much more dangerous, whatever nomenclature is used. Second, there is sufficient evidence that specially trained and tasked troops for peace operations will be necessary in addition to conventional forces being given peace operations as an "add-on" mission. Third, the character of post-Cold War internal wars in failed or failing states suggests that many of these conflicts are less political than they are anomic. That is: the apparent object of the combatants is not the restoration or deposing of a government or political order, but the settling of particularistic scores with clan, tribal, or other enemies; and/or the weakening of political order for self-directed purposes. The ability of militaries to reestablish order from anarchy without destroying vital social and cultural supports for the polity is difficult to create and to maintain under these conditions, and perhaps impossible.

II. THE UNITED STATES AND MILITARY
OPERATIONS APART FROM WAR

Two issues loom when considering operations other than war: defining the nature of the operation and deciding who will command it.

A. Unpeaceful Peace Operations
One of the earliest tests for the post-Cold War cohesion of NATO, and for the willingness of the United States and its NATO allies to support multilateral peace operations, occurred in 1991 in the former Yugoslavia.

The breakup of that multinational state into Serbia, Croatia, Bosnia-Herzegovina, and Slovenia resulted in a variety of uncivil wars involving "ethnic cleansing" and other atrocities. Bosnia itself was eventually torn apart by civil strife. A UN peacekeeping force was established and NATO, in support of UN efforts, was tasked to help isolate the battlefields from outside intervention and maintain as level a playing field as possible among combatant factions. Toward these ends, NATO used its maritime forces to enforce an embargo against the shipment of arms from outside sources into the Yugoslav cauldron. NATO also established a "no-fly" zone over portions of former Yugoslavia, especially over parts of the Bosnia-Herzegovina, to support UN efforts to restore peace there.

By the summer of 1995 it become clear that traditional peacekeeping, based on the assumption that disputant parties are ready to stop fighting, was inadequate as a mechanism for conflict termination in Bosnia; UN forces were an enticing target set for angry sharpshooters not yet disarmed. Accordingly, NATO resolved its internal differences of opinion and intervened with massive, and effective, force to establish an at-least-temporary freezing of the military status quo. Under the terms of the Dayton peace agreement of December, 1995, NATO deployed some 60,000 troops in Bosnia-Herzegovina, of which about 20,000 were Americans, with an objective somewhere between traditional peacekeeping and peace enforcement. NATO's Operation Joint Endeavour tasked its Implementation Force (IFOR) to disarm combatant factions and support an enforced pause in the fighting among Bosnian factions. At the same time, NATO's diplomacy obtained the necessary political and diplomatic acquiescence of Slobodon Milosevic's Serbian government in order to ensure the cooperation of Bosnian Serbs. After IFOR's one-year mandate ended it was replaced by the smaller NATO contingent stabilization force (SFOR) with a mandate permitting more military support for the rebuilding of consensus-based political institutions in Bosnia. SFOR's mission was scheduled to expire in 1998.

The deployment of U.S. forces in support of NATO's mission in Bosnia was controversial on the home front, but not inconsistent with the expectations of U.S. military planners since the end of the Cold War. U.S. national military strategy requires that American forces be prepared for a variety of "contingency operations," defined as military operations that go beyond the "routine deployment or stationing of U.S. forces abroad" but "fall short of large-scale theater warfare."[7] In December, 1994, the U.S. Army published its first field manual devoted to peace operations, and joint service doctrine for the conduct of "military operations other than war" was issued in 1995.[8] Peace operations, as defined by the U.S. Department of Defense, include both peacekeeping and peace enforcement. *Peacekeeping,* according to the Defense department, refers to military or paramilitary operations that are "undertaken with the consent of all major belligerent parties" and are primarily designed to "monitor and facilitate implementation of an existing truce agreement and support diplomatic efforts to reach a long-term political settlement."[9] Peace *enforcement,* on the other hand, involves the application or threat of military force "to compel compliance with generally accepted international norms, resolutions, or sanctions" in order to "maintain or restore peace and support diplomatic efforts to reach a long-term political settlement."[10] Thus, the NATO Implementation Force in Bosnia as of December, 1995, may have a foot in each of two camps: a peacekeeping mission, but with military expectations more attuned to those characteristic of peace enforcement. The DOD terminology is more or less similar to that of the UN Charter, which divides operations into Chapter VI operations and Chapter VII operations. Chapter VI operations are carried out "with the *consent* of belligerent parties in support of efforts to achieve or maintain peace, in order to promote security and sustain life in areas of potential or actual conflict." Operations authorized under Chapter VII, on the other hand, are conducted in order to "restore peace between belligerent parties *who do not all consent* to intervention and may be engaged in combat activities."[11]

The distinction between peacekeeping and peace enforcement is not only semantic.[12] The availability of consent on the part of local belligerent parties may determine the likelihood of success or failure of an intervention. The difficulty is that consent is not a hard line but a vanishing and reappearing fog of indistinct political and military attributes.[13] The range of the zone of intervention is wide: on one side it is bounded by traditional UN Chapter VI peacekeeping, and on the other by large-scale but limited wars like Desert Storm. In between lies a no man's land with plentiful opportunities for self-deception and wishful thinking on the part of outside interveners and their militaries. As Chris Bellamy warns,

It becomes clear that once one moves into the zone of intervention, anything can happen. It is therefore unrealistic and
dangerous to make decisions about the nature of an operation and expect it to conform to one's wishes. It won't.[14]

The participation of great-power forces in peacekeeping and peace enforcement operations is not without difficulties. During the Cold War it
was necessary for American and Soviet forces to be excluded from
United Nations peacekeeping or peace enforcement operations. The exclusion was necessary for obvious reasons: a regional crisis might be
turned inadvertently into a superpower conflict. This difficulty no
longer obtains. The end of the Cold War thus opens the door to Security
Council peacekeeping or peace enforcement operations backed by both
the United States and Russia, among other permanent members.

However, the involvement of U.S. forces in multilateral operations
will not be uncontroversial on the home front. The commitment of U.S.
combat forces under the command of any other governments, even
under the umbrella of an international organization, creates potential
problems of operational integrity and political accountability. These
problems did not really arise in Korea or in the Gulf War of 1991 because, although authorized by the United Nations, they were essentially
U.S.-designed and -directed military campaigns. Both were also collective security, not peacekeeping, missions. Of more typical multinational
peacekeeping operations, a prescient UN general officer once summarized: "Peacekeeping is to war-making what acting is to ballet—the environment is similar but the techniques are very different."[15]

Former Chairman of the Joint Chiefs of Staff Gen. Colin L. Powell
expressed some of the misgivings of the U.S. officer corps about military
involvement in operations other than war in a September, 1993, press
conference. Powell did not dismiss the possibility that policymakers
might call upon armed forces for peacekeeping or other noncombat missions. He emphasized, however, that the main business of the U.S. armed
forces must be war:

> Because we are able to fight and win the nation's wars, be-
> cause we are warriors, we are also uniquely able to do some
> of these other new missions that are coming along—peace-
> keeping, humanitarian relief, disaster relief—you name it,

we can do it . . . but we never want to do it in such a way that we lose sight of the focus of why you have armed forces—to fight and win the nation's wars.[16]

In his testimony before Congress in September, 1993, Col. Harry G. Summers, Jr., also pointed to the concern among U.S. military professionals that an overemphasis on peacekeeping and other nonmilitary operations would erode the military's sense of its core missions and responsibilities.[17] According to Summers, persons calling for massive involvement of U.S. armed forces in peacekeeping, nation building, and additional operations other than war are "unwittingly turning traditional American civil-military relations on its head."[18] Summers is concerned that a preoccupation with social or political tasks may displace a military ethos centered on war, to the detriment of both the U.S. armed forces and American society.

Despite the misgivings of Summers and other traditionalists, demands for U.S. military involvement in peace operations are certain to increase in the aftermath of the Cold War. State disintegration brought about by ethno-nationalist, religious, and other politically combustible forces leads to revolutionary wars, irredentist claims, and humanitarian disasters that invite outside intervention. If the United Nations cannot act to reestablish order in internal wars, then authority and effective control will devolve onto local warlords, terrorists, revolutionists, or dictators. The U.S. military offers unique capabilities in intelligence, logistics, and other assets to support peace operations. With the United States as a bystander, the United Nations' credibility in peacekeeping and peace enforcement is diminished, perhaps to the vanishing point. On the other hand, U.S. participation in multinational peace operations raises problems of command and control, as discussed below.

B. Conducting Peace Operations: Who Commands?

When U.S. military involvement outside the United States is proposed, problems of military mission pluralism are often compounded by the need to coordinate the activities of several national forces. Knowing this, U.S. and allied NATO military leaders have been reluctant dragons when intervention in other states' civil strife has been proposed as a coalition task. In the 1994 version of its annual report to the Congress, the U.S.

Department of Defense was careful to acknowledge the difficulty of command and control for multinational operations and to offer itself a plausible way out:

> The issue of command and control will always be a key factor in deciding whether to deploy U.S. forces as part of a UN peace operation. As a practical matter, if significant combat operations are contemplated, and if American involvement is planned, it is unlikely that the United States would agree to place its forces under the operational control of a UN commander. In these situations, the United States would prefer to rely either on its own resources, on those of a capable regional organization such as NATO, or on an appropriate coalition such as that assembled for Operation Desert Storm.[19]

The Clinton administration policy statement on U.S. participation in multilateral peace operations establishes three sets of criteria.[20] The first set of factors come into play as U.S. leaders decide whether to vote in support of a UN peace operation (whether Chapter VI or Chapter VII). The second, more restrictive, set of standards apply when the participation of U.S. personnel in peace operations is being considered. A third set of even more rigorous factors will be taken into account if the peace operation is a peace enforcement (Chapter VII) exercise likely to involve combat. These criteria are summarized in table 18.

Military professional and political constraints against U.S. involvement in limited war pose problems for America's post-Cold War participation in peace operations. In the case of U.S. involvement in multilateral operations authorized by the United Nations, the requirements of coalition maintenance may preclude the use of maximum force. In addition, peace operations are more like unconventional than conventional warfare: the conventional warfare/overwhelming force mind-set of the American military leadership is potentially ill-suited to the restraint required of peacekeepers. Peace operations impose limitations on both the ends and means of warfare. Even in Chapter VII (enforcement) operations the objective may not be to destroy the entire military power of one or more combatant sides, but to use coalition forces as a persuader to make durable a peace agreement. NATO's tasking to implement the military aspects of the December, 1995, Dayton peace agreement on

Table 18
Clinton Administration Criteria for Deciding Whether the United States Would Vote for, or Participate in, Multilateral Peace Operations

Voting for Peace Operations	Participating in Peace Operations (in addition to preceding column)	Participating in Peace Enforcement (in addition to preceding two columns)
U.S. involvement advances U.S. interest and an international community of interest exists	Participation advances U.S. interests, and both the unique and general risks to U.S. personnel have been estimated and are considered acceptable	A determination exists to commit sufficient forces to achieve clearly defined objectives
A threat to, or breach of, international peace and security exists due to one or more of the following: • international aggression; • urgent humanitarian disaster combined with violence; • sudden interruption of established democracy or gross human-rights violations, combined with violence or threat of violence	Sufficient personnel, funds, and other resources are available	A plan exists to achieve the stated objectives in a decisive manner

Table 18 (Continued)

Voting for Peace Operations	Participating in Peace Operations (in addition to preceding column)	Participating in Peace Enforcement (in addition to preceding two columns)
Clear objectives exist, and it is clearly understood where the mission fits on the spectrum from traditional peacekeeping to peace enforcement	U.S. participation is necessary for the success of the operation	A commitment exists to reassess and adjust, as necessary, the size, disposition, and composition of U.S. forces in order to achieve objectives
For Chapter VI (traditional peacekeeping) operations, a cease-fire should be in place and the consent of parties obtained in advance, before forces are deployed	The role of U.S. forces is tied to clear objectives, and an endpoint for U.S. participation is identified	
Necessary means to accomplish the mission are available, including forces, financing for the operation, and an appropriate mandate for the mission	Domestic political and Congressional support exists, or can be developed	
Political, economic, and humanitarian consequences of inaction have been weighed, and judged unacceptable	Acceptable command and control arrangements exist	

Table 18 (Continued)

Voting for Peace Operations	Participating in Peace Operations (in addition to preceding column)	Participating in Peace Enforcement (in addition to preceding two columns)
Duration of the operation is tied to clear objectives and to realistic criteria for ending the operation for Chapter VII (peace enforcement) operations, the threat to international peace and security is considered to be significant		

Source: U.S. Deparatment of State, *The Clinton Administration's Policy on Reforming Multilateral Peace Operations,* 4–5.

Bosnia is a case in point. NATO preferred to deter with overwhelming presence the need for actual combat operations against one or more of the previously combatant factions in Bosnia, thereby avoiding the negatives attached to shedding Bosnian Muslim, Croatian, or Serbian blood.

Even in unilateral U.S. military peace operations approved by the United Nations, restrained use of force and the reconciliation of competing domestic factions may be as important as the judicious application of firepower. The United Nations authorized a U.S. occupation of Haiti in 1994 in order to depose the illegal military government of Gen. Raoul Cedras and to restore to elected office former President Jean Bertrand Aristide. The U.S. objective in the operation against Haiti required a game plan for post-conflict restoration of political stability.[21] Continued fighting among Haitian factions after U.S. military departure would defeat the purpose of the invasion. Restoration of the dissipated authority of a government or of a state is much more difficult, because more complicated, undertaking than the defeat of an enemy in battle. The U.S. government learned this in the aftermath of the Bush administration invasion of Panama in 1989 to overthrow Manuel Noriega (Operation Just Cause).

Another set of constraints on UN peacekeeping and peace enforcement, pertinent to defining the future U.S. role in those kinds of operations, is inherent in the limitations of UN security resources and organization. For example, the United Nations has no independent intelligence gathering system, nor a round-the-clock operations center to monitor events for the Secretary General. It has no standing forces and it cannot order the forces of member states into action. The UN Secretariat has failed to think through the implications of more frequent and more intensive involvement in aggravated peacekeeping situations such as Somalia in 1992 and 1993. It still relies on reflexes from its experience in traditional peacekeeping.[22]

III. FACES OF NW IN THE POST–COLD WAR WORLD

One great challenge facing the United States and other countries in the post-Cold War era is the question of whether to intervene in crises in order to restore stability to unstable situations. The answer to this question can greatly affect, and be greatly affected by, public opinion at home.

A. Stability Operations

The international security environment, as Lawrence Freedman has noted, is in the process of shifting from one characterized by possible wars of survival or necessity to wars of choice.[23] The United States and its allies will have to consider whether and how to intervene for the purpose of stabilizing a variety of intrastate or interstate controversies caused by exploding social change combined with political pluralism. These stability operations, of which peace operations are one kind, require of field forces more dexterity than firepower in the carrying out of nonwar missions with minimum force and with the cooperation of indigenous political and military elites. It might be argued with equal force, and in tandem with Freedman's argument, that there is a growing frequency of wars fought by nonuniformed personnel using irregular tactics and unaccountable to state political authority (Chechens in Russia, Mujaheddin volunteers in Bosnia and in Tajikistan, Basques in Spain, Palestinians in the Middle East, Kurds in Iraq and Turkey, and so forth). The danger is in assuming that this rising tide of irregular wars means the end or obsolescence of conventional warfare waged on a large scale by state-authorized and -accountable military forces.[24] It is too early for the verdict of conventional military obsolescence; for the moment the conventional and unconventional paradigms coexist in uneasy tension. This tenuous coexistence of two forms of war strains the capacities of policy planners and military commanders alike. As I. William Zartman notes, the coexistence also imposes additional constraints on negotiators who seek to manage or to terminate conflicts:

> Domestic regional and ethnic conflicts and demands should be handled early, by means of normal politics, while government legitimacy is still intact and grievances are manageable. If rebuffed and neglected, such demands cause the aggrieved community to turn inward, consolidate its political organization, challenge the legitimacy of the state, look for neighbors' support and sanctuary, and reject government efforts to meet their grievances as too little too late.[25]

Consider, as one example, the problem of early-warning indicators in a setting that combines NW missions with an urban "Third World" environment. The concept of early warning may have to stretch to include demographic volcanoes waiting to erupt. As populations in West Africa, for example, are driven by ecological, economic, and demographic factors into large cities, a combustible mixture of unemployment, frustration, and poverty confronts political leaders and security professionals. Urban guerrilla warfare or terrorism on a large scale is only one possibility in such an environment.[26] Such warfare might be unlike the classical Maoist model of insurgency, in which the insurgents first build a political and military base in the countryside and only later attempt to encircle and capture cities.[27] It might also be unlike the paradigmatic Leninist model of revolution, in which a sudden coup overthrows the political leadership in the capital and the revolutionaries then gradually consolidate power throughout the countryside.

Twenty-first-century urban guerrilla warfare might follow neither the Maoist nor the Leninist pattern of revolution, but might be some-

thing *sui generis* and for which the customary procedures for indica-
tions and warning would provide few clues. Revolutionary cells might
be dispersed and disaggregated instead of centralized under a single di-
rectorate. According to Gerard Chaliand, an expert on unconventional
conflicts,

> The new factor in contemporary terrorism as compared with
> national liberation movements (some of which also resort to
> terrorism) is the emergence of little groups with no organized
> links with the masses and no movement worthy of the name
> to draw up a political programme. There has been a massive
> increase in the number of minuscule groups which see indis-
> criminate terrorism as both tactic and political line.[28]

Modern computer and communications technologies make this behavior feasible for the revolutionaries and quite appealing as a means of survivability through redundancy and decentralization.[29] Cutting off the
head of the scorpion no longer renders its tail nonlethal. Now take this
the next step: Techno-revolutionaries could use computers and communications along with other covert means to subvert the technologies of
the United States and other G-7 powers at their sources. Hackers have already provided enough scares, with regard to the potential vulnerability
of all nonsecure networks and some secure government ones, to require
little imagination from information and communications terrorists.[30]

B. The Home Front and OOTW: Achilles Heel?

When Russia invaded its rebellious province Chechnya in December, 1994, it was expected in Moscow that Chechen resistance would
rapidly give way to superior Russian forces. From the Russian standpoint
it was not really a war at all, but an internal insurrection that should have
been put down by internal and border troops. When they didn't, Russian
escalated and sent in its army and air force. The Russian army proved
hollow and its poor training and inept tactics trapped it in a Chechen
cauldron that lasted several years instead of several weeks. One of Russia's problems throughout its campaign in Chechnya, from its beginning
in 1994 and continuing until a peace agreement was signed in 1996, was
that the incursion of Russian troops into Chechnya was never popular
among most Russians. This was true even among Russians who agreed

in principle with the Russian government that Chechnya was in fact a part of Russia and could not simply secede by fiat.

It was only partly due to Russia's inept field performance that it lost its campaign in Chechnya and was forced to concede a peace agreement that left open Chechnya's future. Russia's attempt to suppress Chechen rebels was also impeded by the Russian government's inability to maintain the moral high ground throughout the conflict. Russia lost the battle of moral influence for several reasons. First, the leadership of the Russian armed forces was bitterly divided over the prudence of using the security forces of Russia, and especially the Russian army as opposed to internal troops, to impose order on Chechnya. Second, the Russian media thoroughly covered the war, giving a great deal of publicity to Russian and Chechen opponents of the war. Third, Chechens successfully used psychological warfare, including deception operations, to depict favorably their cause and to attempt to intimidate and deceive their opponents. For example, a commander of Russia's North Caucasus Military District complained that the Ministry of Defense had almost totally ignored any preparations for psychological warfare in Chechnya. As a result, the Chechen forces of Dzhokar Dudayev had nearly demoralized the 19th Motorized Rifle Division by sending radio messages to individual officers by name and threatening their wives and children if those officers took part in any attack on Grozny. Another example is the use of Ukrainian nationalists in Chechen deception operations. Ukrainians dressed in Russian uniforms led unsuspected Russian comrades to Dudayev as prisoners of war. Other Ukrainians disguised themselves as members of Doctors without Borders (Medecins sans Frontieres) or the Red Cross in order to question refugees and to obtain other intelligence for Chechen forces.[31] Chechen "psyop" information activities against Russia also exploited perceptions management in order to urge the case against Russian military intervention to Russian and other news media.

Unexpectedly large casualties also helped to turn the Russian public and some of its military leaders against extended operations in Chechnya. One inevitable by-product of the extremely one-sided outcome of the Gulf war of 1991 is increased sensitivity on the part of the U.S. public to casualties. Presidential expectations of nearly cost-free war and public or media aversion to the realities of combat have the potential for strategic miscalculation and for the avoidance of difficult policy issues

Table 19
Worldwide U.S. Active Duty Military Deaths, Selected Military Operations, 1980–96

Operation/Incident	Casualty Type		Total
Iranian hostage rescue, Apr. 25, 1980	hostile	0	8
	nonhostile	0	
Lebanon peacekeeping, Aug. 25, 1982–Feb. 26, 1984	hostile	254	263
	nonhostile	9	
Grenada (Urgent Fury), Oct., 1983	hostile	18	19
	nonhostile	1	
Panama (Just Cause), 1989	hostile	23	23
	nonhostile	0	
Desert Shield, 1990	hostile	0	84
	nonhostile	84	
Desert Storm, 1991	hostile	148	299
	nonhostile	151	
Somalia (Restore Hope, UNOSOM), 1992–94	hostile	29	43
	nonhostile	14	
Haiti (Uphold Democracy), 1994–Aug. 1996	hostile	4	4
	nonhostile	0	
Bosnia (Operations from Dec., 1995–Jul. 17, 1997)	nonhostile	11	11[a]
	hostile	0	

Source: U.S. Department of Defense, August, 1996, from Internet, for all cases except Bosnia.
[a]Bosnian cases include six vehicular and other accidents, three heart attacks, and two self-inflicted wounds.

to which potential force commitments are attached. Arguably the outcome of the Gulf War made it harder, not easier, for the United States and its NATO allies to bite the bullet for IFOR in Bosnia. Were Bosnia to turn uglier and U.S. and allied forces face a more intensive internal shooting war, rising casualties could exhaust public patience and invite Congressional skepticism for continuing the mission. A summary of U.S. military deaths attendant to some recent wartime and "other than war" operations is provided in table 19.

Greater sensitivity to casualties may be a feature of "post-heroic" warfare, according to some military theorists and historians.[32] Other experts feel that the U.S. policy process is, because of cultural traditions or media saturation, exceptionally vulnerable to the political impact of casualties. One French commander of UN forces in Bosnia reportedly stated: "Desert Storm left one awful legacy. It imposed the idea that you must be able to fight the wars of the future without suffering losses. The idea of zero-kill as an outcome has been imposed on American generals. But there is no such thing as a clean or risk-free war. You condemn yourself to inactivity if you set that standard."[33] There is, in addition, the inevitable commingling of civilian noncombatants with hostile armed personnel as part of the background for any use of force to restore civil order against the wishes of one or more intrastate domestic partners. The potential for backlash as a result of inadvertent loss of innocent life is enormous.

On the other hand, the sensitivity of Americans to U.S. armed forces, while a significant variable in sustaining coercive military strategies including peace operations, should not be overstated. The majority of Americans, immediately after the October, 1993, deaths of eighteen U.S. Army Rangers in Somalia, were in favor of sending reinforcements to capture Somali warlord Aideed.[34] U.S. public sensitivity to combat casualties has a direct relationship to at least two other variables: (1) public perceptions of the significance of the conflict; and (2) the expectation that U.S. political and military objectives will be accomplished in a timely manner and at acceptable cost. Of course, the U.S. political leadership plays an important role, especially the president, in mobilizing public support for military intervention, or failing to do so. The irony is that the presidents may have to try a harder sell for nonwar operations in which significant casualties are possible than they find it necessary to argue for traditional wars, since public understanding of the latter is apt to be more intuitive.

By its very nature, unconventional warfare, including covert operations of various sorts, demands things that do not televise well. It sometimes requires that U.S. policymakers ally themselves with disreputable characters among the leaders of other state or nonstate actors. The U.S. government may be required to disown its prior authorship of operations gone afoul of the original intent, or to conceal the role of allies.[35]

Leaders may have to dissemble for reporters or for Congress while an operation is in the planning and hopeful stages in order to avoid compromising security. All of these possible requirements for the successful conduct of covert operations sit poorly with the mind-sets of many, not only in the U.S. Congress and media, but also entrenched in the U.S. intelligence bureaucracy.

U.S. military service intelligence, including that pertinent to unconventional warfare and special operations, is as steeped in a legalistic paradigm as is its civilian counterpart. The jurisprudential paradigm for deciding how and whether to engage in unconventional warfare is an understandable temptation.[36] Any officer or policymaker who lived through the 1970s investigations of U.S. intelligence or the 1980s Iran-Contra flap has developed forgivable protective instincts and a necessary reflex for a backside-covering paper trail. Unfortunately, the behaviors and legalisms that are self-protective in courtrooms or Congressional hearings are not necessarily strategically useful. Peace operations and other operations "other than war" will not escape the constraints of U.S. legalism and formalism in policy making. This means, in all likelihood, that a successful endgame for U.S. participation in peace operations will require the drawing of a clear line between peacekeeping and peace enforcement and staying clear of the nether-world between the two conditions.

CONCLUSION

This chapter has presented some conclusions about operations "other than war." They present challenges that are not altogether unique in technology, personnel, or tasking, compared to other missions. They may require a skillful blending of intelligence collection, analysis, and decision making of a kind highly stressful for the U.S. policy process. Moral influence is a very important aspect of nonwar operations, including peacekeeping, and it is sometimes decisive in making those operations succeed or fail. Moral influence applies on the home front of peacekeepers and peace enforcers as well as in the field. The management of perceptions is a necessary part of any strategy for dealing with omnipresent media that can be used for or against one side of a peace process or internal war.

Operations other than war can quickly and inadvertently become warlike. Outside interveners in civil wars need a clear statement of mission and some reasonable expectations about the endgame. One RAND study published in 1996 concluded that, with respect to U.S. and Russian use of armed forces since the end of the Cold War,

> intervention decisions have been made in both countries from time to time for no more profound reason than the absence of any better ideas. Both the United States and Russia are configured toward unstructured and often shortsighted policy planning, with a tendency to commit forces without clearly articulated aims. In particular, ad hoc and impromptu assessments of "what is at stake" often decide what ultimately gets placed on the U.S. intervention calendar.[37]

Peace operations, as a form of collective security or otherwise motivated, are dependent upon the willingness of the parties to settle sooner or later. If there is nothing about which to compromise, there is little prospect for agreed, or imposed, solutions. Wars among ethnic, racial, and religious factions tend to have this implacable character, and the techniques needed for ending them by enforcement will not always meet the highest standards of military etiquette. Operations other than war are, in the absence of a great deal of luck, merely one step away from blood sport.

Conclusion

Wars are the products of societies and cultures; the American way of war has not been the English, the Japanese, or the Russian. This variety in ways of making war produces equal diversity in the role of coercion in states' military strategies. Although much use of force is coercive, an important question for theory and policy is whether coercion is at the center or the periphery of a state's military strategy. Strategy is a purposeful activity, but it is also a work of art that takes place within a context of historical uncertainty and indeterminacy.[1] Stumbling into the coercive use of force does not count as a strategy, only as a blunder. And when coercion and strategy do go together, policymakers and commanders will find that the coordination and cooperation demanded of them by coercive military strategy is as hard on the nerves in crisis and in wartime as it is on the budget in peacetime.

In this study I argue that coercive military strategy is one aspect of persuasion supported by the threat or use of force.[2] The use of force may not be for the purpose of combat, although it can be. Force can also be used effectively for political purposes by being threatened but not used. Sometimes troops are moved to a border, or ships are steamed toward another country's harbor, simply to send a message. The message can be ambiguous but nevertheless powerful, opening the possibility of violent clashes between armed combatants without closing the door to further negotiation between potential adversaries. Coercive strategy is recognized by its subtlety and dexterity, even when it is necessary to employ a blunt edge. Coercion flows around and envelops a target instead of crushing it. Coercion works on the enemy's mind and brain in the first instance, and on the enemy's "body" of fighting forces and logistics in the second, as a means to mastery of the enemy's soul.

In a sense, all use of force by states is psychological as well as physical. War is not a shooting gallery. States seek power, glory, territory, and other spoils of war, or they seek to induce others to comply with their demands short of war. Nor is the threat or use of force restricted to territorial states. Terrorists, guerrillas, bandits, drug lords, and other nonstate actors have used various forms of violence or threat of violence to induce victims, including blackmailed governments, to comply with their demands. Although some heads of state and some nonstate actors may revel in the use of violence for its own sake, they are the exceptions. By and large, the use or threat of force is political, i.e., purposive. It has an objective related to the gaining, losing, or sharing of power over significant social values.[3]

These introductory paragraphs set the stage for a summary of findings and their implications, which follows in three parts. First is a brief look at some historical cases apart from those explained by previous chapters, in order to show the historical generality as well as the topicality of the problem of military coercion. It has always been there, and it will not go away, but it has not always been recognized for what it is. Second is a description of the general attributes of successful coercive military strategy, with the recognition that coercive or other strategies must be judged as "successful" or not in terms of the prevailing international environment. Third is a review of the major findings from the preceding chapters in support of the general arguments made about the opportunities for and constraints upon the use of military coercion.

I. COERCION IN WAR AND STRATEGY: CASES OF SUCCESS AND FAILURE

A nuanced understanding of the nature of coercion has always been part of a successful war. An attacker who prepares well for war will frequently have induced in the intended victim's leadership and public a feeling of helplessness or inevitable defeat, a feeling worth many divisions. Something like this fatalism may have taken hold of the French political and military leadership in the spring of 1940. An opposite example is provided by Russia's winter war against Finland in 1939–40. The Finns offered unexpected resistance and Stalin was forced to use significant military resources in order to subdue them. The Finns refused to regard their defeat as inevitable, although later historians now say that it was. Perhaps so, but not at a cheap price for Moscow.[4]

Napoleon would have been served well by a coercive strategy to accompany his military campaign against Russia in 1812. Napoleon had assumed that the very fact of invasion would intimidate the Tsar into prompt negotiation and concessions. When this did not happen and Russian resistance proved steadfast, Napoleon lacked a political strategy by which to persuade Russia to make peace. The Tsar would not negotiate with the French so long as French troops occupied his country, and so long as this was the Tsar's policy, French military victory was impossible. Napoleon nevertheless pressed home the military campaign, arriving in Moscow itself. Surely, he reasoned, a French occupation would cause the Russians to see the pointlessness of further resistance.

But the Russians had a military strategy that was proof against Napoleon's form of military coercion. Field Marshal Mikhail Kutuzov allowed Napoleon into Moscow, retreating with his army intact and leaving Napoleon with a "victory" of no political or military use. Napoleon occupied Moscow, dithering there while Kutuzov's army escaped his grasp; his subsequent retreat to the Berezina destroyed the remainder of his own army. Kutuzov outlasted Napoleon instead of outfighting him; the only way Napoleon could have avoided this disaster was by arranging for a peace that eluded him.

Napoleon did employ a coercive strategy in at least one instance, and the case is an interesting one. His Continental System was designed to exclude British trade from continental Europe. The aim was to impose economic privation on Great Britain so that its leadership and citizens would eventually quit the struggle against French hegemony on European territory. Napoleon's system did do some damage to British trade, but it was leaky and his maritime forces were not up to the task of comprehensive enforcement. When Russia defected from the Continental System, because of a need to trade with England, the French Emperor turned against the Russians and set France on the path to invasion.

The Continental System was an example of protracted coercion, or "slow squeeze" to induce compliance with the demands of France against rival powers. In the discipline of political science, the literature on coercive diplomacy has emphasized the role of coercive strategy in crisis management. While this focus is appropriate, it is also important to recognize that coercive strategy may be equally applicable over a period of months or years. Trade wars among states are an example of competitive coercion, and economic competition of this kind can continue for years or even decades. In military affairs, a coercive strategy is often necessary in war or in alliance formation when it is clear that one side cannot reasonably hope to conquer or subdue the other.

For example, the United States and its NATO allies during the Cold War could not reasonably expect to thwart Soviet expansion by attacking Russia and occupying the Kremlin. The physical means were beyond them, and once both the United States and the Soviet Union had developed large nuclear forces, war would have been mutually suicidal. Therefore the United States contrived the strategy of "containment" to accomplish by coercion what could not be taken by force. Containment was a combination of diplomacy and military threat. As articulated by George F. Kennan, the theory of containment drew a line beyond which the forward thrust of Soviet military power would be resisted by force. Having drawn this line, the United States and its allies would wait for the Kremlin's policy objectives and strategies to mellow. The success of containment would show that the historical march of communism across Europe was not inevitable. This was more than a posthumous defeat for Marx's theology; it was also a propaganda and public-diplomacy defeat for the Soviet Union. Western Europe prospered outside of Soviet leaders' grasp while their own citizens' living standards fell further behind.

Containment was a successful, long-term coercive strategy for influencing Soviet behavior while avoiding war. By the time Mikhail Gorbachev assumed the office of General Secretary of the Communist Party of the Soviet Union in 1985, he recognized that containment had already succeeded. His task would not be to expand Soviet frontiers and raise higher levels of military threat against the West. To the contrary, he sought accommodation on security issues and emphasized the need to construct a "new European home" in order to realign the power struggle within Soviet domestic politics. In order to rebuild the Soviet consumer economy, Gorbachev needed to both shift resources from the military and the heavy industrial "metal eaters" into nondefense sectors and encourage the privatization of enterprises. His reforms ultimately acquired their own momentum and gained power unforeseen by the sorcerer himself, causing his own ultimate political demise.

Coercive diplomacy was used as part of coercive military strategy by President Abraham Lincoln in April, 1861, in order to deal with the impasse between the U.S. government and the Confederacy over the status of Fort Sumter, South Carolina. South Carolina had already demanded, during the term of President James Buchanan, that the United States evacuate the fort. Now the garrison was in danger of being starved out unless provisions were shipped in. Lincoln's preferred policy was conciliation without acquiescing in Southern independence. Some of his key advisors, including Comm. Gen. Winfield Scott, opposed either a provisioning or reinforcing expedition to Sumter.[5] Although he was reluctant to force the issue at Sumter, Lincoln was faced with hardening opinion in the North and with steadfast opposition to further concessions to the South within his own party. The Southern seizure of Federal forts had taken place before Lincoln assumed office. Although Lincoln had chosen not to threaten to repossess forts already taken, he had announced in his inaugural address that further surrenders would not be acceptable.

Caught between the proverbial rock (concede Sumter and suffer humiliation) and hard place (reinforce Sumter and possibly provoke war), Lincoln chose a course of action that refused to abandon Sumter but didn't explicitly provoke a war. He ordered two relief expeditions fitted out, one for Sumter and the other for Fort Pickens, Florida. On April 6, 1861, Lincoln sent a State Department emissary to inform the governor of South Carolina that "an attempt will be made to supply Fort Sumter [*sic*] with provisions only; and that, if such attempt be not resisted, no effort to throw in men, arms, or ammunition, will be made, without further notice, or in case of an attack upon the Fort."[6] Some historians charge that Lincoln chose this course of action with the deliberate intent to provoke a war. Historian Charles W. Ramsdell claims that Lincoln, "having decided that there was no other way than war for the salvation of his administration, his party, and the Union, maneuvered the Confederates into firing the first shot in order that they, rather than he, should take the blame of beginning bloodshed."[7]

It may be true that Lincoln sought to provoke a war, but it is also possible that he sought an alternative that offered the Confederacy one last clear chance to avoid war. His nonbelligerent reinforcement of the Fort was a symbolic defiance of Southern claims to it, but not an overt military provocation equivalent to military reinforcement or attack against the Southern artillery batteries at nearby Cummings Point and Sullivan Island. Lincoln's move to reprovision Sumter prefigures

Kennedy's choice of a blockade instead of immediate air strike or invasion to remove the Soviet missiles deployed in Cuba in 1962. Kennedy tightened the screw on Khrushchev, reinforcing the Soviet leader's perception of Kennedy's resolve to accomplish removal of the missiles. Kennedy also left it up to Khrushchev to decide whether to run the blockade, with a high likelihood of war, or turn back his ships. Lincoln similarly left the Confederacy the option whether to acquiesce to his "turn of the screw" or escalate, and in so doing, precipitate a war. The Confederacy and Khrushchev made different choices. Whether Lincoln's overture resulted in an outcome he intended, it was consistent with his objective to avoid a humiliating diplomatic defeat without accepting the responsibility for the breakdown of peace.[8]

The preceding examples show the universality of the problem of adapting strategy and war planning to the specific and immediate context of war and diplomacy, taking into account the enemy's plans and intentions. We now proceed beyond examples to generalize across specific actors, times, and places and develop some propositions about coercive military strategy and its implications for military and political leaders and for theorists. We recognize that differences in existential perspective remain, as between persons living through events and scholars considering those events, even as we can offer concepts as a bridge or connection between them.

II. ATTRIBUTES OF COERCIVE MILITARY STRATEGY

In the international environment of the Cold War, technology (nuclear weapons) compelled interest in coercive military strategy. Politics (bipolarity and U.S.-Soviet interest in avoiding a third world war) was an enabling force for the enhancement of interest in, and capability for, coercive strategy. In the post-Cold War international system, politics is a compelling force, and technology an enabling force, for the development of coercive military strategy. Politics (the end of the Soviet Union, the removal of threat of global war) compels more attention to the development of capabilities and doctrine for fighting smaller wars, and for the use of military power in support of operations "other than war," including peacekeeping. Also in the post-Cold War international system, technology (precision weapons; automated systems for command and control; and enhanced capabilities for intelligence, surveillance, and re-connaissance in real time) now enables the United States and other major powers to use force selectively, but still decisively, for coercive purposes.

A well-formulated coercive military strategy can be recognized by at least five attributes or characteristics, explained below. Each of these at-tributes or characteristics is best thought of as a behavioral space in three dimensions (visualize a cube). The first dimension involves the goals and means used toward those goals by one party to a conflict. The second dimension represents the goals and means of the second party to the same conflict. The third dimension in this hypothetical "cube" is the environment within which the competitive interaction between the two sides is taking place. Of course, if the conflict expands from two to *n* parties, this three-sided figure expands into one of *n* + 1 sides.[9] A two-dimensional representation of this simple three-dimensional space ap-pears in table 20.

A. Influencing the Will

A coercive military strategy has as its *primary* objective the task of influencing the opponent's *will*. This does not preclude military opera-tions intended to destroy the capabilities of the opponent, when and if required. In one sense, all war is about influencing the will of the enemy, but the point here is not truistic in that sense. A coercive military strat-egy uses carefully calibrated, but not necessarily *small* amounts of de-struction, in order to *change the other side's calculus* about its own risks and potential costs if it continues on the present, undesired, path. This influence process takes place through "negotiation" by use of force and/or threat of force at two levels. Side A attempts to influence Side B's estimate of Side A's intentions and capabilities; Side A also attempts to influence Side B's estimates of its *own* intentions and capabilities as the fighting continues.

This abstraction can be made quite concrete with an example. Dur-ing the American Civil War, the Confederacy launched two daring inva-sions of the North in 1862 and 1863; the first was rebuffed in a standoff battle at Antietam in September, 1862, and the second was turned aside at Gettysburg during the first three days of July in the following year. The Confederate invasions had political aims as much as military aims. Nei-

Table 20
Behavioral "Space" of Coercive Strategy

	Goals and Means of First Actor	Goals and Means of Second actor	Environment (enabling or compelling)
Attribute A			
Attribute B			
Attribute C			
Attribute D			
Attribute E			

Source: Author.

ther Gen. Robert E. Lee, in command of the Army of Northern Virginia, nor Confederate President Jefferson Davis expected to conquer and occupy the North. Their hope was to disillusion Northern publics and politicians by dealing a temporary and embarrassing setback to Yankee forces on their home territory. The object lesson that the South could strike unexpectedly into the Union heartland and upset its citizens' day-to-day routines would, according to this logic, encourage those in the North to settle for a compromise peace instead of total victory.

Southern strategy for invasion of the North was also influenced by President Lincoln and Commanding Gen. Henry W. Halleck's known obsession about defending Washington at all costs, including their willingness to insist upon military maldeployments from other theaters of operation as had taken place in the summer of 1862. Lee's invasion of the North was also influenced by his and Davis's estimates of their own capabilities present and future. Moving the fighting away from war-ravaged Virginia would provide relief for citizens of that state already much deprived by war's exertions, and it would permit Lee's forces to take advantage of the comparatively well-off farms and workshops of Maryland and Pennsylvania. (The battle of Gettysburg was the unintended result of a Confederate brigade having been sent to that town to forage for shoes.)[10]

Implicit in a coercive military strategy is a willingness *sometimes* to settle for less than total victory, and perhaps, less than one's original war aim. The political object of unconditional surrender, and the military object of total defeat of the opposed armed forces in battle, are not *necessarily* in conflict with a coercively appropriate military strategy. Circumstances sometimes preclude limitation on the ends and means of fighting until a regime is toppled or the fighting power of its armies is totally destroyed. Revisionist historians to the contrary, any compromise short of unconditional surrender with Hitler was impossible. His trail of broken promises prior to the outbreak of World War II and his publicly proclaimed racial criteria for political legitimacy made a compromise peace with Germany dangerous and impractical.[11]

Ironically, civil wars, although sometimes described in the literature as "low-intensity" conflicts or small wars, frequently have this totality of uncompromising goals on one or both sides. Two sides are in conflict for control of a regime or territory and neither may believe that the prize is divisible. The flexible tactics of civil wars may also prolong them. Fighting can simmer below the level of conventional military conflict within acts of terror, sabotage, and revolutionary "justice" in the interim periods between conflict by designated combat forces.[12] Terror and counterterror in turn inflame the population for and against the government. Algeria in the mid-1990s was reminiscent of French Algeria in the mid-1950s in this explosive cycle of terror and counterterror that prolonged a civil war.

B. Openness to Revision

Coercive strategy often requires an openness to *revising* one's own initial political or military objectives without necessarily conceding to the opponent its objectives. The reason for this requirement is that the opposed side has its own definitions of relative gains and losses relative to various objectives, its and yours. Coercive strategy relies upon the *interdependence* of actors' gains and losses. Of course, objectives may have to be revised upward or downward, becoming more ambitious, or less. Many are the heads of state and military planners who embarked on war with expectations that it would be short and relatively cheap in blood and treasure, only to be summarily disappointed. The major combatants in World War I expected a war that would end by Christmas, and they were correct: it did end by Christmas, but in 1918, not 1914.

Other historical examples make the same point, such as that of the American Civil War. The initial expectations of both sides in 1861 when the conflict erupted was that it would be a short war, a matter of months instead of years. And in this short war, both sides expected to emerge victorious.[13] Only well into 1862, as the casualty figures multiplied, did it become clear that a protracted war with unprecedented costs was in progress, one that would resist any negotiated settlement short of total military defeat for the armed forces of the loser.[14] The political and social coercion of secession and emancipation hardened against any solution short of total war as the costs of war mounted and the symbolism of war's aims became more divisive. The North and South were no longer mere adversaries: they had become conflicting ways of life and alternate visions of the American future. Military tactics and campaign strategies were adapted to, and in turn caused by, this hardening of hearts and minds.

C. Perspective Taking

Related to the ability to rethink one's goals and objectives is *perspective taking,* the ability and willingness to see into the other side's objectives and motives and appreciate their sources. This does not necessarily imply agreement with, or sympathy for, those motives. For example, a state may take a position in a controversy because of strong domestic constituencies that have to be appeased, as in the union of Junker and industrialist in Wilhelmine Germany prior to World War I. Or, a state may feel that its reputation for resolve is on the line if it fails to stand firm against deterrent or compellent threats posed by an adversary.

One of the difficult aspects of interstate rivalry is that states can come to believe that their commitments are so interdependent that the renegotiation of one commitment will place all others into jeopardy. This image of "falling dominoes" is one that academics and military theorists may deride, but it is a familiar one to heads of state who fear losing their offices. Even if the dominoes are not really that tightly coupled and the loss of one ally does not entail immediate jeopardy to another, the party out of power can exploit the domino image for gain at the ballot box at the expense of the party in power. This perceived "domino effect" is one reason why empires, having been acquired, are so difficult to get rid of.

D. Symbolic Manipulation

An important aspect of coercive strategy is the ability to master the *manipulation of symbols and information* in support of one's political and military objectives. Because reality is often what people think it is, changing the perception of reality can, under the right conditions, be tantamount to changing the "objective," disinterested reality that might be seen by the proverbial visitor from Mars. An example of manipulation of symbols and information is former Soviet leader Mikhail Gorbachev's campaign to reform the communist order from 1985 to 1988. Succeeding all too well, Gorbachev effectively stripped the facade of invincibility and inevitability from the Soviet approach to a planned economy and from the rule of the Communist Party. Gorbachev did not anticipate the side effects; into the sudden vacuum moved nationalists, democrats, and others with the larger agenda of ending the Soviet Union itself.

One type of manipulation of symbols and information pertinent to strategy is *perceptions management.* Sometimes confused with propaganda, perceptions management is more inclusive, and frequently more subtle. It includes any statements, decisions, and actions taken by one state in order to influence another state's assumptions about the first state's intentions and capabilities. Intelligence, and especially the intelligence discipline called "counterintelligence," is very much about the manipulation of adversary perceptions in a direction favorable to one's own interests. The importance of the counterintelligence function to states lies in the centrality of counterintelligence for perceptions management.[15] For example, the Aldrich Ames case revealed that Soviet capture of a key CIA counterintelligence operative permitted Moscow to control the images and information flowing from the USSR back to Washington.

The entire Cuban missile crisis resulted in part from a two-way failure in perceptions management, related to the inability of the Soviet and American leaderships to engage in constructive perspective taking. Khrushchev's rocket-rattling diplomacy was based on hubristic boasts about U.S. military weakness relative to that of the Soviet Union, on the assumption that this talk might intimidate the Eisenhower and Kennedy administrations. The effect was the opposite: increased domestic support in the United States for a nuclear and other military buildup. A comparable U.S. failure was to boast publicly in October, 1961, about U.S. nuclear strategic superiority, a communication intended to intimidate Khrushchev and to defang his own nuclear diplomacy. The U.S. action had the opposite effect: Suddenly put on the defensive, the Soviet leader looked to his Cuban missile gambit as part of a short-term solution. Then, too, Khrushchev may have misread Kennedy's unwillingness to invade Cuba during the Bay of Pigs fiasco, and Kennedy's apparent willingness to tolerate both the Berlin Wall and Khrushchev's browbeating at Vienna in 1961, as signs of an irresolute or weak president who would be easy to push around.[16]

Perspective taking requires getting to know the opponent better. Consider, for example, the case of U.S. bargaining with Imperial Japan in 1945 over the terms for Japanese surrender. The United States obviously held the military cards, but the Japanese could make the process of surrender more or less costly to the allies. There remained, even after Germany's defeat and Japan's total isolation against history's greatest wartime coalition, a residual capability on the part of Japan to surrender with various degrees of resistance. This continuum of Japanese surrender options ran from maximum resistance, requiring U.S. and allied invasion of the Japanese home islands, to a surrender by the Japanese government that stood down their armed forces and dissolved their government, but retained Emperor Hirohito as a national symbol. The U.S. decision to permit the Japanese to retain their emperor as a unifying national symbol made postwar occupation and the acceptance of military defeat easier for Japanese to accept.

On the other hand, Japanese perspective taking near the end of the war was fatally flawed in ways that only increased the likelihood of the harshest possible surrender terms. Japanese efforts in 1945 to use the Soviet Union as an intermediary with its American and British allies in order to arrange favorable terms for peace, as defined by Japan, were not treated seriously by Stalin, who used the pretense of good offices in relaying Japanese overtures in order to ingratiate himself with Washington and London and in order to set up Japan for the Soviet Union's ultimate entry into the war. Japan's expectation that Stalin would help to conciliate his wartime allies on Japan's behalf was the equivalent of grasping at the straws of imaginary allied disagreement in order to avoid facing the more fundamental and depressing truth of Japanese defeat.

E. Moral Influence

A final characteristic of coercive military strategy is that *moral influence* is a very important, perhaps the most important, aspect of strategy. The idea is not a new one. Sun Tzu Wu, Chinese philosopher of war and attributed author of the classic study *The Art of War,* said that moral influence is the first of five fundamental factors by which war should be appraised.[17] Sun Tzu defined moral influence as "that which causes the people to be in harmony with their leaders, so that they will accompany them in life and unto death without fear of mortal peril."[18] This idea has several implications. It implies popular support for war aims and for the methods used to make war. It also implies that the armed forces will not be demoralized by being misused or permitted to be torn apart by political factionalism. And, those who find themselves in uniform must feel that, consistent with military discipline and tradition, they are treated with dignity and respect. In each of these aspects of moral influence, the successful manipulation of symbols and information, previously discussed, is very important.

Popular support for armies is often thought necessary only in democracies. But history shows that all armed forces and the governments that must provide them rely in the long run on popular support. Coercion can only go so far before leaders are strung up, and guns and ammunition dry up. Consider the situation in post-Communist Russia from 1992 through 1997. The Russian armed forces disintegrated once the Soviet Union dissolved, not only because funds were scarce, but also because the legitimacy of the armed forces was called into question after the Soviet Union fell. The Soviet military had, along with the security services and the party organs, been the major props of the communist state. When the state fell, the military drifted into an abyss, unsure of its focus and divided into political factionalism. Although most of the Russian military leadership had no desire to establish military rule in Russia, they became unwilling arbiters of Russia's political fate when they became caught up in internal power struggles in 1991 and in 1993.

The disintegration of moral influence in the Russian armed forces became so acute by 1994 that Russia was unable to fight an effective military campaign against rebels in Chechnya.[19] Former Defense Minister Pavel Grachev had boasted in the autumn of 1994 that Russia need send only a few airborne divisions in order to rout Chechen separatists and reestablish Russian control in Grozny, the Chechen capital. Russia's military performance, however, was below even the level set by prewar pessimists. Troops were sent into the fighting with inadequate training, units were poorly coordinated, and leadership at the sharp end of the tactical spear was abysmal. But most important, Russia's intervention had no moral backing. Russia's public opinion largely condemned it, and even officers assigned to the invading troops openly opposed it. Some officers resigned during the campaign, and mothers of troops conscripted and sent to Chechnya appeared in the battle zone to demand the return of their sons and a halt to the war.[20] Had Marshal Georgi Zhukov, chief of the general staff of Soviet forces in World War II and triumphant victor of the Battle of Berlin that ended Hitler's Reich, lived to see Russian military operations in Chechnya from 1994 through 1996, he would have returned his numerous medals in shame.

The United States in Vietnam also discovered the importance of moral influence in war. American public ambivalence toward the war in 1965 and 1966 turned to angst in 1967 and to widespread and growing popular opposition by 1968. The Tet offensive was a public-relations disaster for the Johnson administration, and Johnson's decision not to run for reelection signaled his recognition that middle America was tired of a war that he could not bring to a successful conclusion. Lack of public support filtered out to the theater of operations in Vietnam, where troops engaged in mutinous and insubordinate behavior against their own officers. There were many causes for U.S. political and military setbacks in Vietnam, but among them one must number the moral ambiguity of U.S. military operations in the minds of many Americans and in the minds of the fighting forces. The U.S. president and the Congress had somehow contrived to engage America in a major war without mobilizing the kind of popular support necessary to sustain any U.S. force.

Another example of the importance of moral influence was provided by President Abraham Lincoln during the Civil War. Lincoln recognized that emancipation of the slaves was not only the right thing to do, but also a very politic move on the part of the North. He ran the risk of immediate political opposition and the creation of divided opinion within the Union: many soldiers and politicians from midwestern and border states, in particular, did not want any part of a war with the objective of liberation. On the other hand, if the immediate controversy over emancipation could be gotten over, the long-term benefits for Northern public diplomacy and for the symbolism of the Union cause would be enormous. Defining the war as a crusade for freedom, as well as a fight to retain the Union intact, added to the ideological fervor necessary to persevere in fighting the Confederacy to the bitter end in 1865.[21]

The issue of moral influence is related not only to the ability of political leaders to affirm objectives that obtain popular support for the military but to the affirmation of faith in military leadership and in the military institution by those who must risk their lives in combat. The Union troops who experienced incompetent military leadership at Fredericksburg and the "mud march" that followed in January, 1863, must surely have felt as dispirited as those Russians sent into Grozny in January, 1995. Russia's present-day military troubles are in part due to poor living conditions among enlisted personnel, including rotten food and substandard medical care. But Russians have for centuries fought for empire and state under worse conditions.[22] Worse for the moral legitimacy of Russia's military is that an estimated three-to-four thousand soldiers died each year in the mid-1990s from accidents or hazing, or by suicides related to hazing. A Russian Academy of Sciences report in 1994 noted that a young man entering the armed forces had an 80 percent chance of being beaten up, and a 30 percent chance of being beaten in "a particularly savage or humiliating way."[23]

Russia has strayed very far from its best traditions. One of Tsarist Russia's greatest military leaders, Aleksandr Suvorov, was distinguished by his concern for the relationship between officers and the men they led. His training emphasized repeated explanation of orders and the reasons for them to the rank and file. He mixed a tough and realistic training regimen with hands-on supervision of his troops' well-being in camp, including meals, sanitation, and medical care. Suvorov's eccentricities often led him to be less respectful to peers and superiors than to subordinates. But his instinct about the essence of the relationship between military leaders and followers was exceptional, and sound. His troops would travel faster and fight harder than any of their contemporaries other than Napoleon's own elite forces. The moral force that emanated from Suvorov's leadership is apparent in the following description by one of his biographers:

There is no doubt that Suvorov was happier in the company
of the ordinary soldier than he was in that of the rich or the
noble. . . . He did not stand on his dignity; he did not pa-
tronize. The relationship was one of human equality, in
which class prejudice played no part, as on another level it
was one of a father and his children. Suvorov created a family
spirit, a relationship built upon mutual trust.[24]

These five major attributes of successful coercive military strategy can
be supplied to the matrix in table 20 in order to complete the three-
dimensional space for each, as indicated in table 21.

III. THE FACES OF MILITARY COERCION

The preceding chapters examine cases of military coercion and its successful or unsuccessful exploitation that have seemed interesting to
scholars and practitioners of the military art. By no means are these
cases exhaustive, and they are not explained by the "case study" method
used in business schools. That method is appropriate and useful for
some purposes, but not for an understanding of the connection between strategy and politics, or war and policy. Coercive military strategy is politico-military competition short of war, or a politico-military
strategy within war itself. The emphasis here on "politico-military" is
deliberate. It is the complexity of that connection between the political
and the military that makes coercion interesting, complicated, and
frustrating for analysts and operators alike.

Chapter 1 argued that the United States learned about limited war
and coercive military strategy the hard way, one war or crisis at a time,
during the disillusioning Cold War years. The Cold War forced rethinking of basic diplomatic and strategic concepts by which peacetime U.S.
presidents had previously operated. The United States was essentially
denied the option of withdrawal from responsibility for Europe's security. Substantial U.S. forces stationed in Europe, backed up by the threat
of nuclear retaliation, became part of the coercive strategy of Cold War
diplomacy. The Korean war presented another kind of challenge for
which U.S. diplomacy and strategy were not fully prepared. It was necessary to fight a costly, but limited, war in a single theater of operations

Table 21
Attributes of Coercive Military Strategy

	Goals and Means of First Actor	Goals and Means of Second actor	Environment (enabling or compelling)
Emphasis on influencing will of opponent			
Openness to revising political and military objectives			
Ability to engage in perspective taking			
Manipulation of symbols and information (including perceptions management)			
Moral influence (including popular support for war aims)			

without escalation to world war and without overcommitment of U.S. and allied resources. It was also necessary to negotiate overtly with North Korea and covertly with China and the Soviet Union in order to terminate the war.

Unfortunately for many U.S. military planners and policymakers, the Korean war was treated as an aberration or even as a "loss." Few lessons were learned from it, and it did not spark an effort to think about how, or whether, a more effective use of coercive strategy might have affected the outcome. For this and for other reasons, the United States blundered into escalation in Vietnam overly dependent upon a military strategy heavily bound up with coercive diplomacy, Cuban missile crisis style. The Johnson administration's "slow squeeze" of off-and-on bombing of North Vietnam and escalated ground fighting in South Vietnam failed to threaten North Vietnam with unacceptable losses or the fear of uncontrollable costs. North Vietnam and its National Liberation Front allies, facing no decisively compellent threat, outlasted the toleration of the U.S. home front for the war.

Chapter 2 discussed the Cuban missile crisis of 1962 as an example of coercion. For the first decade or so after the crisis, it was generally held in the academic literature as a triumph of coercive diplomacy for the United States against Soviet military adventurism. More recent scholarship has called those earlier judgments into question. A series of conferences among Soviet and American participants in the crisis was held in the latter 1980s and early 1990s. When the resulting first-person testimonies were added to additional archival research being done, both before and after the end of the Cold War, by Russian and Western scholars, a different picture began to emerge.

The Cuban missile crisis now appears more inadvertent than deliberate in its causes, and more a question of shared nuclear danger than successful nuclear deterrence. This much is not a novel finding. However, the recognition that mutual disaster was avoided in Cuba is insufficient for a full appreciation of the implications of this case for crisis management, one form of politico-military coercion widely touted in the nuclear age. The findings here are as follows. First, nuclear coercion is *sui generis*, because of the greater mutual risks involved and therefore, a greater degree of shared interest between opponents. Second, crisis management works only under very favorable conditions, including close monitoring by political leaders of military operations with potential to confuse the signals being sent to the other side. Third, crisis management depends upon the willingness of both parties to engage in creative perspective taking, as described earlier; to see the other side as it sees itself. Notice that this is *different* from the classical and valid military maxim "Know thy enemy." The object of that venerable warning is to know the enemy's intent in order to prevail in battle. Crisis management has a different object: preferably to *avoid* battle, especially nuclear battle, while preserving important national interests.

One can find in U.S. and Soviet Cold War policy pronouncements the same misperceptions, cognitive biases, and decision-making pathologies that one finds in the July crisis of 1914 set in motion by the assassination of Archduke Ferdinand in Sarajevo. The fact that Kennedy and Khrushchev were hindered by misperception and bias prior to October, 1962, is evident in Khrushchev's mistaken assumption that Kennedy would swallow the missile deployments with only a diplomatic protest. Additional evidence of misperception and cognitive closure, from the other side, is provided by Kennedy's acceptance of Soviet reassurances that no "offensive" missiles would be deployed to Cuba, as if in Soviet and Cuban eyes the *American* distinction between offensive and defensive weapons would be meaningful.

The precrisis misperceptions of October, 1962, were rapidly cleared up by nuclear exigency, to be sure, but also by the coercive strategy employed by Kennedy that allowed time for first impressions to be replaced by calmer assessments. On the basis of instinct immediately after the United States had discovered the Soviet missiles in Cuba, Kennedy might have attacked the missile sites or invaded Cuba. Khrushchev, faced with Kennedy's sudden public exposure of his Cuban missile deployments, might have followed through on his threat to run the U.S. blockade and precipitated a violent clash in the Caribbean, or worse. The coercive strategy allowed time for perspective taking on the part of Kennedy and Khrushchev and for perceptions management for, not against, conciliation by each leader within his respective government. On the other hand, the advantage of a coercive strategy in slowing things down almost caused a breakdown in perspective taking, by allowing the Soviet leadership to misjudge, at least temporarily, Kennedy's sense of urgency about resolving the crisis in good time.

The U.S. and allied coalition war against Iraq in 1991, caused by Iraq's invasion of Kuwait in August, 1990, has seemingly little to do with the subtleties of military coercion. The coalition won a quick and decisive victory, exploiting its superiority in high-technology weapons. For many military professionals, the dramatic success of the Gulf War seemed to show the benefits of overwhelming force and the comparative limitations of graduated escalation. This reading of the Gulf War was tendentious, and misleading as to the relationship between force and coercion. Chapter 3 argued the case that coercion was very much a part of U.S. and allied coalition war strategy.

The U.S. strategy for the Gulf War was bipartite, and the problem of coercion dominated its first part. Attempts at deterrence having failed to prevent Iraq's occupation of Kuwait, the U.S. problem became one of marshaling compellent threats sufficient to cause Saddam Hussein to withdraw his troops without war. The first step was to make available sufficient forces in the immediate theater of operations to deter Iraq from expanding its attack into Saudi Arabia. Fortunately Iraq did not test the U.S. and allied forces early in their deployment period. The second step, once President Bush had decided upon the need for an offensive military option to expel Iraq from Kuwait, created the forces, logistics, and command and control necessary for a coalition of some 700,000 personnel assigned to ground, air, or naval maritime arms of service. With this compellent option in place, Bush, supported by UN authorization and belated U.S. congressional resolutions, applied the diplomatic squeeze to Iraq.

Iraq did not respond even though its leadership must have known that, in the event of war, they were operating at a significant disadvantage. But perhaps this is mere after-the-fact reasoning; Iraq's leaders might have engaged in wishful thinking, failing to take into account the perspective of the United States and its allies that the latter were in a position to impose their will in Iraq. The possibility that Iraq failed in perspective taking is enhanced by President Bush's closely held hand, until the very moment when Operation Desert Storm was set in motion on January 17, 1991. Bush repeatedly stated his policy that Iraq must withdraw from Kuwait but also emphasized that the United States was willing to negotiate the details and timing of any such withdrawal. Saddam might have mistaken this implied flexibility about details for a willingness to give on the essential issue of continued Iraqi occupation of Kuwait.

President Bush knew that it would not suffice to take American forces into war with only foreign governments in support of his war aims, however many governments he lined up. Thus he also sought to maintain public support for Operation Desert Shield, the defensive buildup from August through December, 1990, and if necessary for Desert Storm, the liberation of Kuwait in 1991. Bush took several actions to make certain that he would not find his hands tied by adverse public opinion as Lyndon Johnson had upon escalation of U.S. involvement in Vietnam. First, Bush avoided even mentioning the draft, except in passing and in response to reporters' queries on that specific subject. When asked, Bush stated that no thought was being given to returning to the draft. Second, Bush repeatedly stated, in a cue that Saddam Hussein and some U.S. domestic audiences missed, that this "would not be another Vietnam." Some took this to mean that Bush would not engage in gradual escalation if the United States went to war, that he would follow the "Powell doctrine" (the point of view of Chairman of the Joint Chiefs of Staff Gen. Colin Powell), authorizing the use of all necessary force in order to accomplish the stated military and political objectives.[25] Bush did mean that, but he also meant three other things. First, he would not fight without allies. Second, he would not cede the initiative to the opponent. And, third, he would make the U.S. Congress stand up and be counted, for or against an offensive military option against Iraq.

Bush's political strategy isolated Iraq from allies and his Congressional opponents from public support adverse to Bush policy. This favorable political platform for waging war allowed Bush to face down Saddam Hussein knowing that he had closed off all of Iraq's exits in the Middle East and in Washington. Neither on the home front nor in the theater of operations could Iraq outflank U.S. strategy. Even with domestic political support, on the other hand, Bush's compellent threat against Iraq failed to cause Saddam to withdraw his forces from Kuwait without war. Operation Desert Storm was set in motion.

Appreciation of coercion had much to do with the operational aspects of Desert Storm as well as with the attempt by Bush to use compellence prior to war. The U.S. air strategy was not one of mass destruction of indiscriminate targets, but sequential attention to a matrix of high-priority targets that served as the base on which Iraq's entire war machine rested. Therefore, the air war emphasized the prompt destruction of air defenses and command, control, and communications from the center to the ganglia of Saddam's armed forces. Strikes against leadership facilities were included in these early counter-command attacks. The next priority was to gain air superiority by strikes against runways, shelters, and fighter-interceptor and fighter-bomber aircraft. Also included in the first waves of coalition air strikes were attacks on electric power grids, petroleum manufacturing plants, key transportation nodes, and known chemical, biological, and nuclear facilities.

The essence of this strategy was persuasive, not destructive, although many targets were destroyed. But they were deliberately destroyed, not indiscriminately, and the pattern of destruction was intended to send a message as much as to render the targets inoperable. The message was: You have lost effective centralized control over your forces, your air force is out of action, and your ability to see and to hear the flow of battle has been disrupted. In short, continuation of this one-sided struggle can only result in further destruction of your armed forces and, perhaps, of your political leadership. (U.S. officials vigorously denied that any attacks had been authorized specifically to kill Saddam Hussein, but all acknowledged that there would be no American complaints if the Iraqi leader accidentally walked under a cruise missile.)

U.S. strategy did not envision the entire destruction of Iraq's armed forces, nor the disestablishment by coalition warfare of the Saddam Hussein regime from power in Baghdad. Bush did indicate that he would be delighted to see the Iraqi military overthrow Saddam in the aftermath of Iraq's humiliating defeat, but the charge that Bush had counted on this and so deceived the American public in this regard is unfair. It *is* fair to say that U.S. intelligence about the durability of Saddam's regime was inadequate and overly optimistic, and Bush's wishful thinking undoubtedly reflected that. Bush expected that being pushed out of Kuwait and having much of his offensive military power blunted would be a jolt to Saddam Hussein's "face" within his own country, and a national humiliation sufficient to cause his downfall. But Iraq in 1991 was not Tsarist Russia in 1917, and Saddam had surrounded himself with willing sycophants and relatives totally dependent upon his personal whim. Bush's hope that defeat in battle might coerce Saddam's departure from power in humiliation was disappointed.

Bush had authorized extensive force within the theater of operations, but he worked to control the expansion of the conflict because he felt that expansion would work to Saddam's advantage, not to that of the United States and its allies. Saddam launched missile attacks on Israeli cities in the expectation that he could draw Israel into the war, thereby complicating the U.S.-led coalition's relations with its Arab members. Israel resisted the temptation after the United States agreed to provide Tel Aviv with Patriot missile defenses to knock down the attacking Iraqi SCUD surface-to-surface missiles. Had the political strategy of keeping Israel on the sidelines not worked successfully, the accomplishment of U.S. and allied military objectives in Kuwait and in southern Iraq would have been all the harder. In the case of Israel, the United States also employed coercion along with conciliation: Patriot missiles were provided but preparations were made to deny IFF (identify friend or foe) codes for Israeli aircraft that might decide to enter combat on the allied side, and the plan for denial was made known to Israel.

Chapter 4 considered whether coercive military strategy contributed to the inability of the United States to accomplish its political and military objectives in Vietnam. The perspectives of Robert S. McNamara were used as filters to ascertain whether, and to what extent, coercive strategy was responsible for U.S. failures in policy and strategy. The verdict was that coercive military strategy, properly understood, was not really tried in Vietnam. Coercive strategy does not necessarily imply a gradualist approach to escalation. And a gradual instead of dramatic and sudden use of escalation was at best a minor chord in a larger symphony of policy and strategic misconceptions that bedeviled the United States in Vietnam. A truly gradualist approach would have been based on modesty in expectation about favorable outcomes in battle and in diplomacy. U.S. expectations in Vietnam, at least from 1965 through 1967, were anything but modest. U.S. leaders expected to reform the South Vietnamese government, deter a North Vietnamese invasion, defeat the NLF insurgency and avoid expansion of the war to include China and Russia, while conducting business as usual on the home front.

McNamara's hubris led to the expectation that the methods for success in business, applied in military logistics, budgeting, and weapons purchase, could yield equal success in military strategy and operations, i.e., in the conduct of war. Unfortunately, as Clausewitz had warned, preparation for war is not the same thing as war itself. The social and cultural dimensions of the war in Vietnam, which turned out to be fundamental to the task of devising an effective military strategy, could not be addressed in the statistical computations of body counts and hamlets secured. In effect, the U.S. methodology in Vietnam measured *our own activity* instead of measuring the effect of our actions on the enemy's strategy and determination to persevere. Coercive military strategy would have emphasized perspective taking and a clearer understanding of the opponent's view of war and politics. The expectation that the opponent was a small state and/or insurgent movement, with a readily discernible strategic calculus of pain and privation, led U.S. policymakers into a debacle in Vietnam and on the home front. In the end, the United States inadvertently coerced itself into military stalemate and political defeat in Vietnam.

The theory of collective security, discussed in chapter 5, places the responsibility for world order and stability on the willingness of the great powers to emphasize their collaborative interests over their conflictual ones. Collective security implies a willingness on the part of individual states to balance against any aspiring hegemon, regardless of preexisting political, social, religious, or other ties. This condition is hard to meet in the real world, but collective security theory has spawned some experiments that have at least moderated the frequency of war and the destructiveness of those wars that were not avoided. Collective security did not prevent the Second World War, for example, nor did it guarantee U.S.-Soviet harmony during the Cold War. But, as expressed through the United Nations in the years from 1945–90, a "Concert" model of collective security did operate to create spaces of cooperation between the predominant U.S. and Soviet Cold War adversaries.

Collective security is not the same as collective defense. Collective defense is represented by an alliance with standing peacetime military forces and pointed at a particular, probable source of aggression. Collective defense is deliberately exclusive: one side's sphere of influence is not to be shared with the other. Collective security is supposed to work on the basis of realistic altruism: up to a point, it's all for one and one for all. No particular disturber of the peace is identified before the fact. Any state is theoretically capable of aggression, and after the fact of aggression all perpetrators are equally deserving of punishment. Thus, the use of the terms "security" and "defense" as synonyms may have a propaganda or heuristic purpose, but it cannot be accurate to conflate the two in discussions of collective state action or alliance decision making.

One of the interesting controversies of the post–Cold War era will be whether NATO can or should transform itself from a collective defense into a collective security organization. Some argue that NATO, demonstrably the most successful peacetime military alliance in modern history, is the best focal point for organizing a new security order in Europe. Others doubt that NATO, given its military focus and its origins as an anti-Soviet pact, can serve as the focal point for a new European security architecture. Those holding the second view would prefer to see the new European security pyramid based in an organization with membership more inclusive than NATO, and whose definition of security is more inclusive of conflict prevention and crisis management than that of NATO.

The West European Union (WEU) has been given new life after the Cold War as the potential military arm of a European pillar for transAtlantic defense. However, it would have to cooperate closely with NATO in order to obtain necessary logistics and intelligence support, and it is not a plausible candidate for a more inclusive security community from the Atlantic to the Urals. Some favor the Organization for Security and Cooperation in Europe (OSCE) as the best institutional expression of a new Eurasian security order. OSCE's inclusiveness is its strong point, but it is based on consensus decision making and lacks its own military support. NATO decided in July, 1997, to offer membership to three potential new member states in 1999 (its fiftieth anniversary): Poland, the Czech Republic, and Hungary; the door is apparently open to further enlargement of NATO's membership. NATO enlargement is predicated on the assumption of elongation in NATO's mission portfolio to emphasize the newer missions of conflict prevention and reduction.

Chapter 6 examined the increasing demand for U.S. and other great powers to participate in "operations other than war" (OOTW) due to a variety of causes inherent in the political disorder of the post-Cold War world. These causes include ethno-national and religious wars within and between states, humanitarian disasters, terrorism, civil strife, and disorder of various kinds, as well as the socio-economic consequences of the political anarchy resulting from failed states. As a result of these and other forces, the United States and the United Nations have found themselves engaged in an unprecedented number of military peace operations. These range from NATO's extensive commitment of its implementation force in Bosnia in support of the December, 1995, peace agreement, to the U.S./UN restoration of the democratically elected government of Haiti from 1994 through 1996. Peace operations are an especially interesting form of coercive military strategy, frequently requiring a very high degree of self-restraint in the application of force. Peace operations also can lead to vexatious problems of coalition management and command and control whether undertaken with UN or other multinational sponsorship.

CONCLUSION

Having established that the theory of coercion has some applicability to military affairs, can we use it to say anything useful to policymakers or to military professionals? I would argue "yes" on both counts. Coercive military strategy is a very "real-world" topic once it has been relieved of its socio-psychological abstractions and applied to pertinent examples. Alexander L. George, who has contributed much to the exposition of coercive diplomacy (one aspect of coercive military strategy as I have described it), acknowledges that coercive diplomacy is a body of ideas rooted in the experience of policymakers.[26] Thomas C. Schelling revolutionized the theory of strategy by emphasizing the significance of coercive, compared to destructive, use of military power.[27] These and other writers who have developed theories about the coercive use of military force have done so as a result of a focus rooted in contemporary problems: reducing the risks of war, limiting the costs of wars that do occur, avoiding inadvertent war or escalation, preventing states from misperceptions that are contributory to surprise attacks, and so forth.

In addition to its insights for nuclear deterrence and the fighting of conventional wars, coercive theory is also pertinent to the problem of adjusting U.S. military doctrine and training to a set of security challenges dominated by unconventional conflicts. The U.S. military tradition is steeped in the concepts of Baron A. H. Jomini, noted early-nineteenth-century Swiss military theorist and author of the most celebrated military handbook of the time, and Clausewitz (for land warfare); Alfred Thayer Mahan, U.S. proponent of sea power by means sufficient to seek out and destroy the opponent's battle fleet (for maritime strategy); and Giulio Douhet, early-twentieth-century Italian

military theorist and advocate of victory through strategic air bombardment (for air strategy).[28] For example, Clausewitz's classic study
On War is a complex study rich in insights about many aspects of warfare, but few would disagree with the argument that the center of gravity in Clausewitz's understanding of war is the decisive defeat of the
enemy's armed forces.[29] While this perspective might be applicable to
conventional wars dominated by regular forces, it lacks another dimension of insight into unconventional conflicts in which political and social factors are more important than military. Unconventional conflicts
are therefore better understood according to the ideas about war outlined in the work of the great Chinese strategic thinker, Sun Tzu Wu.[30]
According to one writer:

> American military leaders, because of a fixation on "vic-
> tory" and "winning wars," have too often viewed conflict as
> a zero-sum game in which a gain for one side results in a cor-
> responding loss by the other and thus have frequently failed
> to provide the kind of politico-military advice a crisis situa-
> tion requires. . . . Rather than thinking in terms of a variety
> of conflict management techniques . . . too many military
> leaders continue to focus on conflict as a contest to be "won"
> rather than an international malady that requires flexible
> and imaginative management.[31]

The gist of the preceding statement is to offer a warning against one-
dimensional thinking about the use of force. As it stands, however, it
comes dangerously close to social-scientific naïveté that would blur the
essential line between war and all else. The strength of Clausewitz is his
comprehension of the uniqueness of war as a social phenomenon: its at-
mosphere of danger, its idiom of uncertainty, and its openness to the
fickle influence of probability and chance. The use of force even for
"peace operations" crosses a threshold beyond which lies the unknown.
Coercive military strategy is not a panacea, and not a substitute for the
other ingredients required for the mastery of policy related to strategy.
Nor is it an anodyne for the realities of combat seen up close and personal. As Gen. Colin Powell once said during a discussion of the differences between the "limited war" and "all-out war" schools:

For the man and woman in combat . . . such academic niceties are moot. I am reminded of the famous Bill Mauldin cartoon that shows two GIs—Willie and Joe—flat on the ground while machine-gun tracers lick overhead and exploding artillery rounds light up the night sky. Joe says to Willie: "I can't git no lower, Willie. Me buttons is in th' way."[32]

Notes

INTRODUCTION:
MILITARY STRATEGY AND COERCION

1. Illustrations of the usefulness of coercive thinking with respect to prob-lems of military innovation, including research and development, appear in Stephen Peter Rosen, *Winning the Next War: Innovation and the Modern Military,* esp. 8–52 and 243–45.
2. Sun Tzu, *The Art of War,* 77–78.
3. Ibid., 82–83.
4. Bevin Alexander, *How Great Generals Win,* 187–208, is especially good on the period from 1927 to 1935, which culminated in the Long March and the arrival, against great odds, of the First Army in Yan'an.
5. Alexander, *The Future of Warfare,* 160–75.
6. James M. McPherson, *Battle Cry of Freedom: The Civil War Era,* 570–75.
7. Sun Tzu, *The Art of War,* 63.
8. Ibid., 64.
9. Karl von Clausewitz, *On War,* ed. and trans. Michael Howard and Peter Paret.
10. Ibid., 89. Also see Michael I. Handel, *Sun Tzu and Clausewitz: "The Art of War" and "On War" Compared,* 20.
11. Clausewitz, *On War,* ed. and trans. Michael Howard and Peter Paret, 113–14, 119–21, and passim.
12. Ibid., 108.
13. Unexpected forward deployment of the Union Third Corps by its com-mander, Gen. Daniel Sickles, placed the Union left flank in the air and created the opportunity for an almost separate battle of Little Round Top to develop on the late afternoon of July 2. According to one historian of the battle: "The occupation of Little Round Top at the right time and right place by Vincent's [Col. Strong Vincent of the 83rd Pennsylvania, in command of Third Brigade, First Division, Fifth Army Corps until mor-tally wounded at Gettysburg] was the result of a combination of circum-stances and a stroke of rare good luck for which no one person in the Union high command could claim the credit, and in fact none tried to." Edwin B. Coddington, *The Gettysburg Campaign: A Study in Command,* 390. See also Jesse Bowman Young, *The Battle of Gettysburg: A Compre-hensive Narrative,* 384–449, for rosters of the Army of the Potomac and Army of Northern Virginia with biographical notes.

14. Joshua Lawrence Chamberlain, "The State, the Nation and the People," speech given at the dedication of Maine monuments at Gettysburg, Oct. 3, 1889, cited in Alice Rains Trulock, *In the Hands of Providence: Joshua L. Chamberlain and the American Civil War*, 446, fn. 87.

15. Strategy is the realm of paradox. See Edward N. Luttwak, *Strategy: The Logic of War and Peace*, passim.

16. Richard N. Haass, *Intervention: The Use of American Military Force in the Post-Cold War World*, 68.

17. Amplification can be obtained in Thomas C. Schelling, *Arms and Influence*, esp. 92–125.

18. See I. William Zartman, ed., *Collapsed States: The Disintegration and Restoration of Legitimate Authority*, esp. chaps. 5 and 10; and Donald M. Snow, *Uncivil Wars: International Security and the New Internal Conflicts*, 93–114.

19. Kenneth Allard, *Command, Control, and the Common Defense*, esp. 273–303.

20. For expert assessments on this topic, see Stuart E. Johnson and Martin C. Libicki, eds., *Dominant Battlespace Knowledge: The Winning Edge*.

21. Alexander L. George, "Coercive Diplomacy: Definition and Characteristics."

22. Ibid., 9.

23. Ibid. On the concept of compellence, see Schelling, *Arms and Influence*, 70–72. Although George's exclusion of deterrence and compellence from coercive diplomacy has the virtue of emphasizing nonaggressive or nonmilitary approaches to conflict resolution, both terms belong in any viable concept of coercive *military* strategy. See, in support of the last point: Robert Jervis, *The Meaning of the Nuclear Revolution: Statecraft and the Prospect of Armageddon*, esp. 237–57 and chap. 5 passim.

24. George, "Coercive Diplomacy," 10.

25. Ibid.

26. Jervis, *The Meaning of the Nuclear Revolution*, 137.

27. Clausewitz, *On War*, trans. Colonel J. J. Graham, vol. 1, book 1, chap. 11, 40.

28. Robert A. Pape, Jr., *Bombing to Win: Air Power and Selection in War*, 4. Pape's definition of coercion is too narrow for some social scientific usage, but not inappropriate in a context for defining the uses of force.

29. Ibid., 18–19 and 58–86. My summary follows the original with the addition of the requirement in denial strategies for being able to deny the opponent its objectives *at an acceptable cost*, but this is fully consistent with the overall thrust of Pape's argument.

30. See Schelling, *Arms and Influence*, 26–34, and Bernard Brodie, *War and Politics*, 375–432.

31. Brodie, *War and Politics*, 426.

CHAPTER 1. THE COLD WAR AND U.S. LIMITED WAR STRATEGY

1. Russell F. Weigley, *Towards an American Army: Military Thought from Washington to Marshall;* Samuel P. Huntington, *The Soldier and the State;* Stephen J. Cimbala, "United States."

2. For pertinent documentation, see Walter Lafeber, *America, Russia, and the Cold War, 1945–1975.* On the development of U.S. Cold War policy, see John Lewis Gaddis, *The United States and the Origins of the Cold War, 1941–1947.* For Soviet policy, see Vojtech Mastny, *Russia's Road to the Cold War: Diplomacy, Warfare, and the Politics of Communism, 1941–45.*

3. John Lewis Gaddis, *The Long Peace: Inquiries into the History of the Cold War,* 114.

4. Robert Endicott Osgood, *Limited War: The Challenge to American Strategy.*

5. Henry A. Kissinger, *Nuclear Weapons and Foreign Policy.*

6. Thomas C. Schelling, *The Strategy of Conflict.* See also Schelling, *Arms and Influence.*

7. William W. Kaufmann, *The McNamara Strategy.*

8. Maxwell D. Taylor, *The Uncertain Trumpet.*

9. Robert A. Doughty et al., *Military Operations Since 1871,* 913.

10. A critique of U.S. experiences with covert action is provided in D. Michael Shafer, *Deadly Paradigms: The Failure of U.S. Counterinsurgency Policy.* See also Douglas S. Blaufarb, *The Counterinsurgency Era: U.S. Doctrine and Performance, 1950 to the Present.* For other evaluations, see John Prados, *Presidents' Secret Wars: CIA and Pentagon Covert Operations Since World War II,* and Roy Godson, ed., *Covert Action,* vol. 4 of *Intelligence Requirements for the 1980s.* An assessment of the impact of low-intensity conflict on American military professionalism appears in Sam C. Sarkesian, *Beyond the Battlefield: The New Military Professionalism,* chaps. 4–7.

11. Harry G. Summers, Jr., *On Strategy II: A Critical Analysis of the Gulf War,* 72–73.

12. Charles Krauthammer, "The Unipolar Moment," 298.

13. See Secretary of Defense William J. Perry's *Annual Report to the President and the Congress,* 5.

14. Michael Klare, *Rogue States and Nuclear Outlaws: America's Search for a New Foreign Policy,* 109–10.

15. For diverse views on this, see contributions by Don M. Snider and Andrew J. Kelly, and Lawrence J. Korb, in my *Clinton and Post-Cold War Defense.*

16. U.S. Congressional Budget Office, *An Analysis of the Administration's Future Years Defense Program for 1995 through 1999,* 18.

17. Ibid., 4–5.

18. Martin Van Creveld, *The Transformation of War.*

19. Clausewitz, *On War.*

20. For an excellent discussion, see John A. English, *Marching through Chaos: The Descent of Armies in Theory and Practice*, 36–37.

21. K. J. Holsti, *The State, War, and the State of War*, 24–25.

22. Ibid., 25.

23. Robert J. Art, "A Defensible Defense: America's Grand Strategy After the Cold War."

24. Ibid. passim. Art offers a deliberately narrow and specific definition of security: the ability of the United States to protect its homeland from attack, conquest, invasion, or destruction. (See ibid., 7.)

25. John Lewis Gaddis, *The United States and the End of the Cold War: Implications, Reconsiderations, Provocations*, 193–94.

26. Andrew J. Krepinevich, Jr., *The Army and Vietnam*, esp. 164–93.

27. Sam C. Sarkesian suggests that the term *unconventional* conflict is preferable to *low-intensity* conflict. Unconventional conflicts are nontraditional and not in conformity with the American way of war. These kinds of conflicts emphasize social and political variables, especially the problem of revolution and counterrevolution, rather than the military dimensions of conflict. See Sarkesian, "U.S. Strategy and Unconventional Conflicts: The Elusive Goal."

28. Sarkesian, *Beyond the Battlefield*, chaps. 4–6.

29. Sun Tzu, *The Art of War*, 45–56. For an assessment of literature on many important aspects of unconventional warfare, see John Shy and Thomas W. Collier, "Revolutionary War," 815–62.

30. Summers, *On Strategy*, argues that the United States should have followed a conventional military strategy in Vietnam, leaving counterinsurgency, civic action, and the like to the South Vietnamese. In his view, U.S. strategy failed in Vietnam because it strayed from military traditionalism into politico-military amateurism, especially graduated escalation and counterinsurgency. Sarkesian, *America's Forgotten Wars: The Counterrevolutionary Past and Lessons for the Future*, 194–218, provides a different assessment, contending that the military aspects of the war were especially complex and involved an unusual mixture of conventional and unconventional campaigns.

31. Sarkesian, "U.S. Strategy and Unconventional Conflicts," 199. See also Leslie H. Gelb with Richard K. Betts, *The Irony of Vietnam: The System Worked*, for an argument that bad foreign policy resulted from a U.S. domestic policy-making process that worked as it was designed to. For counterpoint to the Gelb-Betts arguments, see Shafer, *Deadly Paradigms*, esp. 260–61.

32. Weigley, "American Strategy from Its Beginnings through the First World War," 410–12, and *The American Way of War: A History of United States Military Strategy and Policy*.

33. Weigley, "American Strategy from Its Beginnings," 412.

34. Ibid., 410, and Sarkesian, *America's Forgotten Wars,* 107.
35. Sarkesian, *America's Forgotten Wars,* 110.
36. On the development of the strategy of annihilation in German military thinking, see Larry H. Addington, *The Blitzkrieg Era and the German General Staff, 1865–1941,* esp. 3–27. On the development of the distinction between strategies of annihilation (*Niederwerfungsstrategie*) and strategies of exhaustion (*Ermattungsstrategie*) by German historian Hans Delbruck, see Gordon A. Craig, "Delbruck: The Military Historian," esp. 341. An important Russian contribution on the difference between annihilation- and attrition-oriented strategies is Aleksandr A. Svechin's *Strategy,* 240–50.
37. Mao Tse-tung (Zedong), *Basic Tactics,* esp. 67–89.
38. The strategic concept of the Gulf War, covered in another chapter, also involved important elements of selective military strategy, as explained therein.
39. For an assessment of threats to U.S. security remaining after the Cold War, see Art, "A Defensible Defense," 23ff.
40. A collection of essays speaking to these and other issues pertinent to future U.S. defense planning is Davis, ed., *New Challenges for Defense Planning: Rethinking How Much Is Enough,* esp. chaps. 2 and 4.
41. Davis, "Planning Under Uncertainty Then and Now: Paradigms Lost and Paradigms Emerging," 31.
42. The point is emphasized in Michael J. Mazarr, Don M. Snider and James A. Blackwell, Jr., *Desert Storm: The Gulf War and What We Learned,* 162–68.
43. Ibid., 175.
44. The term *reconnaissance-strike complexes* originated in Russian/Soviet military discourse to describe combinations of increasingly accurate conventional munitions, improved target identification and location, and enhanced control and communications systems for directing the employment of munitions against selected targets. See V. G. Reznichenko, I. N. Vorob'yev, and N. F. Miroshnichenko, *Taktika (Tactics),* 24, which notes: "In the opinion of foreign specialists, reconnaissance-strike (fire) complexes are the most effective form of high-precision weapon. High-precision reconnaissance resources and high-precision weapons are coordinated by an automated control system making it possible to carry out reconnaissance and destruction missions practically in real time." The issue continues to preoccupy the Russian military, although it will struggle to maintain the military-industrial base for future modernization. See John Erickson, "Quo Vadis? The Changing Faces of Soviet/Russian Forces and Now Russia."
45. According to one source, "various offices in the Pentagon are battling for control of a dramatic new initiative for nonlethal warfare. By using blind-

ing lasers and chemical immobilizers to stun foot soldiers, and munitions with "entanglement" warheads to stop armored vehicles on land or ships at sea, it is hoped by some that the United States could some day fight a war that did not involve death, or at least few deaths." Mazarr, Snider, and Blackwell, *Desert Storm*, 172. Life imitates art, or at least, simulation.

CHAPTER 2. COERCIVE STRATEGY IN THE CUBAN MISSILE CRISIS

1. My distinction between these two concepts is explained in the introduction.
2. Alexander L. George, "The Cuban Missile Crisis, 1962."
3. See George, "Coercive Diplomacy," esp. 8–9, and "The Cuban Missile Crisis: Peaceful Resolution Through Coercive Diplomacy," both of which appear in George and William E. Simons, eds., *The Limits of Coercive Diplomacy.*
4. Khrushchev, quoted in Graham T. Allison, *Essence of Decision: Explaining the Cuban Missile Crisis,* 64–65.
5. See the comments of Dean Rusk on this point in James G. Blight and David A. Welch, *On the Brink: Americans and Soviets Reexamine the Cuban Missile Crisis,* 174–75.
6. Raymond L. Garthoff, *Reflections on the Cuban Missile Crisis,* 73–74.
7. George, "The Cuban Missile Crisis, 1962," 133.
8. Ibid., 133–34. See also George, "The Cuban Missile Crisis: Peaceful Resolution Through Coercive Diplomacy," 115. As George notes, "the practice of deliberately slowing up and spacing out military actions, which crisis management requires, may be difficult to reconcile with the need to generate the sense of urgency for compliance" ("The Cuban Missile Crisis, 1962," 134). For further background on this and other crisis management issues, see Ole R. Holsti, "Crisis Decision Making"; and Phil Williams, *Crisis Management.* Pertinent to the Cuban missile crisis is the discussion in Albert and Roberta Wohlstetter's "Controlling the Risks in Cuba."
9. M. A. Neale and M. H. Bazerman, "The Role of Perspective-Taking in Negotiating Under Different Forms of Arbitration," *Industrial and Labor Relations Review* 36 (1983): 378–88, cited in Daniel Druckman and P. Terrence Hopman, "Behavioral Aspects of Negotiations on Mutual Security," note 116.
10. Ibid.
11. The various editions of the Pentagon's *Soviet Military Power* throughout the Reagan years provide ample evidence for my point here. For an overview of this issue, see Robert L. Arnett, "Soviet Attitudes Towards Nuclear War: Do They Really Think They Can Win?"
12. For evidence, see the President's Commission on Strategic Forces (Scowcroft Commission) *Report.*
13. See John Lewis Gaddis, *We Now Know: Rethinking Cold War History,* esp.

222–23 and 235–36, on Khrushchev's strategy for exploiting fictive nuclear superiority.

14. *Pravda*, Jan. 15, 1961.

15. Talensky said that it was necessary to "emphasize that a future war, if the aggressors succeeded in unleashing it, will lead to such an increase in human losses on both sides that its consequences for mankind might be catastrophic" (*Kommunist 7* [1960]: 31–41). Talensky drew an explicit comparison between the destruction of Soviet cities at the hands of Nazi Germany and the destruction attendant to nuclear rocket war, arguing that the degree of destruction in nuclear war would be "magnified a thousand times" compared to World War II and extended over whole continents (*Mezhdunarodnaya zhizn'* 10 [1960]: 33). Both articles are cited in Arnold L. Horelick and Myron Rush, *Strategic Power and Soviet Foreign Policy*, 78–79.

16. Horelick and Rush, *Strategic Power and Soviet Foreign Policy*, 78–79.

17. Ibid., 80.

18. Ibid.

19. Ibid., 83.

20. Gilpatric, quoted in ibid., 84.

21. Malinovsky, quoted in Richard Ned Lebow and Janice Gross Stein, *We All Lost the Cold War*, chap. 2.

22. Horelick and Rush, *Strategic Power and Soviet Foreign Policy*, 85.

23. Ibid., 86–87. Kennedy had actually said that he would not rule out the possibility of a U.S. first strike under some conditions, which was consistent with previous U.S. policy guidance for nuclear weapons employment in the Eisenhower administration.

24. Khrushchev, quoted in *Pravda*, July 11, 1962, cited in Horelick and Rush, *Strategic Power and Soviet Foreign Policy*, 87.

25. Horelick and Rush, *Strategic Power and Soviet Foreign Policy*, 87.

26. I have admittedly collapsed a wide spectrum of opinion into two boxes here. For more complete discussion, see Robert Jervis, *The Meaning of the Nuclear Revolution;* Colin S. Gray, *Nuclear Strategy and National Style;* and David W. Tarr, *Nuclear Deterrence and International Security: Alternative Nuclear Regimes.*

27. *Granma*, Dec. 2, 1990, 3. Letter from Castro to Khrushchev, Oct. 26, 1962. I am grateful to Ned Lebow for first calling this correspondence to my attention.

28. Ibid. Italics supplied.

29. Ibid. Italics supplied.

30. Letter from Khrushchev to Castro, Oct. 28, 1962, *Granma*, Dec. 2, 1990, 3.

31. Ibid.

32. Ibid.

33. David N. Schwartz, *NATO's Nuclear Dilemmas*, chap. 4, esp. 62–66 and

73–74. The Gaither Report had also advocated overseas U.S. IRBM deployments even before Sputnik (Ibid., 65). U.S. Jupiter missiles were formally handed over to the Turks on October 22, the day of President Kennedy's televised address announcing U.S. discovery of the Soviet missiles in Cuba and the decision to impose the quarantine in response (Blight and Welch, *On the Brink*, 172).

34. McGeorge Bundy, transcriber, and James G. Blight, editor, "October 27, 1962: Transcripts of the Meetings of the ExComm."

35. Ibid., 36–37.

36. Ibid., 38–39.

37. Blight and Welch, *On the Brink*, 170–71, 173.

38. McNamara, quoted in Blight and Welch, *On the Brink*, 187.

39. Ibid., 153.

40. Bundy and Blight, "October 27, 1962," 72ff.

41. Ibid., 75.

42. Numerous arguments to this effect by members of the ExComm appear in Bundy and Blight, "October 27, 1962," passim.

43. In his memoirs, Khrushchev noted that "In addition to protecting Cuba, our missiles would have equalized what the West likes to call 'the balance of power.' The Americans had surrounded our country with military bases and threatened us with nuclear weapons, and now they would learn just what it feels like to have enemy missiles pointing at you; we'd be doing nothing more than giving them a little of their own medicine." Strobe Talbott, *Khrushchev Remembers*, 494. A summary of ExComm deliberations on Khrushchev's possible motives for the deployment appears in Roger Hilsman, *The Cuban Missile Crisis: The Struggle Over Policy*, 79–81.

44. It will be important for U.S. and Soviet scholars to work together to establish more confidence in such arguments, admittedly tentative. Some Soviet scholars are now applying modeling and simulation techniques to the analysis of the Cuban missile crisis. See, for example, V. P. Akimov, et al., "Karibskiy krizis: opyt modelirovaniya" ("The Caribbean Crisis: Experience of Modelling").

CHAPTER 3. COERCIVE MILITARY STRATEGY AND DESERT STORM: LIMITATION WITHOUT RESTRAINT

1. Perhaps the United States was dealing with more than one "Saddam" personality. Or, it may be prudent for future policymakers to model more than one personality type for adversary leaders. See Davis and John Arquilla, *Deterring or Coercing Opponents in Crisis: Lessons from the War with Saddam Hussein*, esp. 14. Deterrence as practiced during the Cold War may not be very meaningful for dealing with post-Cold War rogue

states or terrorists, especially for those acquiring weapons of mass destruction. See Keith B. Payne, *Deterrence in the Second Nuclear Age*, 56–58.

2. Named for Gen. Colin Powell, Chairman of the Joint Chiefs of Staff under President George Bush and formerly military assistant to then Secretary of Defense Caspar Weinberger in 1984, when Weinberger promulgated a list of highly restrictive guidelines for when and how the United States should get into a war. Powell is widely thought to have been the actual author of the "Weinberger doctrine," as it was initially known.

3. Powell's role in revising U.S. national military strategy during the Bush administration is described in Stephen J. Cimbala, "The Role of Military Advice: Civil-Military Relations and Bush Security Strategy."

4. According to one analysis of U.S. Gulf War aims, "Many of those who loudly applauded the Bush administration's inexorable march toward a military confrontation with Saddam Hussein later roundly condemned the White House for what they regarded as a premature cease-fire, and for Bush's failure to support post-cease-fire Kurdish and Shi'a uprisings against Baghdad and to use force again to compel Saddam's compliance with cease-fire terms." Jeffrey Record, *Hollow Victory: A Contrary View of the Gulf War*, 52.

5. For example, on the use of "denial" versions of coercive air strategy, see Pape, *Bombing to Win*, 69–79.

6. U.S. Secretary of State Dean Acheson is said to have raised doubts about the importance of Korea in a January, 1950, speech in which he defined a number of U.S. vital interests in Asia, but did not specifically mention Korea. His was not, however, a formulation which excluded the possibility of a U.S. response to North Korean aggression, as North Korean Premier Kim Il Sung and Soviet General Secretary Joseph Stalin soon learned.

7. Robert Jervis, "What Do We Want to Deter and How Do We Deter It?" 118.

8. Geoffrey Blainey, *The Causes of War*, 146–56.

9. I am grateful to Paul Davis for emphasizing this point in a critique of an earlier draft of this manuscript.

10. On Saddam's motives, see Richard Herrmann, "Coercive Diplomacy and the Crisis over Kuwait," 234–35.

11. Michael R. Gordon and General Bernard R. Trainor, *The Generals' War: The Inside Story of the Conflict in the Gulf*, 331.

12. Bruce W. Jentleson, *With Friends Like These: Reagan, Bush, and Saddam, 1982–1990*.

13. In "War by Miscalculation," 198, Bernard E. Trainor notes that the U.S. track record for deterrence over the preceding four decades was successful against the main threat of Soviet aggression but less successful against lesser threats, as a number of regional and local wars attests.

14. Testimony of John Kelly, Assistant Secretary of State, July 31, 1990, to U.S.

Congress, House Foreign Affairs Committee, cited in Davis and Arquilla, *Deterring or Coercing Opponents in Crisis,* 67–68.

15. John Keegan, "The Ground War," 77.

16. The difference between "perspective taking" and "mirror imaging" should be noted here. Perspective taking implies the awareness of the opponent's motives in his or her own terms, regardless whether they correspond to one's one assumptions and motives. Where mirror imaging leads to closure and bias, perspective taking leads to openness and objectivity.

17. The White House, Office of the Press Secretary, *Address by the President to the Nation,* Aug. 8, 1990.

18. Ibid.

19. Alexander L. George, "The Development of Doctrine and Strategy," 1–35.

20. Schelling, *Arms and Influence,* 69–73.

21. Schelling, *Arms and Influence,* 78.

22. Richard K. Betts, *Nuclear Blackmail and Nuclear Balance,* 31–47.

23. *Time,* Sept. 24, 1990, 31–35. This raised the total of French forces committed to the immediate theater of operations to 7,800.

24. George, "The Development of Doctrine and Strategy," passim.

25. In the example of the Cuban missile crisis discussed at length in Chapter 2, the "try and see" variation was the blockade imposed against further shipments of missiles into Cuba; the blockade could preclude additional shipments of medium- or intermediate-range ballistic missiles, but it could not by itself cause the Soviet Union to remove the missiles. Only the additional pressure of an ultimatum that the missiles had to be removed within 24 hours, coupled with the warning that if the Soviets could not do so the United States would, finally forced Khrushchev's hand on October 28.

26. Dan Balz and R. Jeffrey Smith, "Bush Ordered Escalation to Show Resolve, Aide Says," *Philadelphia Inquirer,* Nov. 11, 1990, 16-A.

27. Ibid. By Christmas, however, Vice President Dan Quayle was stating in public that sanctions had failed to dislodge Saddam from Kuwait. It now seems apparent that President Bush had determined to expel Iraq from Kuwait by means of force, if necessary, by mid-November at the latest. According to Jeffrey Record, by the fall of 1990 it was an open secret in Washington that "the Bush administration's worst nightmare was a voluntary Iraqi withdrawal from most or all of Kuwait, which would have effectively eliminated war as an administration option." Record, *Hollow Victory,* 40.

28. Ibid.

29. *New York Times,* Nov. 30, 1990, A1.

30. However, the vote was very close; the Senate vote to authorize force, for example, was 52–47 in favor. This supports the point made earlier that Saddam's apparent hardheadedness about not withdrawing from Kuwait

voluntarily was not as irrational or unreasonable as some now depict it to have been. See Davis and Arquilla, *Deterring or Coercing Opponents in Crisis,* 54.

31. Rick Atkinson, "Hussein, Baghdad Would be Air Force's Top Targets," *Philadelphia Inquirer,* Sept. 17, 1990, 10-A.

32. Ibid.

33. Ibid.

34. Paul Bracken, *The Command and Control of Nuclear Forces,* 92–93.

35. See George H. Quester, *Deterrence before Hiroshima: The Airpower Background to Modern Strategy.*

36. Kenneth Allard, "The Future of Command and Control: Toward a Paradigm of Information Warfare," 188. This passage has the virtue of benign overstatement, but makes a nevertheless valid point. Command systems are not literally weapons of destruction, but a bad command system can be the medium for self-destruction through ossified command channels, poor situation awareness, confused intelligence assessment, and so on.

37. Eliot A. Cohen, "The Mystique of U.S. Airpower," 63.

38. A generalization aptly documented in Martin Van Creveld's *Command in War.*

39. Fred Charles Ikle, *Every War Must End,* 59–83.

40. Ibid., 66.

41. Gen. Michael Dugan, "The Air War," *U.S. News and World Report,* Feb. 11, 1991, 26.

42. Gordon and Trainor, *The Generals' War,* passim., esp. 212, and Dugan, "The Air War." General Dugan's description of the phased air campaign notes that the phases were overlapping and not altogether sequential.

43. Cohen, "The Mystique of U.S. Airpower," 61.

44. For comparison, see the analysis of U.S. air power in Robert A. Pape, Jr., "Coercive Air Power in the Vietnam War."

45. An argument to this effect appears in ibid. passim.

46. Ikle, *Every War Must End,* 60–83.

47. George, "The Development of Doctrine and Strategy," 1–35.

48. The argument holds even if the actual Bush objectives were more ambitious, including the dethronement of Saddam Hussein. The large numbers of tactical sorties and the uncontested control of airspace over Iraq by the coalition can be read to suggest a massive, indiscriminate air war of attrition for the purpose of destroying Iraq's military capability. However, the United States, perhaps mistakenly, did not seek to disestablish the Iraqi regime by direct application of military force (*hoping* for Saddam Hussein's internal overthrow does not constitute a politico-military objective), nor was the destruction of Iraq's *defensive* capabilities intended. A smaller, user-friendly Iraq was the political postwar objective, not a power vacuum in the Middle East that Iran would exploit. Although the expectation that

Saddam would be overthrown by his own praetorian guard overestimated his vulnerability to domestic pressure, that U.S. and allied intelligence misestimate does not carry any weight in the argument whether the United States waged a limited, or unlimited, air and ground war.

49. Thomas A. Keaney and Eliot A. Cohen, Directors, *Gulf War Air Power Survey* (Washington: U.S. Government Printing Office, 1993), chaps. 3, 21; cited in Air Vice Marshal Tony Mason's *Air Power: A Centennial Appraisal*, 301.

50. *Gulf War Air Power Survey*, chaps. 3, 21, and 25, cited in Mason, *Air Power*, 301.

51. Mason, *Air Power*, 272.

52. Robert A. Pape, Jr., "Coercion and Military Strategy: Why Denial Works and Punishment Doesn't."

53. The charge has been laid against the U.S. 1965–68 bombing campaign in Vietnam from by military critics. See Mark Clodfelter, *The Limits of Air Power: The American Bombing of North Vietnam*, esp. 77–88.

54. U.S. Secretary of State James A. Baker, III, outlined postwar U.S. objectives for the Gulf and Middle East regions in testimony before the U. S. Congress House Foreign Affairs Committee, Feb. 6, 1991. His statement hinted at a continued U.S. military presence in the region, and included among five major goals the economic reconstruction of Iraq. Baker was noncommittal on insisting that Saddam Hussein resign as a precondition for U.S. postwar aid. *New York Times*, Feb. 7, 1991, A-17.

55. This objective was not as impractical is it now seems. According to one expert assessment, low U.S. and allied casualties in Desert Storm were the result of a fortuitous synergism between new technology and the imbalance in skills between Iraq and its opponents. In the absence of *either* Iraqi mistakes or new technology effective at proving ground levels, U.S. and friendly casualties "would likely have reached or exceeded prewar expectations." See Stephen Biddle, "Victory Misunderstood: What the Gulf War Tells Us about the Future of Conflict," note 140.

CHAPTER 4. VIETNAM AND COERCIVE STRATEGY

1. Harry G. Summers, Jr., *On Strategy: A Critical Analysis of the Gulf War*, esp., 49–50, 98–99, and 103.

2. On U.S. coercive *diplomacy* against North Vietnam, see William E. Simons, "U.S. Coercive Pressure on North Vietnam, Early 1965," 133–73. On U.S. attempted coercion of North Vietnam in individual campaigns, see Pape, *Bombing to Win*, esp. 174–94.

3. Robert S. McNamara with Brian VanDeMark, *In Retrospect: The Tragedy and Lessons of Vietnam*.

4. Charles J. Hitch and Roland N. McKean, *The Economics of Defense in the Nuclear Age*, 105–32.

5. A balanced appraisal of the "new scientific strategists" and of systems analysis appears in Brodie, *War and Politics*, 453–78.

6. The difference between the qualities of thinking needed for weapons procurement and for strategic thinking are explained in Colin S. Gray, *Weapons Don't Make War: Policy, Strategy, and Military Technology*, esp. 65–89.

7. Three interesting studies that make this point in the context of contemporary military strategy are: William T. Johnsen, et al., *The Principles of War in the 21st Century*, esp. 4–6; Gordon R. Sullivan and Anthony M. Coroalles, *The Army in the Information Age*, passim.; and David Jablonsky, *Strategic Rationality Is Not Enough: Hitler and the Concept of Crazy States*, esp. 5–8.

8. Clausewitz, *On War*, ed. and trans. Michael Howard and Peter Paret, chap. 2, book 2, 141. The point is made within the larger context of Clausewitz's discussion of the environment of warfare and its inclusion of uncertainty, danger, and hostile feelings. (Ibid., 136–40.)

9. Allan R. Millett and Peter Maslowski, *For the Common Defense: A Military History of the United States of America*, 555.

10. Ibid. McNamara's own views appear in his book, *The Essence of Security*. A favorable view of McNamara's impact on Pentagon decision making is presented in Kaufmann, *The McNamara Strategy*. A sensible appreciation of this matter appears in Brodie, *War and Politics*, 473–79.

11. Avinash Dixit and Barry Nalebuff, *Thinking Strategically: The Competitive Edge in Business, Politics, and Everyday Life*.

12. Eliot A. Cohen and John Gooch, *Military Misfortunes: The Anatomy of Failure in War*, 239. See also Rosen's *Winning the Next War*, 4, which contends that "no good explanation of bureaucratic innovation exists."

13. McNamara with VanDeMark, *In Retrospect*, 239, cited in Harold P. Ford, "Thoughts Engendered by Robert McNamara's *In Retrospect*," 95–109, note 106. Westy is Gen. William C. Westmoreland, head of U.S. Military Assistance Command, Vietnam (MACV) during the heaviest U.S. buildup of forces in Vietnam.

14. I gratefully acknowledge an anonymous reader of this manuscript for this point.

15. Taylor, *The Uncertain Trumpet*. See also Osgood, *Limited War*. For the U.S. shift to flexible response strategy that emphasized preparedness for wars below the nuclear threshold, including subconventional wars, see Millett and Maslowski, *For the Common Defense*, 553ff; and Krepinevich, *The Army and Vietnam*, esp. 28–29.

16. Doughty, et al., *Military Operations Since 1871*, 912–14.

17. Historian Crane Brinton notes that even an apparently "abortive" revolution at one time may "mold the defeated revolutionary group to an even more heroic determination" and pave the way for continued resistance and plotting. Brinton, *The Anatomy of Revolution*, 23.

18. Pape, *Bombing to Win*, 174–210.

19. Ibid., 182–84.

20. Although his other assessments of Rolling Thunder are convincing, Pape give insufficient emphasis to this point.

21. Pape, *Bombing to Win*, 209 and passim.

22. Deborah D. Avant, *Political Institutions and Military Change: Lessons From Peripheral Wars*, 57. Gen. Maxwell D. Taylor served in a variety of posts in the Kennedy administration, including special military advisor to the President and Ambassador to South Vietnam.

23. The first formal definition of U.S. "assured destruction" requirements was presented by McNamara in his Fiscal Year 1966 budget statement of February, 1965: "But, it seems reasonable to assume the destruction of, say, one-quarter to one-third of its population and about two-thirds of its industrial capacity . . . would certainly represent intolerable punishment to any industrialized nation and thus should serve as an effective deterrent." McNamara, cited in Desmond Ball, "The Development of the SIOP, 1960–1983," 69.

24. Raymond L. Garthoff, *Deterrence and the Revolution in Soviet Military Doctrine*, 24–28. See also David Holloway, *The Soviet Union and the Arms Race*, 34–58.

25. Lawrence Freedman, *The Evolution of Nuclear Strategy*, 235. 26. For evidence that McNamara's view of this issue influenced his recommendations on U.S. Vietnam strategy, see the final chapter of *In Retrospect*.

26. For evidence that McNamara's view of this issue influenced his recommendations on U.S. Vietnam strategy, see the final chapter of *In Retrospect*.

27. Stephen M. Meyer, "Soviet Nuclear Operations," esp. 476–97 and 497–512. See also Lt. Gen. A. I. Yevseev, "O nekotorykh tendentsiyakh v izmenii soderzhaniya i kharaktera nachal'nogo perioda voiny," *Voenno-istoricheskii zhurnal* 11 (Nov., 1985), 10–20; Meyer, "Soviet Perspectives on the Paths to Nuclear War."

28. Adherence by U.S. military professionals to the belief that a campaign of annihilation against North Vietnam would have accomplished our war aims at lower cost dies a slow death. Krepinevich's discussion of this strategic option is seminal and worth quoting in its entirety:

> That this strategic war of annihilation against North Vietnam still evokes support in some Army quarters reinforces the notion that for some the learning process proceeds at a glacial pace, if at all. The alternative strategy of invasion focused not on combating the insurgency in South Vietnam but on trying to fit the war to the needs of the Army's *modus operandi*. By failing to materially assist the South Vietnamese against the VC, the invasion proponents

would not have brought any significant respite for the GVN against the insurgents. Certainly Army casualties resulting from an invasion and prolonged occupation of the North would have been heavier than those suffered under the attrition strategy. Erosion of U.S. public support for the war effort would have proceeded at an accelerated pace, and prospects for a long-term U.S. military presence in the region would have diminished.

Krepinevich, *The Army and Vietnam*, 262. For counterpoint, see Summers, *On Strategy*, 130–31.

CHAPTER 5. COLLECTIVE SECURITY AND COERCION

1. See Inis L. Claude, Jr., *Swords Into Plowshares: The Problems and Progress of International Organization*, 223–60.
2. John J. Mearsheimer, "The False Promise of International Institutions," note 27.
3. Charles A. Kupchan and Clifford A. Kupchan, "The Promise of Collective Security," note 54. For counterarguments, see Mearsheimer, "The False Promise of International Institutions," 30–32.
4. Mearsheimer, "The False Promise of International Institutions," 31.
5. Davis and Arquilla, *Deterring or Coercing Opponents in Crisis*.
6. Mearsheimer, *Conventional Deterrence*, 23–66.
7. Kupchan and Kupchan, "The Promise of Collective Security," 55. For counterpoint, see Mearsheimer, "The False Promise of International Institutions," 30–34. Mearsheimer's and other realist views are critiqued in Robert O. Keohane and Lisa L. Martin, "The Promise of Institutionalist Theory." The argument by Kupchan and Kupchan cited in this footnote is based on principles of structural realism, although the authors' piece is intended primarily as a critique of realism in defense of collective security. This is one illustration of the essential covariation, not antithesis, between collective security and realist theory. Collective security theory does not imply the rejection of realist assumptions as does, for example, critical theory: see Richard K. Ashley, "The Poverty of Neorealism."
8. Paul R. Pillar, *Negotiating Peace: War Termination as a Bargaining Process*.
9. Ibid., 14–15.
10. J. David Singer and Melvin Small, *The Wages of War 1816–1965*. Interstate wars are those wars in which at least one member of the state system fights on each side. Extrasystemic wars are usually colonial or imperial wars with a member of the state system on only one side.
11. In this regard, civil wars may not be unusual. According to Zartman, "scarcely any violent conflict in the post-World War II world has been resolved or even managed by direct negotiations by the parties themselves." See his "Bargaining and Conflict Resolution," note 271.

12. A seminal discussion of the problem of terminating civil wars appears in Roy C. Licklider, "How Civil Wars End: Preliminary Results from a Comparative Project." For case studies of UN efforts in war termination, see Sydney D. Bailey, *How Wars End: The United Nations and the Termination of Armed Conflict, 1946–1964.*

13. K. J. Holsti, *The State, War, and the State of War*, 36. See also Van Creveld, *The Transformation of War*, 206.

14. K. J. Holsti, *The State, War, and the State of War*, 189. Holsti's discussions of the political culture of failed states is important and avoids much of the neglect of essential political variables all too typical of literature on "Third World" conflicts.

15. The list is from K. J. Holsti, *The State, War, and the State of War*, 190–91, revised by the author for use here.

16. Richard Ned Lebow, *Nuclear Crisis Management: A Dangerous Illusion.*

17. Michael E. Brown, "The Flawed Logic of NATO Expansion," esp. 37.

18. In *Arms and Influence*, 70–73, Schelling explains the distinction between deterrence and compellence. The concept of compellence is among Schelling's many original contributions to politico-military theory that will outlast the end of the Cold War.

19. The terminology and distinction appear in K. J. Holsti, *The State, War, and the State of War*, passim.

20. Jennifer Morrison Taw and Bruce Hoffman's "Operations Other Than War" provides a good discussion of OOTW and provides pertinent references.

21. Victor A. Kremenyuk and Zartman, "Prospects for Cooperative Security and Conflict Resolution," 336.

22. Lawrence Freedman, "Bosnia: Does Peace Support Make Any Sense?"

23. Ibid., 20. See also Christopher Bellamy, *Knights in White Armour: The New Art of War and Peace*, esp. 30–35.

24. Freedman, "Bosnia: Does Peace Support Make Any Sense?" 23.

25. Alvin and Heidi Toffler, *War and Anti-War: Survival at the Dawn of the 21st Century.*

26. See John Arquilla and David Ronfeldt, *Cyberwar Is Coming!* for useful clarification of some of the terminology related to information warfare. Carl H. Builder has emphasized that developments in technology are related to, and interpreted within, the framework of military service culture, including self-image. See Builder, *The Masks of War*, esp. 23–24, for a discussion of "toys versus the arts."

27. Johnson and Libicki, *Dominant Battlespace Knowledge.*

28. See U.S. Navy Admiral William A. Owens' "The Emerging U.S. System of Systems," 7.

29. Michael Sovereign, "DBK with Autonomous Weapons," 123–24.

30. Ibid., 123.

31. Two useful commentaries on RMA are: Earl H. Tilford, Jr., *The Revolution in Military Affairs: Prospects and Cautions;* and Steven Metz and James Kievit, *Strategy and the Revolution in Military Affairs: From Theory to Policy.* Note the placement of information warfare within the larger RMA spectrum in this study. Russian perspectives on the future Revolution in Military Affairs are noted in C. J. Dick, *Russian Views on Future War.*

32. Roger C. Molander, Andrew S. Riddile, and Peter A. Wilson, *Strategic Information Warfare,* xiv.

33. David S. Alberts, *The Unintended Consequences of Information Age Technologies: Avoiding the Pitfalls, Seizing the Initiative,* 11.

34. Owens, "The Emerging U.S. System of Systems," 4–5.

35. Winn Schwartau, *Information Warfare: Chaos on the Electronic Superhighway,* 17–22 and 258–311.

36. Both anti-Russian rebels in Chechnya and Taliban revolutionaries in Kabul in 1996 had World Wide Web pages. Others seek interconnections with less publicity: see Boris F. Kalachev, "The Illegal Proliferation of Narcotics in Russia: Internal Trends and the Impact on the International Situation," 117–28.

37. See General Wayne A. Downing's "New National Security Challenges," esp. 95–96.

38. J. F. Holden-Rhodes and Peter A. Lupsha, "Horsemen of the Apocalypse: Gray Area Phenomena and the New World Disorder," 218.

39. The potential for an expanded WEU and OSCE (formerly CSCE) to contribute to an effective new European security order is addressed in Richard Ullman, *Securing Europe,* 63–79.

CHAPTER 6. OPERATIONS "NOT WAR" AND COERCIVE MILITARY STRATEGY

1. Daniel J. Kaufman, "The Army," 49–50. I have combined two of the items from the original list into one.

2. James B. Motley, "Noncombat Operations," 375.

3. Colin S. Gray, *Explorations in Strategy,* 212.

4. Snow, *Uncivil Wars,* esp. 144–46.

5. On the concept of failed states, see K. J. Holsti, *The State, War, and the State of War,* 119–22.

6. Zartman, "Introduction: Posing the Problem of State Collapse." See also K. J. Holsti, *The State, War, and the State of War,* 116–17.

7. K. J. Holsti, *The State, War, and the State of War,* 21. See also chap. 5.

8. Ibid., 23.

9. Ibid., 22.

10. Ibid.

11. UN Chapter VI and VII citations are from Bellamy, *Knights in White Armour,* 156. Italics supplied.

12. My colleague Donald M. Snow objects to the locution "peace enforcement" as an oxymoron. Snow argues that the critical line is between "peacekeeping," which occurs with the consent of previously combatant parties and "peace imposition," which involves a settlement imposed over the objections of one or more combatants by outsiders. See Snow, *Uncivil Wars,* 132–33.

13. Chris Bellamy's discussion of this point is very insightful. See *Knights in White Armour,* 155–61 and passim.

14. Ibid., 160. I have defined the zone of intervention a little more narrowly than does Bellamy, who puts major coalition wars at the other end of the spectrum; the concept is useful either way.

15. Bruce F. Macdonald, "A Canadian Serviceman Looks at United Nations Peace-Keeping Operations," quoted in Larry L. Fabian, *Soldiers without Enemies: Preparing the United Nations for Peacekeeping* (Washington, D.C.: Brookings Institution, 1971), 28.

16. Gen. Colin L. Powell, then Chairman of the Joint Chiefs of Staff, press conference Sept. 1, 1993, cited in statement by Col. Harry G. Summers, Jr., USA (Ret.) before the U.S. House of Representatives, Committee on Foreign Affairs, Subcommittee on International Security, International Organizations and Human Rights, Sept. 21, 1993, and reprinted in *Strategic Review* 4 (Fall, 1993): 70.

17. Summers, statement before Committee on Foreign Relations subcommittee, 69–72.

18. Ibid., 71. The significance of these contrasting views about peace operations is also noted in chapter 1.

19. See Secretary of Defense Les Aspin's *Annual Report to the President and the Congress,* 67.

20. U.S. Department of State, *The Clinton Administration's Policy on Reforming Multilateral Peace Operations.*

21. For post-conflict missions, see Richard H. Shultz, Jr., "Conflict Resolution: Post-Conflict Reconstruction Assistance Missions."

22. Ibid., 244.

23. Freedman, "Bosnia: Does Peace Support Make Any Sense?"

24. For example, Van Creveld takes a valid argument too far in *The Transformation of War,* esp. 29 and 205–206.

25. Zartman, "Bargaining and Conflict Reduction," note 284. Italics omitted from original.

26. Taw and Hoffman, "Operations Other Than War," 228. See also Urbano, *Fighting in the Streets: A Manual of Urban Guerrilla Warfare,* esp. 10–18.

27. Donald M. Snow, *Distant Thunder: Third World Conflict and the New International Order,* 67–69.

28. Gerard Chaliand, *Terrorism: From Popular Struggle to Media Spectacle,* 117.

29. In *War and Anti-War,* 90, Toffler and Toffler argue for a similar concept: "distributed threats."

30. Ibid., 149–52.

31. Timothy L. Thomas, "The Caucasus Conflict and Russian Security: The Russian Armed Forces Confront Chechnya III. The Battle for Grozny, 1–26 January 1995," esp. 60–64.

32. Edward Luttwak, "Toward Post-Heroic Warfare." See also, on the nature of "unheroic" and "post-heroic" military leadership and command styles, John Keegan, *The Mask of Command,* chap. 3 and 311–51.

33. Gen. Philippe Morillon, quoted in Payne, *Deterrence in the Second Nuclear Age,* 14, note 23.

34. I am grateful to Professor Peter Viggo Jakobsen for calling this point to my attention. He bears no responsibility for arguments here.

35. Roy Godson, *Dirty Tricks or Trump Cards: U.S. Covert Action and Counterintelligence,* 158–80.

36. The temptation is for scholars as well as for soldiers, with the result that there is little written about the *strategic* character of special operations, covert action, or other unconventional means. A useful corrective appears in Gray, *Explorations in Strategy,* 163–88.

37. Jeremy R. Azrael, Benjamin S. Lambeth, Emil A. Payin, and Arkady A. Popov, "Russian and American Intervention Policy in Comparative Perspective."

CONCLUSION

1. See Donald Kagan, *On the Origins of War and the Preservation of Peace,* esp. 566–73, and John Keegan, *A History of Warfare.*

2. See, in particular, Schelling, *Arms and Influence.* Also see other references in the introduction to this book.

3. In this regard, force has something in common with the process of negotiation. See Linda P. Brady, *The Politics of Negotiation: America's Dealings with Allies, Adversaries, and Friends,* esp. 36–39.

4. Field Marshal Lord Carver, *Twentieth Century Warriors: The Development of the Armed Forces of the Major Military Nations in the Twentieth Century,* 223.

5. J. G. Randall and David Donald, *The Civil War and Reconstruction,* 168–72.

6. Ibid., 174.

7. Quoted in Richard N. Current, *The Lincoln Nobody Knows,* 125.

8. According to Current, Lincoln's strategy was "shrewd" because he knew that mounting the expedition, and giving advance notice of it, would have different meanings to Northern and Southern audiences. The former

would see a provisioning expedition as innocent; the latter, as a provocation. Ibid., 125–26.

9. The typology in tables 20 and 21 is inspired by a variety of sources, but the final result is my own responsibility. See, for example: Alexander L. George and Richard Smoke, *Deterrence in American Foreign Policy: Theory and Practice;* George, ed., *Avoiding War: Problems of Crisis Management;* George, Hall, and Simons, eds., *The Limits of Coercive Diplomacy: Laos, Cuba, Vietnam;* George and Simons, eds., *The Limits of Coercive Diplomacy;* Craig and George, *Force and Statecraft: Diplomatic Problems of Our Time,* 189–204; Schelling, *The Strategy of Conflict* and *Arms and Influence;* Robert Jervis, Richard Ned Lebow, and Janice Gross Stein, eds., *Psychology and Deterrence;* Jervis, *Perception and Misperception in International Politics;* Jervis, "Deterrence and Perception"; Lebow, *Between Peace and War: The Nature of International Crisis;* Lebow, "Windows of Opportunity: Do States Jump Through Them?"; Lebow, "The Soviet Offensive in Europe: The Schlieffen Plan Revisited?"; Lebow, *Nuclear Crisis Management: A Dangerous Illusion;* and Lebow and Janice Gross Stein, "Rational Deterrence Theory: I Think, Therefore I Deter."

10. Coddington, *The Gettysburg Campaign,* 159 and 263.

11. Imaginative writers have claimed that Hitler only wanted to subdue continental Europe and would have been glad, subsequent to the defeat of France in 1940, to arrange a negotiated peace based on the status quo of June, 1940. Hitler mused over various possibilities after his unexpectedly quick victory in France, no doubt, but the testimony of his own actions (waging war on two fronts) and statements (too numerous to mention) shows that negotiated peace and limited war were not what Hitler was about. Stalin understood Hitler clearly on this point, and two of Stalin's responses are symbolically indicative: he permitted the revival of religion in Russia; and, he reinstated the order of (Aleksandr) Suvorov (1729–1800), precommunist Russia's legendary military icon, as a combat decoration.

12. As in the former states of the Confederacy subsequent to their defeat in the American Civil War.

13. This fallacy in prewar estimation of war's duration and outcome is a historical commonplace. See Blainey, *The Causes of War,* 35–56.

14. The battle of Shiloh, for example, on April 6–7, 1862, was the most costly battle fought in the Western Hemisphere to that date: The killed and wounded on each side exceeded 1,700 and 8,000, and some 2,000 eventually died from wounds. Shiloh was a preview of worse to come. See James M. McPherson, *Ordeal by Fire: The Civil War and Reconstruction,* 225–29.

15. Godson, *Dirty Tricks or Trump Cards,* esp. 184–200.

16. Kagan, *On the Origins of War and the Preservation of Peace,* 497.

17. Sun Tzu, *The Art of War,* 63.

18. Ibid., 64. See also introduction.
19. Thomas, "The Caucasus Conflict and Russian Security."
20. Various organizations representing soldiers' mothers have engaged in political activism in post-Soviet Russia. Perhaps the best known in the West is the Soldiers' Mothers of St. Petersburg, which documents abusive treatment of recruits and conscripts and other violations of military law and discipline that result in soldiers' deaths, injuries, or resignations from the armed forces.
21. McPherson, *Ordeal by Fire*, 296–97.
22. Philip Longworth, *The Art of Victory: The Life and Achievements of Field-Marshal Suvorov, 1729–1800*, esp. 32–36.
23. C. J. Dick, "A Bear Without Claws: The Russian Army in the 1990s."
24. Longworth, *The Art of Victory*, 222–23.
25. The "Powell doctrine" has become code for the statement of Department of Defense views by former Defense Secretary Caspar Weinberger on whether and how the United States should use, or avoid the use of, force. Powell was Weinberger's military assistant at the time and was widely credit with having influenced the contents of Weinberger's policy. See: excerpts from remarks by Secretary of Defense Caspar W. Weinberger to the National Press Club, Washington, D.C., Nov. 28, 1984, in Haass, *Intervention*, 173–81. Compare with Powell's own statement of his views in ibid., 191–97.
26. See, among his many contributions, Alexander L. George, "A Provisional Theory of Crisis Management." Also very pertinent are: Richard Smoke, *War: Controlling Escalation;* George, Hall, and Simons, *The Limits of Coercive Diplomacy;* Williams, *Crisis Management;* and George's discussion of coercive diplomacy, in "Strategies for Crisis Management," 384–87. This chapter also outlines other approaches to crisis management, some partaking of coercion in various forms.
27. Schelling, *The Strategy of Conflict* and *Arms and Influence*.
28. See Paret's *Makers of Modern Strategy,* esp. the following contributions: Weigley's "American Strategy from Its Beginnings through the First World War," Philip A. Crowl's "Alfred Thayer Mahan: The Naval Historian," and David MacIsaac's "Voices from the Central Blue: The Air Power Theorists."
29. Clausewitz, *On War,* trans. Col. J. J. Graham, book 1, chap. 2, 40: "The combat is the single activity in War; in the combat the destruction of the enemy opposed to us is the means to the end; it is so even when combat does not actually take place; . . . It follows, therefore, that the destruction of the enemy's military force is the foundation-stone of all action in War, the great support of all combinations, which rest upon it like the arch on its abutments. . . The decision by arms is, for all operations in War, great and small, what cash payment is in bill transactions."

30. Sun Tzu is not, of course, the entire key to understanding unconventional warfare, and some experts would dispute whether he deserves pride of place. Great commanders have taken the best ideas from a variety of military thinkers and applied them in a mix appropriate to the exigent circumstances: Vo Nguyen Giap, Vietnam's master strategist and the architect of many of Ho Chi Minh's victories, was admittedly more of a student of Clausewitz than of Sun Tzu. Giap's strategy is discussed in Alexander, *The Future of Warfare*, 160–75. Giap was, of course, also influenced more immediately by the works and actions of Mao Zedong. My appreciation of the entire topic of unconventional warfare owes much to Sam C. Sarkesian. See, esp., his *America's Forgotten Wars* and *The New Battlefield: The United States and Unconventional Conflicts*.

31. Stanley E. Spangler, *Force and Accommodation in World Politics* (Maxwell AFB, Alabama: Air University Press, Aug. 1991), 5–6, cited in Sarkesian, *Unconventional Conflicts in a New Security Era: Lessons from Malaya and Vietnam*, 191.

32. Gen. Colin L. Powell, "U.S. Forces: Challenges Ahead," 193.

Bibliography

Addington, Larry H. *The Blitzkrieg Era and the German General Staff, 1865–1941.* New Brunswick, N.J.: Rutgers University Press, 1971.

Akimov, V. P., V. B. Lukov, P. B. Parshin, and V. M. Sergeyev. "Karibskiy krizis: opyt modelirovaniya" ("The Caribbean Crisis: Experience of Modelling"). *SShA: politika, ekonomika, ideologiya* 5 (1989): 36–49.

Alberts, David S. *The Unintended Consequences of Information Age Technologies: Avoiding the Pitfalls, Seizing the Initiative.* Washington, D.C.: National Defense University, Institute for National Strategic Studies, Apr. 1996.

Allard, Kenneth. *Command, Control, and the Common Defense.* Rev. ed. Washington, D.C.: National Defense University, 1996.

———. "The Future of Command and Control: Toward a Paradigm of Information Warfare." In *Turning Point,* ed. Ederington and Mazarr, 161–92.

Alexander, Bevin. *The Future of Warfare.* New York: W. W. Norton, 1995.

———. *How Great Generals Win.* New York: W. W. Norton, 1993.

Allison, Graham T. *Essence of Decision: Explaining the Cuban Missile Crisis.* Boston: Little, Brown, 1971.

Allison, Graham T., Albert Carnesale, and Joseph S. Nye, Jr., eds., *Hawks, Doves, and Owls.* New York: W. W. Norton, 1985.

Arnett, Robert L. "Soviet Attitudes Towards Nuclear War: Do They Really Think They Can Win?" *Journal of Strategic Studies* 2 (September, 1979): 172–91.

Arquilla, John, and David Ronfeldt. *Cyberwar Is Coming!* Santa Monica, Ca.: RAND, 1992.

Art, Robert J. "A Defensible Defense: America's Grand Strategy After the Cold War." *International Security* 4 (Spring, 1991): 5–53.

Art, Robert J., and Kenneth N. Waltz, eds. *The Use of Force.* Boston: Little, Brown, 1971.

Ashley, Richard K. "The Poverty of Neorealism." *International Organization* 2 (Spring, 1984): 225–86.

Aspin, Les. *Annual Report to the President and the Congress.* Washington, D.C.: U.S. Government Printing Office, Jan., 1994.

Avant, Deborah D. *Political Institutions and Military Change: Lessons from Peripheral Wars.* Ithaca, N.Y.: Cornell University Press, 1994.

Azrael, Jeremy R., Benjamin S. Lambeth, Emil A. Payin, and Arkady A. Popov. "Russian and American Intervention Policy in Comparative Perspective." In *U.S. and Russian Policymaking with Respect to the Use of Force,* ed. Azrael and Payin, http://www.RAND.org/PUBS/index.html.

Azrael, Jeremy R., and Emil A. Payin, eds. *U.S. and Russian Policymaking with Respect to the Use of Force.* Santa Monica, Calif.: RAND, 1996.

Bailey, Sydney D. *How Wars End: The United Nations and the Termination of Armed Conflict, 1946–1964.* Vol. 2. Oxford: Clarendon Press, 1982.

Ball, Desmond. "The Development of the SIOP, 1960–1983." In *Strategic Nuclear Targeting,* ed. Ball and Richelson, 57–83.

Ball, Desmond, and Jeffrey Richelson, eds. *Strategic Nuclear Targeting.* Ithaca, N.Y.: Cornell University Press, 1986.

Bellamy, Christopher. *Knights in White Armour: The New Art of War and Peace.* London: Hutchinson, 1996.

Betts, Richard K. *Nuclear Blackmail and Nuclear Balance.* Washington, D.C.: Brookings Institution, 1987.

Biddle, Stephen. "Victory Misunderstood: What the Gulf War Tells Us about the Future of Conflict." *International Security* 2 (Fall, 1996): 139–79.

Blainey, Geoffrey. *The Causes of War.* 3rd ed. New York: The Free Press, 1988.

Blank, Stephen J., and Jacob W. Kipp, eds. *The Soviet Military and the Future.* Westport, Conn.: Greenwood Press, 1992.

Blaufarb, Douglas. *The Counterinsurgency Era: U.S. Doctrine and Performance, 1950 to the Present.* New York: The Free Press, 1977.

Blight, James G., and David A. Welch. *On the Brink: Americans and Soviets Reexamine the Cuban Missile Crisis.* New York: Hill and Wang, 1989.

Bracken, Paul. *The Command and Control of Nuclear Forces.* New Haven, Conn.: Yale University Press, 1983.

Brady, Linda P. *The Politics of Negotiation: America's Dealings with Allies, Adversaries and Friends.* Chapel Hill: University of North Carolina Press, 1991.

Brinton, Crane. *The Anatomy of Revolution.* Englewood Cliffs, N.J.: Prentice-Hall, 1965.

Brodie, Bernard. *War and Politics.* New York: Macmillan, 1973.

Brown, Michael E. "The Flawed Logic of NATO Expansion." *Survival* 1 (Spring, 1995): 34–52.

Builder, Carl H. *The Masks of War.* Baltimore, Md.: Johns Hopkins University Press, 1989.

Bundy, McGeorge, transcriber, and James G. Blight, editor, "October 27, 1962: Transcripts of the Meetings of the ExComm." *International Security* 3 (Winter, 1987/88): 30–92.

Carter, Ashton B., John D. Steinbruner, and Charles A. Zraket, eds., *Managing Nuclear Operations.* Washington, D.C.: Brookings Institution, 1987.

Chaliand, Gerard. *Terrorism: From Popular Struggle to Media Spectacle.* London: Saqi Books, 1987.

Cheney, Dick. *Annual Report to the Congress.* Washington, D.C.: U.S. Government Printing Office, 1991.

Cimbala, Stephen J. "Military Persuasion and the American Way of War." *Strategic Review* 4 (Fall, 1994): 33–43.

————. "The Role of Military Advice: Civil-Military Relations and Bush Security Strategy." In *U.S. Civil-Military Relations: In Crisis or Transition?* ed. Snider and Carlton-Carew, 88–112.

————. "United States." In *The Political Role of the Military: An International Handbook,* ed. Constantine P. Danopoulos and Cynthia Watson, 420–39. Westport, Conn.: Greenwood Press, 1996.

————, ed. *Clinton and Post-Cold War Defense.* Westport, Conn.: Praeger, 1996.

Cimbala, Stephen J., and Sidney R. Waldman, eds. *Controlling and Ending Conflict: Issues Before and After the Cold War.* Westport, Conn.: Greenwood Press, 1992.

Claude, Inis L., Jr. *Swords Into Plowshares: The Problems and Progress of International Organization.* New York: Random House, 1964.

Clodfelter, Mark. *The Limits of Air Power: The American Bombing of North Vietnam.* New York: The Free Press, 1989.

Coddington, Edwin B. *The Gettysburg Campaign: A Study in Command.* New York: Charles Scribner's Sons, 1984.

Cohen, Eliot A. "The Mystique of U.S. Airpower." In *Turning Point,* ed. Ederington and Mazarr, 53–64.

Cohen, Eliot A., and John Gooch. *Military Misfortunes: The Anatomy of Failure in War.* New York: Vintage Books, 1991.

Craig, Gordon. "Delbruck: The Military Historian." In *Makers of Modern Strategy,* ed. Paret, 326–53.

Craig, Gordon, and Alexander L. George. *Force and Statecraft: Diplomatic Problems of Our Time.* New York: Oxford University Press, 1983.

Crowl, Philip A. "Alfred Thayer Mahan: The Naval Historian." In *Makers of Modern Strategy,* ed. Paret, 444–80.

Currant, Richard N. *The Lincoln Nobody Knows.* New York: Hill and Wang, 1958.

Davis, Paul K. "Planning Under Uncertainty Then and Now: Paradigms Lost and Paradigms Emerging." In *New Challenges for Defense Planning,* ed. Davis, 15–58.

Davis, Paul K., ed. *New Challenges for Defense Planning: Rethinking How Much Is Enough?* Santa Monica, Calif.: RAND, 1994.

Davis, Paul K., and John Arquilla. *Deterring or Coercing Opponents in Crisis: Lessons from the War with Saddam Hussein.* Santa Monica, Calif.: RAND, 1991, R-4111-JS.

Dick, C. J. "A Bear Without Claws: The Russian Army in the 1990s." *Journal of Slavic Military Studies* 1 (Mar., 1997), 1–10.

————. *Russian Views on Future War.* Camberley: Conflict Studies Research Centre, Royal Military Academy Sandhurst, June 8, 1993.

Dixit, Avinash, and Barry Nalebuff. *Thinking Strategically: The Competitive Edge in Business, Politics, and Everyday Life.* New York: W. W. Norton, 1991.

Doughty, Robert A. et al. *Warfare in the Western World.* Vol. 2, *Military Operations Since 1871.* Lexington, Mass.: D. C. Heath, 1996.

Downing, Wayne A. "New National Security Challenges." In *Managing Contemporary Conflict: Pillars of Success,* chap. ed. Manwaring and Olson, 91–102.

Druckman, Daniel, and P. Terrence Hopman. "Behavioral Aspects of Negotiations on Mutual Security." In *Behavior, Society, and Nuclear War,* ed. Tetlock, et al., 1:85–173.

Ederington, L. Benjamin, and Michael J. Mazarr, eds. *Turning Point: The Gulf War and U.S. Military Strategy.* Boulder, Colo.: Westview Press, 1994.

English, John A. *Marching through Chaos: The Descent of Armies in Theory and Practice.* Westport, Conn.: Praeger Publishers, 1996.

Erickson, John. "Quo Vadis? The Changing Faces of Soviet/Russian Forces and Now Russia." In *The Soviet Military and the Future,* ed. Blank and Kipp, 33–58.

Fabian, Larry L. *Soldiers without Enemies: Preparing the United Nations for Peacekeeping.* Washington, D.C.: Brookings Institution, 1971.

Ford, Harold P. "Thoughts Engendered by Robert McNamara's *In Retrospect.*" In *Studies in Intelligence, No. 5* (Washington, D.C.: Central Intelligence Agency, 1996.

Freedman, Lawrence. "Bosnia: Does Peace Support Make Any Sense?" *NATO Review* 6 (Nov., 1995): 19–23.

———. *The Evolution of Nuclear Strategy.* New York: St. Martin's Press, 1981.

Gaddis, John Lewis. *The Long Peace: Inquiries into the History of the Cold War.* New York: Oxford University Press, 1987.

———. *The United States and the End of the Cold War: Implications, Reconsiderations, Provocations.* New York: Oxford University Press, 1992.

———. *The United States and the Origins of the Cold War, 1941–1947.* New York: Columbia University Press, 1972.

———. *We Now Know: Rethinking Cold War History.* Oxford: Clarendon Press, 1997.

Garthoff, Raymond L. *Deterrence and the Revolution in Soviet Military Doctrine.* Washington, D.C.: Brookings Institution, 1990.

———. *Reflections on the Cuban Missile Crisis.* Revised Edition. Washington, D.C.: Brookings Institution, 1989.

Gelb, Leslie H., with Richard K. Betts. *The Irony of Vietnam: The System Worked.* Washington, D.C.: Brookings Institution, 1979.

George, Alexander L. "Coercive Diplomacy: Definition and Characteristics." In *The Limits of Coercive Diplomacy,* ed. George and Simons, 7–12.

———. "The Cuban Missile Crisis: Peaceful Resolution Through Coercive

Diplomacy." In *The Limits of Coercive Diplomacy,* ed. George and Simons, 111–32.

———. "The Cuban Missile Crisis, 1962." In *The Limits of Coercive Diplomacy: Laos, Cuba, Vietnam,* ed. George, Hall, and Simons, 86–143.

———. "The Development of Doctrine and Strategy." In *The Limits of Coercive Diplomacy,* ed. George, Hall, and Simons, 1-35.

———. "A Provisional Theory of Crisis Management." In *Avoiding War,* ed. George, 22–30.

———. "Strategies for Crisis Management." In *Avoiding War,* ed. George, 377–94.

———, ed. *Avoiding War: Problems of Crisis Management.* Boulder, Colo.: Westview Press, 1991.

George, Alexander L., David K. Hall, and William E. Simons, eds. *The Limits of Coercive Diplomacy: Laos, Cuba, Vietnam.* Boston: Little, Brown, 1971.

George, Alexander L., and William E. Simons, eds. *The Limits of Coercive Diplomacy.* 2d ed. Boulder, Colo.: Westview Press, 1994.

George, Alexander L., and Richard Smoke. *Deterrence in American Foreign Policy: Theory and Practice.* New York: Columbia University Press, 1974.

Godson, Roy. *Dirty Tricks or Trump Cards: U.S. Covert Action and Counterintelligence.* Washington, D.C.: Brassey's, 1995.

———. *Intelligence Requirements for the 1980s.* Vol. 4, *Covert Action.* Washington, D.C.: National Strategy Information Center, 1983.

Gordon, Michael R., and General Bernard R. Trainor. *The Generals' War: The Inside Story of the Conflict in the Gulf.* Boston: Little, Brown, 1995.

Gray, Colin S. *Explorations in Strategy.* Westport, Conn.: Greenwood Press, 1996.

———. *Nuclear Strategy and National Style.* Lanham, Md.: Hamilton Press, 1986.

———. *Weapons Don't Make War: Policy, Strategy, and Military Technology.* Lawrence: University Press of Kansas, 1993.

Handel, Michael I. *Sun Tzu and Clausewitz: "The Art of War" and "On War" Compared.* Carlisle Barracks, Pa.: Strategic Studies Institute, 1991.

Haass, Richard N. *Intervention: The Use of American Military Force in the Post-Cold War World.* Washington, D.C.: Carnegie Endowment for International Peace, 1994.

Herrmann, Richard. "Coercive Diplomacy and the Crisis over Kuwait." In *The Limits of Coercive Diplomacy,* ed. George and Simons, 234–35.

Hilsman, Roger. *The Cuban Missile Crisis: The Struggle Over Policy.* Westport, Conn.: Praeger Publishers, 1996.

Hitch, Charles J., and Roland N. McKean. *The Economics of Defense in the Nuclear Age.* New York: Atheneum, 1969.

Holden-Rhodes, J. F., and Peter A. Lupsha. "Horsemen of the Apocalypse:

Gray Area Phenomena and the New World Disorder." *Low Intensity Conflict and Law Enforcement* 2 (Autumn, 1993): 212–26.

Holloway, David. *The Soviet Union and the Arms Race.* Second Edition. New Haven: Yale University Press, 1984.

Holsti, Kalevi J. *The State, War, and the State of War.* Cambridge: Cambridge University Press, 1996.

Holsti, Ole R. "Crisis Decision Making." In *Behavior, Society, and Nuclear War,* vol. 1, ed. Tetlock, et al., 8–84.

Horelick, Arnold L., and Myron Rush. *Strategic Power and Soviet Foreign Policy.* Chicago: University of Chicago Press, 1966.

Huntington, Samuel P. *The Soldier and the State.* Cambridge: Belknap Press/Harvard University Press, 1957.

Ikle, Fred Charles. *Every War Must End.* New York: Columbia University Press, 1971.

Jablonsky, David. *Strategic Rationality Is Not Enough: Hitler and the Concept of Crazy States.* Carlisle Barracks, Pa.: Strategic Studies Institute, August, 1991.

Jentleson, Bruce W. *With Friends Like These: Reagan, Bush, and Saddam, 1982–1990.* New York: W. W. Norton, 1994.

Jervis, Robert. "Deterrence and Perception." In *Strategy and Nuclear Deterrence,* ed. Miller, 57–84.

———. *The Meaning of the Nuclear Revolution: Statecraft and the Prospect of Armageddon.* Ithaca, N.Y.: Cornell University Press, 1989.

———. *Perception and Misperception in International Politics.* Princeton: Princeton University Press, 1976.

———. "What Do We Want to Deter and How Do We Deter It?" In *Turning Point: The Gulf War and U.S. Military Strategy,* ed. Ederington and Mazarr, 117–36.

Jervis, Robert, Richard Ned Lebow, and Janice Gross Stein, eds. *Psychology and Deterrence.* Baltimore: Johns Hopkins University Press, 1985.

Johnsen, William T., Douglas V. Johnson, II, James O. Kievit, Douglas O. Lovelace, Jr., and Steven Metz. *The Principles of War in the 21st Century.* Carlisle Barracks, Pa.: Strategic Studies Institute, U.S. Army War College, August, 1995.

Johnson, Stuart E., and Martin C. Libicki, eds. *Dominant Battlespace Knowledge: The Winning Edge.* Washington, D.C.: National Defense University Press, 1995.

Kagan, Donald. *On the Origins of War and the Preservation of Peace.* New York: Doubleday, 1995.

Kalachev, Boris F. "The Illegal Proliferation of Narcotics in Russia: Internal Trends and the Impact on the International Situation." *Low Intensity Conflict and Law Enforcement* 2 (Autumn, 1996): 117–28.

Kaufman, Daniel. J. "The Army." In *America's Armed Forces,* ed. Sarkesian and Connor, 33–62.

Kaufmann, William W. *The McNamara Strategy.* New York: Harper and Row, 1964.

Keaney, Thomas A., and Eliot A. Cohen, Directors. *Gulf War Air Power Survey.* Washington: U.S. Government Printing Office, 1993. Republished as Thomas A. Keaney and Eliot A. Cohen, *Revolution in Warfare? Air Power in the Persian Gulf* (Annapolis, Md.: Naval Institute Press, 1995).

Keegan, John. "The Ground War." In *Turning Point: The Gulf War and U.S. Military Strategy,* ed. Ederington and Mazarr, 65–78.

———. *A History of Warfare.* New York: Alfred A. Knopf, 1993.

———. *The Mask of Command.* New York: Penguin Books, 1987.

Keohane, Robert O., and Lisa L. Martin. "The Promise of Institutionalist Theory." *International Security* 1 (Summer, 1995): 39–51.

Kissinger, Henry A. *Nuclear Weapons and Foreign Policy.* New York: Harper and Row, 1957.

Klare, Michael. *Rogue States and Nuclear Outlaws: America's Search for a New Foreign Policy.* New York: Hill and Wang, 1995.

Kolodziej, Edward A., and Roger E. Kanet, eds. *Coping with Conflict after the Cold War.* Baltimore: Johns Hopkins University Press, 1996.

Krauthammer, Charles. "The Unipolar Moment." In *Rethinking America's Security,* ed. Graham Allison and Gregory F. Treverton, 295–306. New York: W. W. Norton, 1992.

Kremenyuk, Victor A., and I. William Zartman. "Prospects for Cooperative Security and Conflict Resolution." In *Cooperative Security: Reducing Third World Wars,* ed. Zartman and Kremenyuk.

Krepinevich, Andrew, Jr. *The Army and Vietnam.* Baltimore: Johns Hopkins University Press, 1986.

Kupchan, Charles A., and Clifford A. Kupchan. "The Promise of Collective Security." *International Security* 1 (Summer, 1995), 52–61.

Lafeber, Walter. *America, Russia, and the Cold War, 1945–1975.* 3rd ed. New York: John Wiley and Sons, 1976.

Lebow, Richard Ned. *Between Peace and War: The Nature of International Crisis.* Baltimore: Johns Hopkins University Press, 1981.

———. *Nuclear Crisis Management: A Dangerous Illusion.* Ithaca, N.Y.: Cornell University Press, 1987.

———. "The Soviet Offensive in Europe: The Schlieffen Plan Revisited?" *International Security* 4 (Spring, 1985), 44–78.

———. "Windows of Opportunity: Do States Jump Through Them?" *International Security* 1 (Summer, 1984): 147–86.

Lebow, Richard Ned, and Janice Gross Stein. "Rational Deterrence Theory: I Think, Therefore I Deter." *World Politics* 2 (Jan., 1989): 208–24.

———. *We All Lost the Cold War.* Princeton: Princeton University Press, 1994.

Licklider, Roy C. "How Civil Wars End: Preliminary Results from a Comparative Project." In *Controlling and Ending Conflict: Issues Before and After the Cold War,* ed. Cimbala and Waldman, 219–38.

Longworth, Philip. *The Art of Victory: The Life and Achievements of Field-Marshal Suvorov, 1729–1800.* New York: Holt, Rinehart and Winston, 1965.

Lord Carver, Field Marshal. *Twentieth Century Warriors: The Development of the Armed Forces of the Major Military Nations in the Twentieth Century.* New York: Weidenfeld and Nicolson, 1987.

Luttwak, Edward N. *Strategy: The Logic of War and Peace.* Cambridge: Harvard University Press, 1987.

———. "Toward Post-Heroic Warfare." *Foreign Affairs* 3 (May-June, 1995): 109–22.

MacIsaac, David. "Voices from the Central Blue: The Air Power Theorists." In *Makers of Modern Strategy,* ed. Paret, 624–47.

Manwaring, Max G., and William J. Olsen, eds. *Managing Contemporary Conflict: Pillars of Success.* Boulder, Colo.: Westview Press/Harper Collins, 1996.

Mao Tse-tung (Zedong), *Basic Tactics.* Trans. Stuart R. Schram. New York: Frederick A. Praeger, 1967.

Mason, Tony. *Air Power: A Centennial Appraisal.* London: Brassey's, 1994.

Mastny, Vojtech. *Russia's Road to the Cold War: Diplomacy, Warfare, and the Politics of Communism, 1941–45.* New York: Columbia University Press, 1979.

Mazarr, Michael J., Don M. Snider, and James A. Blackwell, Jr. *Desert Storm: The Gulf War and What We Learned.* Boulder, Colo.: Westview Press, 1993.

McNamara, Robert S. *The Essence of Security.* New York: Harper and Row, 1968.

McNamara, Robert S., with Brian VanDeMark. *In Retrospect: The Tragedy and Lessons of Vietnam.* New York: Times Books, 1995.

McPherson, James M. *Battle Cry of Freedom: The Civil War Era.* New York: Oxford University Press, 1988.

———. *Ordeal by Fire: The Civil War and Reconstruction.* New York: Alfred A. Knopf, 1982.

Mearsheimer, John J. *Conventional Deterrence.* Ithaca, N.Y.: Cornell University Press, 1984.

———. "The False Promise of International Institutions." *International Security* 3 (Winter, 1994/95): 5–49.

Metz, Steven, and James Kievit. *Strategy and the Revolution in Military Affairs: From Theory to Policy.* Carlisle Barracks, Pa.: U.S. Army War College, Strategic Studies Institute, 1995.

Meyer, Stephen M. "Soviet Nuclear Operations." In *Managing Nuclear Operations,* ed. Carter, Steinbruner, and Zraket, 470–534.

———. "Soviet Perspectives on the Paths to Nuclear War." In *Hawks, Doves and Owls,* ed. Allison, Carnesale, and Nye, 167–205.

Miller, Steven E., ed. *Strategy and Nuclear Deterrence.* Princeton: Princeton University Press, 1984.

Millett, Allan R., and Peter Maslowski. *For the Common Defense: A Military History of the United States of America.* New York: The Free Press, 1994.

Molander, Roger C., Andrew S. Riddile, and Peter A. Wilson. *Strategic Information Warfare.* Santa Monica, Calif.: RAND, 1996.

Motley, James B. "Noncombat Operations." In *America's Armed Forces,* ed. Sarkesian and Connor, 363–86.

Nye, Joseph S., Jr., and Roger K. Smith, eds. *After the Storm: Lessons from the Gulf War.* New York: Madison Books/Aspen Institute, 1992.

Osgood, Robert Endicott. *Limited War: The Challenge to American Strategy.* Chicago: University of Chicago Press, 1957.

Owens, William A. "The Emerging U.S. System of Systems: Introduction." In *Dominant Battlespace Knowledge,* ed. Johnson and Libicki, 3–18.

Pape, Robert A., Jr. *Bombing to Win: Air Power and Coercion in War.* Ithaca, N.Y.: Cornell University Press, 1996.

———. "Coercion and Military Strategy: Why Denial Works and Punishment Doesn't." *Journal of Strategic Studies* 4 (Dec., 1992): 423–75.

———. "Coercive Air Power in the Vietnam War." *International Security,* 2 (Fall, 1990): 103–46.

Paret, Peter, ed. *Makers of Modern Strategy.* Princeton: Princeton University Press, 1976.

Payne, Keith B. *Deterrence in the Second Nuclear Age.* Lexington: University Press of Kentucky, 1996.

Perry, William J. *Annual Report to the President and the Congress.* Washington, D.C.: U.S. Government Printing Office, 1996.

Pfaltzgraff, Robert L., Jr., and Richard H. Shultz, Jr. *Ethnic Conflict and Regional Instability: Implications for U.S. Policy and Army Roles and Missions.* Carlisle Barracks, Pa.: Strategic Studies Institute, U.S. Army War College, 1993.

Pillar, Paul R. *Negotiating Peace: War Termination as a Bargaining Process.* Princeton: Princeton University Press, 1983.

Powell, Colin L. "U.S. Forces: Challenges Ahead." In *Intervention,* by Haass, 191–97.

Prados, John. *Presidents' Secret Wars: CIA and Pentagon Covert Operations Since World War II.* New York: William Morrow, 1986.

President's Commission on Strategic Forces (Scowcroft Commission). *Report.* Washington, D.C.: The White House, 1983).

Quester, George H. *Deterrence before Hiroshima: The Airpower Background to Modern Strategy.* New York: John Wiley and Sons, 1966.

Randall, J. G., and David Donald. *The Civil War and Reconstruction.* 2d ed. Boston: D.C. Heath, 1961.

Record, Jeffrey. *Hollow Victory: A Contrary View of the Gulf War.* Washington, D.C.: Brassey's, 1992.

Reznichenko, V. G., I. N. Vorob'yev, and N. F. Miroshnichenko. *Taktika (Tactics).* Moscow: Voenizdat, 1987.

Rosen, Stephen Peter. *Winning the Next War: Innovation and the Modern Military.* Ithaca, N.Y.: Cornell University Press, 1991.

Sarkesian, Sam C. *America's Forgotten Wars: The Counterrevolutionary Past and Lessons for the Future.* Westport, Conn.: Greenwood Press, 1984.

———. *Beyond the Battlefield: The New Military Professionalism.* New York: Pergamon Press, 1981.

———. *The New Battlefield: The United States and Unconventional Conflicts.* Westport, Conn.: Greenwood Press, 1986.

———. "Special Operations, Low Intensity Conflict (Unconventional Conflicts), and the Clinton Defense Strategy." In *Clinton and Post-Cold War Defense,* ed. Cimbala.

———. *Unconventional Conflicts in a New Security Era: Lessons from Malaya and Vietnam.* Westport, Conn.: Greenwood Press, 1993.

———. "U.S. Strategy and Unconventional Conflicts: The Elusive Goal." In *The U.S. Army in a New Security Era,* ed. Sarkesian and Williams, 195–216.

Sarkesian, Sam C., and Robert E. Connor, Jr. *America's Armed Forces: A Handbook of Current and Future Capabilities.* Westport, Conn.: Greenwood Press, 1996.

Sarkesian, Sam C., and John Allen Williams, eds. *The U.S. Army in a New Security Era.* Boulder, Colo.: Lynne Rienner, 1990.

Schelling, Thomas C. *Arms and Influence.* New Haven: Yale University Press, 1966.

———. *The Strategy of Conflict.* Cambridge: Harvard University Press, 1960.

Schwartau, Winn. *Information Warfare: Chaos on the Electronic Superhighway.* New York: Thunder's Mouth Press, 1994.

Schwartz, David N. *NATO's Nuclear Dilemmas.* Washington, D.C.: Brookings Institution, 1983.

Shafer, D. Michael. *Deadly Paradigms: The Failure of U.S. Counterinsurgency Policy.* Princeton: Princeton University Press, 1988.

Shultz, Richard H., Jr. "Conflict Resolution: Post-Conflict Reconstruction Assistance Missions." In *Ethnic Conflict and Regional Instability: Implications for U.S. Policy and Army Roles and Missions,* ed. Pfaltzgraff and Shultz, 299–316.

Shy, John, and Thomas W. Collier. "Revolutionary War." In *Makers of Modern Strategy,* ed. Paret, 815–62.

Simons, William E. "U.S. Coercive Pressure on North Vietnam, Early 1965." In *The Limits of Coercive Diplomacy,* ed. George and Simons, 133–73.

Singer, J. David, and Melvin Small. *The Wages of War 1816–1965.* New York: John Wiley and Sons, 1972.

Smoke, Richard. *War: Controlling Escalation.* Cambridge: Harvard University Press, 1977.

Snider, Don M., and Miranda A. Carlton-Carew, eds. *U.S. Civil-Military Relations: In Crisis or Transition?* Washington, D.C.: Center for Strategic and International Studies, 1995.

Snow, Donald M. *Distant Thunder: Third World Conflict and the New International Order.* New York: St. Martin's Press, 1993.

———. *Uncivil Wars: International Security and the New Internal Conflicts.* Boulder, Colo.: Lynne Rienner, 1996.

Sovereign, Michael. "DBK with Autonomous Weapons." In *Dominant Battlespace Knowledge,* ed. Johnson and Libicki, 121–32.

Sullivan, Gordon R., and Anthony M. Coroalles. *The Army in the Information Age.* Carlisle Barracks, Pa.: Strategic Studies Institute, U.S. Army War College, March, 1995.

Summers, Harry G., Jr., *On Strategy: A Critical Analysis of the Vietnam War.* New York: Dell Books, 1984.

———. *On Strategy II: A Critical Analysis of the Gulf War.* New York: Dell Publishing Co., 1992.

Sun Tzu. *The Art of War.* Ed. and trans. Samuel B. Griffith. New York: Oxford University Press, 1963.

Svechin, Aleksandr A. *Strategy.* Ed. and trans. Kent D. Lee. Minneapolis, Minn.: East View Publications, 1991. (Translated from the original work, *Strategiya,* 2d ed. [Moscow: Voennyi vestnik, 1927].)

Talbott, Strobe, ed. and trans. *Khrushchev Remembers.* Boston: Little, Brown, 1970.

Tarr, David W. *Nuclear Deterrence and International Security: Alternative Nuclear Regimes.* White Plains, N.Y.: Longman Publishing Group, 1991.

Taw, Jennifer Morrison, and Bruce Hoffman. "Operations Other Than War." In *New Challenges for Defense Planning: Rethinking How Much Is Enough?* ed. Davis, 223–49.

Taylor, Maxwell D. *The Uncertain Trumpet.* New York: Harper and Bros., 1959.

Tetlock, Philip E., Jo L. Husbands, Robert Jervis, Paul C. Stern, and Charles Tilly, eds. *Behavior, Society, and Nuclear War,* vol. I. New York: Oxford University Press, 1989.

Thomas, Timothy L. "The Caucasus Conflict and Russian Security: The Russian Armed Forces Confront Chechnya III. The Battle for Grozny, 1–26 January 1995." *Journal of Slavic Military Studies* 1 (Mar., 1997): 50–108.

Tilford, Earl H., Jr. *The Revolution in Military Affairs: Prospects and Cautions.* Carlisle Barracks, Pa.: U.S. Army War College, Strategic Studies Institute, 1995.

Toffler, Alvin, and Heidi Toffler. *War and Anti-War: Survival at the Dawn of the 21st Century.* Boston: Little, Brown, 1993.

Trainor, Bernard E. "War by Miscalculation." In *After the Storm: Lessons from the Gulf War,* ed. Nye and Smith.

Trulock, Alice Rains. *In the Hands of Providence: Joshua L. Chamberlain and the American Civil War.* Chapel Hill: University of North Carolina Press, 1992.

Ullman, Richard. *Securing Europe.* Princeton: Princeton University Press, 1991.

Urbano, *Fighting in the Streets: A Manual of Urban Guerrilla Warfare*. Fort Lee, N.J.: Barricade Books, 1991.

U.S. Congressional Budget Office. *An Analysis of the Administration's Future Years Defense Program for 1995 through 1999*. Washington, D.C.: CBO Papers, 1995.

U.S. Department of State. *The Clinton Administration's Policy on Reforming Multilateral Peace Operations*. Washington, D.C.: State Department, May 1994.

Van Creveld, Martin. *Command in War*. Cambridge: Harvard University Press, 1985.

———. *The Transformation of War*. New York: The Free Press, 1991.

Von Clausewitz, Karl. *On War*. Trans. Colonel J. J. Graham, new and revised edition, Vol. I. London: Routledge and Kegan Paul, 1966.

———. *On War*. Ed. and trans. Michael Howard and Peter Paret. Princeton: Princeton University Press, 1976.

Waller, Douglas. "Onward Cyber Soldiers." *Time*, Oct. 21, 1995, 38–46.

Weigley, Russell F. "American Strategy from Its Beginnings through the First World War." In *Makers of Modern Strategy*, ed. Paret, 408–43.

———. *The American Way of War: A History of United States Military Strategy and Policy*. New York: Macmillan, 1973.

———. *Towards an American Army: Military Thought from Washington to Marshall*. New York: Columbia University Press, 1962.

Williams, Phil. *Crisis Management*. New York: John Wiley and Sons, 1976.

Wohlstetter, Albert, and Roberta Wohlstetter. "Controlling the Risks in Cuba." In *The Use of Force*, ed. Art and Waltz, 234–73.

Young, Jesse Bowman. *The Battle of Gettysburg: A Comprehensive Narrative*. Carlisle, Pa.: John Kallman Publishers, 1996. Originally published in 1913.

Zartman, I. William. "Bargaining and Conflict Resolution." In *Coping with Conflict after the Cold War*, ed. Kolodziej and Kanet, 271–90.

———. "Introduction: Posing the Problem of State Collapse." In *Collapsed States*, ed. Zartman, 1–11.

———, ed. *Collapsed States: The Disintegration and Restoration of Legitimate Authority*. Boulder, Colo.: Lynne Rienner, 1995.

Index

Note: Pages with tables are indicated by italics.